CLEVELAND

Ethnic Eats

A Guide to the <u>Authentic</u>
Ethnic Restaurants and Markets
of Greater Cleveland

Laura Taxel

GRAY & COMPANY, PUBLISHERS
CLEVELAND

Gray & Company, Publishers
11000 Cedar Avenue
Cleveland, Ohio 44106
(216) 721-2665

ISBN 0-963-1738-7-1
Printed in the United States of America
10 9 8 7 6 5 4 3 2 1

This book is my way of expressing appreciation to all the members of the ethnic communities who so graciously opened their doors to me. It is dedicated to those people who generously shared their ideas, insights, suggestions, and stories, and to the restaurant owners, managers, merchants, chefs, and shopkeepers who were so hospitable and helpful. My thanks to each of you.

Acknowledgements

If you've never done it, it's hard to imagine just what it takes to pull all the pieces of a book like this together. Trust me when I say that it is hard work, requiring long hours. My husband Barney, my three sons Ezra, Nathan, and Simon, and my parents, Elliott and Mitzi Faye gave me an immeasurable quantity of enthusiastic support for my efforts and patient tolerance of my absences, both physical and mental. Their encouragement and good humor kept me going. Their willingness to try almost anything made everything else possible.

To my loyal, fearless, and always hungry band of eating adventurers, I can only tell you what you surely have already realized: I couldn't have done it without you. Many people ate out with me and for me, and though I am not listing them by name, they know who they are. They traveled far and wide, sampled dishes that lesser folk might shrink from, and stuffed themselves beyond the call of duty.

I also want to give special recognition to my tireless and meticulous research assistant, Anna McCormack, and to *Avenues Magazine*, where I first began to explore the Cleveland's ethnic eats in my monthly coulumn Thoughts for Food.

Contents

Contents (*continued*)

Foreword

I come from a family that discussed what to have for dinner while eating breakfast. I have a hearty appreciation for all good food and a special feeling for my own ethnic heritage and the dishes that are a part of it.

My upbringing, coupled with my role as the City of Cleveland's Ethnic and International Affairs Liaison, has made me an ethnic foods aficionado. I enjoy the taste of all ethnic specialties, everything from the Eastern European pierogi I grew up with to a Chinese eggroll or a Mexican flan, and I'm aware of the rich history that's behind every dish I sample.

We are fortunate here in Greater Cleveland to have a city that is home to dozens of different nationality groups, and we can be thankful that our citizens refuse to let go of their ethnic past. This diversity makes Cleveland a wonderful place to live, work, and visit. It is also a great city in which to eat.

Laura Taxel's guide will help you plan culinary adventures. You can find a new place for an Italian dinner one night, Lebanese the next, and then thumb through the guide to find a type of food you've never tried before for another meal out. You can plan trips to grocery stores that will take you, not only from the East Side to the West, but from the East to the West in search of rare spices and tropical fruits. In a month's time you could easily travel from restaurant to restaurant, store to store, and feel as though you have traversed the globe. And you won't even have to contend with jet lag!

Because of my personal and professional interest in ethnic foods and in this city, I am proud to have been asked not only to write this foreword, but also to provide illustrations for Cleveland Ethnic Eats. In any given week, I dine in at least one of the restaurants featured in the Guide, attend an ethnic festival, or am a guest at an ethnic celebration, and I drew upon my personal knowledge of these cultures and cuisines to create the images that are part of each chapter.

If you relish good food like I do, and have a taste for a truly international experience, then *Cleveland Ethnic Eats* is for you. Bon Appetito! Smacznego! Prosit! Buen Gusto! Enjoy!

Richard J. Konisiewicz
Liaison for Ethnic and International Affairs,
City of Cleveland

Introduction

I N THIS DETAILED GUIDE to the authentic ethnic restaurants, bakers, butchers, and grocers of Greater Cleveland, you'll find out who still makes strudel dough and sausages by hand—the Old World way; who sells imported Basmati rice, loquats, or dates; and the only place in town that serves Moroccan sheriya bahara (noodles sweetened with sugar and cinnamon). Researching the book, I spoke with a true United Nations of Clevelanders, individuals who have a strong sense of their own ethnic background. I asked them to tell me where they and other people from their "home" country eat and shop for authentic meals. Housewives and community leaders were my expert advisors. With their help I was able to uncover the vast multicultural food world of greater Cleveland. Even a quick flip though the pages of this book testifies to how interesting and varied a world it is.

More than a directory, Cleveland Ethnic Eats is a guide to eating as an adventurous experience. It's about where to go when you're looking for an alternative to typical American fare or have a yen for the taste of faraway places. It lets you know what to expect when you get there. It offers no guarantees that you'll like what you find, but every place I visited was in its own way worth the trip. Some offer the kinds of dishes your mother or your grandmother made. Others present foods you may never have seen or even imagined people eating. Almost everything—from pierogis to pakoras, linguini to lo mein—is available in Cleveland. It may surprise you to find out just how easy it is to get a bowl of real phad Thai noodles or Jamaican goat curry.

There are spots, hidden behind nondescript storefronts and tucked away in innocuous strip malls, where shopkeepers wear saris; menus, posted on the walls, are written in beautiful Oriental calligraphy; and friendly smiles rather than English may be the only common language. Without flying across an ocean, you can sample Ethiopian yebug alicha (lamb stew) under a thatched roof or sit at a Japanese sushi bar and watch a master slice and wrap raw fish. You can cross a threshold, and leave the sights and sounds of this city behind you as you enter stores filled with exotic smells and unfamiliar foods, close to home and yet as foreign to most of us as a Middle Eastern shouk (bazaar).

I know a couple who have made shopping in Cleveland's ethnic markets a lifelong hobby. They say it's exciting, like a visit to another country, and the foods they encounter always give them new ideas to use in their own kitchen. Eating in ethnic restaurants, they told me, is also a low-cost way to "travel," a chance to soak up the flavor of the people and the culture along with the sauce. After spending almost two years investigating more than 30 of the area's ethnic food communities, I have to agree with them.

Shopping was an outing, not a chore. Many of the markets, family-owned and operated, offer the hospitality and personal service of an old-fashioned corner store. Eating out became more than just a meal in a restaurant; it was an opportunity to take a little trip into parts unknown, break away from the usual, and enlarge my view of what Cleveland is all about. I discovered that this is truly a cosmopolis, a city inhabited by people from all parts of the world, and it's this variety that can make living here so much fun.

Discovering Cleveland's Ethnic Communities

In addition to being a dining guide, this is also a chronicle of the unique mix of peoples and cultures that come together in northeast Ohio. Immigrants, representing more than fifty different nations, have contributed to the growth of Cleveland from its earliest days, changing it from a pioneer backwater to a thriving, culturally rich urban center. They have come with strong backs, skilled hands, and great minds that have helped to build this city and its institutions. And even as they forged new American identities, they kept alive the spirit of their homelands. The shops and restaurants they opened represent the need that each immigrant group has always had for a taste of home. The fact that as a country we've developed an appreciation for many of their distinctive dishes shows what a profound influence their presence has had on our national consciousness.

Some, like the Puerto Ricans and the Vietnamese, are relative newcomers, arriving in this region in significant numbers only within the past 25 years. Others, like the Germans and the Irish, were among the earliest settlers. The census of 1890 showed that more than half of the city's population was foreign born. The Haymarket area southwest of Public Square was called "Baghdad on the Cuyahoga" because so many different languages were spoken there. When Cleveland celebrated its 150th anniversary in 1946, the theme was One World. The Chinese, Czechs, English, Finns, French, Germans, Greeks, Hungarians, Irish, Jews, Italians, Lithuanians, Poles, Scots, Slovaks, Slovenians, Spanish, Swiss, and Ukrainians living here all made floats for the parade.

But we don't have it all. Guides to eating ethnic in other cities include restaurants that feature the foods of Guatemala and Chile, Malaya and Tunis. Although Greater Cleveland boasts residents from Turkey, Armenia, and Cuba, those countries are not represented among our restaurants. There are a few thousand Filipinos living here, but the only source of this unusual cuisine is one lone caterer. An active community interest in ethnic foods demonstrates that we're not just a meatloaf and mashed potatoes town, as some have said, and will encourage other nationality groups to open restaurants and share their food with us.

Nowadays, most ethnic communities are defined not so much by geographic boundaries as by a shared heritage. But in years past, nationality groups clustered in specific neighborhoods. There was Big and Little Italy, Greek Town, the Cabbage Patch and Chicken Village (Czech), Warszawa (Polish), and Chinatown. Remnants of some of those neighborhoods can still be found, and often that's also where there are still many stores and little hole-in-the-wall restaurants that offer foods unlike anything to be found on the shelves of an ordinary supermarket or under a heat lamp at a drive-thru. But special shops and restaurants are located in newer suburbs and shopping malls, too.

That means this book is also a kind of road map, showing you how to escape from the confines of your usual stomping grounds and explore parts of the city and the surrounding communities you may know little about or rarely have occasion to visit.

How the Restaurants and Markets were Chosen

My criteria for choosing what to include were ethnicity, authenticity, and personal recommendations from those who know the food best. This is a book with a theme, not a yellow pages, and that means there are many restaurants that I didn't include. That's not to say they aren't very good, but they didn't fit my definition. If I've missed a place you feel should be included, use the form at the back to tell me about it so I can check it out and possibly add it to the next edition.

There are no national chains in this guide, no places that offer only one or two ethnically inspired dishes, or places that feature what's lately been described as "fusion cuisine" (but which I define as blue corn pasta in peanut salsa with a side of herbed collard greens). I was looking for traditional food made with integrity and respect for the eating style of the culture from which it springs. I stretched my definition of ethnic as far as I could comfortably go, in an effort to include places that honor the foods, flavors, and preparation techniques of a particular geographic region or cultural group.

I didn't pass judgement on the restaurants I've included, or rate them with stars. That's for you to do, though I have to admit that many times I decided that there really was no reason for me to ever cook again. I wanted to offer information, not evaluations, and encourage readers to investigate and experiment. That's what I did, and I had a wonderful time; so did the all the folks who helped me. We met many fine people who are proud of where they come from, determined to link the best from their past with the present, and eager to share their customs and traditions. Hearing their stories and tasting their distinctive cuisines has been a process of building bridges, making connections, and opening doors.

Many of these cuisines almost qualify as endangered species. The "Americanization" of eating, with its emphasis on fast foods, continues to make inroads into traditional practices and lifestyles in Cleveland and around the world. Recognizing the value of Cleveland's ethnic restaurants and markets and patronizing these establishments is a way to preserve them and insure that the unique contribution each makes to the community will continue to nourish us.

"Through its food," Salvador Gonzalez, owner of Cleveland's Mexican Folkarte Gallery, told me, "you can come to know the culture of any country." *Cleveland Ethnic Eats* is an invitation to participate in that fascinating cultural exploration, a journey around the world that can begin and end in northeast Ohio.

Using This Book

How This Book is Organized

This book is divided into eight broad geographic regions. I've established areas that reflect physical proximity and kitchen commonalities rather than political affiliations or national borders. Within each of those chapters, ethnic groups are listed alphabetically. For each group, there is a section of restaurants and another of stores introduced with information about the specific ingredients that define the cuisine of that country or culture. In her cookbook, *All Around the World*, author Sheila Lukins likens these staples and seasonings to a painter's palette, with each cuisine having its own collection of foods and flavorings that set it apart from all others. Of course, these tend to be general descriptions, and there are always distinctive regional differences within every country.

The listings themselves go beyond just names, addresses, and telephone numbers. They'll tell you about parking, identify landmarks that make places easier to locate, and let you know when to call ahead for reservations and special orders. The market information makes rare and hard-to-find ingredients accessible, and points the way to one-of-a-kind treats like homemade meat pies and handmade dumplings. The restaurant information lets you know what sort of dress is appropriate, whether or not it's a good spot to bring the kids, and explains what goes into some of the foods featured on the menu. Using the descriptions you can pick out a fancy, sophisticated place that serves bouillabaisse (a Mediterranean fish soup), an inexpensive little neighborhood hang-out that has huevos rancheros (Mexican eggs), or a bar *cum* restaurant that offers moussaka (Greek eggplant) along with late night jazz.

Some of the stores are big, brightly lit, and modern. Some are quaint, with a charming old-world ambience. Others are irritatingly small, or inconveniently hidden away on back streets, but they're open seven days a week and you're sure to find that jar of kimchi (pickled cabbage), essential for the Korean meal you want to prepare.

The same is true of the restaurants. A few may be well known to the general public and even qualify as trendy, but many serve mostly their own countrymen and a group of loyal fans who think of them as their own special secret "find." There are places that seat 120 and others that squeeze seven tables and a kitchen into a space not much bigger than the average living room. At one end of the spectrum are down-and-dirty joints where the linoleum is cracked and pinball machines provide the only background music; at the other, elegant, stylish dining rooms with well-dressed servers who bring artfully arranged food to your linen-covered table. And there is every variation in between. Some restaurants are located in neighborhoods that diners who come from beyond its borders might not consider the best. Many are unpretentious places, where a dollar goes a long way and the food makes you feel well fed and satisfied. Whether you're looking for upscale or downscale, this book is meant to help you find what you want.

Use it to figure out just how far you'd have to go in order to sample Vietnamese bun ga sao (stir fried chicken) or see what's available, ethnically speaking, in Parma (how about vushka, little meat dumplings, at the Ukrainian Kitchen?). Whether you've a hankering for a cannoli and a loaf of crusty fresh-from-the-oven Italian bread or need green bananas and hot Scotch Bonnet peppers for a Caribbean dish you want to prepare, this book can help you find them.

If you've not been much of an eating adventurer, preferring steak and an iceberg lettuce salad, the predictability of a food franchise, or the familiarity of your own part of town, then this book can help you feel comfortable getting started as you venture out into the frontiers of new taste sensations. It's full of the kind of information that makes everybody an insider. And who knows, new places may soon become your old favorites.

What to Wear? Atmosphere and Attire

Atmosphere is one of the categories of information included in these restaurant listings. The term refers both to the style of dress that seems to be the general rule at a restaurant and to the decor and tone of the place. These are intimately connected: how the patrons dress is part of every dining room's particular ambience. Tank tops and shorts set one kind of mood; suits and ties, another. And if you know how people dress when they go to a particular restaurant, you'll have some idea of what to expect from the surroundings.

Different regions of this country have different standards. Though on the West Coast informality may be the ultimate style—and while there is no denying that we're becoming a dress-down society in general—around Cleveland tradition still reigns supreme. Here, "dressing up" has never meant a jacket with jeans.

In order to establish guidelines that would be useful to Cleveland-area restaurant-goers, I solicited advice from our town's own fashion maven, Janet McCue of *The Plain Dealer*. With her help, I've created a four-step scale that reflects local attitudes and standards for attire: Relaxed, Casual, Dressy, and Formal.

(You may notice below that I have tended to define attire in terms of men's clothing. Please don't read into this any statements about politics or power. It's just a simpler way to make things clear. "Men," explains McCue, "have so few options that it's easier and less confusing to use their clothes as a guideline for both genders.")

Relaxed, for the purposes of this book, means almost anything goes, short of being barefoot and shirtless. Neither the management nor the other diners have any expectations you must meet. On the night I visited one such eatery, the couple ahead of me were dressed in warm-up suits; the woman behind me was wrapped in an ankle-length fur coat. The criterion to go by is what makes you comfortable—knowing, in advance, that it's next to impossible to be underdressed.

Casual is one step up. Comfort is still the aim and informality the norm, but the unspoken, unwritten code definitely calls for better than just a no-holes, clean-clothes style. Picture the look in terms of upscale play attire—what folks in the trendy mail-order catalogs and magazine ads wear when they're having fun. You can get away with wearing a t-shirt, but it shouldn't sport stains, brand names, or lewd remarks. Turtlenecks, sweaters, and jeans are all acceptable, but you'd still fit in if you chose to spruce up just a bit.

Dressy is what was once commonly called business attire and implies a moderate level of formality. It's an office look: shirts with collars, pressed slacks, and sport jackets. Ties are optional. In times past I think this look was described as "nice," as in your mother saying "Why don't you change into something nice?" or "Don't you have anything nicer than that?" before you went out on a date.

Formal indicates that coat and tie are required or strongly suggested. This means that male and female patrons dress up and dress well when they dine at such establishments, moving beyond looking merely nice to looking very nice. "The 'Tie required or suggested' criteria," says McCue, "is a good take-off point for women; they know how to choose a corresponding outfit, whether it's a dress or trousers and a silk blouse, from among the many different kinds of clothes available to them."

Prices

I've used a scale of one to five dollar signs to indicate the relative cost of an average meal at each of the restaurants:

$$$$$	much lower than average
$$$$$	slightly lower than average
$$$$$	about average
$$$$$	slightly higher than average
$$$$$	much higher than average

Obviously, one person's "average meal" varies from another's— even at the same restaurant—depending on what and how much you order. To give a reasonable standard, though, I based my rating on the average dinner entree price from each restaurant's standard menu. I also considered other factors, such as whether entrees come with appetizer, or whether it's the kind of place that's intended for for a lavish multi-course meal rather than a simple sit-down dinner.

Spelling

Throughout the listings, you may notice many different spellings for the same word. That's the nature of transliteration. There's often more than one way to create the English equivalent of a foreign word. In general, I took my cues from the people I spoke with. So one store owner suggested I write "filo" dough while another spelled it out for me as "phyllo," and when I checked, I found both are used in other books. I also adopted a policy of matching my spellings to those that appear on the menu of each establishment I was writing about, except where there were obvious English misspellings.

Location

I've divided Greater Cleveland roughly into seven geographic areas: Downtown, Near West Side, Far West Side, Near East Side, Far East Side, Southeast, and Southwest. This is to help you tell from a glance at the listings approximately where a restaurant or market is located

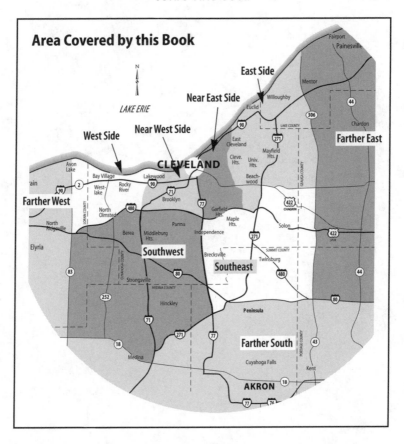

relative to where you live or plan to visit. The map above shows how these areas are divided. An area is indicated at the top right of each restaurant and market listing. Below it are listed specific city and street address information, as well as phone numbers so you can call for directions.

Don't Forget to Call Ahead!
Keep in mind that although the information is as accurate and up-to-date as possible, things can and will change. Hours don't always stay the same, policies and practices are altered, businesses come and go, and new owners often have new ideas.

It is *always* best to call first.

CLEVELAND
Ethnic
Eats

CHAPTER 1

Pacific Rim

THE REGION KNOWN AS THE PACIFIC RIM includes the vast and varied terrain of more than 10 different Far Eastern countries. The Cleveland area is home to markets and restaurants from the Rim nations of Cambodia, China, Japan, Korea, the Philippines, Thailand, and Vietnam.

The Chinese were the first Asian group to come to Cleveland, and their numbers began to grow significantly in the late 1800s. In its early days, Cleveland's Chinese community was made up primarily of immigrants from the southern Cantonese province of Guangdong who came by way of the West Coast. Later it came to include people from northern and central China, Hong Kong, and Taiwan. Cleveland's Chinatown, along Rockwell Avenue between 24th and 21st streets, was once densely populated with immigrants. Though small by the standards of New York or San Francisco, it is nonetheless the historical heart of the community. Now Chinese live in all parts of Greater Cleveland, but the recent $2.3 million renovation of an old warehouse into Asia Plaza on Payne created a modern, bustling Asian shopping and dining center that is a new hub for the old neighborhood.

The Organization of Chinese Americans of Greater Cleveland, which networks with other local groups like The Asian Pacific Federation, is a tightly knit association active in cultural education. "We feel that our traditions are very rich," said Frances Namkoong, Organization President, "and they are important to us. Most Chinese Americans live with a foot in both worlds. We continue to be close to our immigrant ancestors and a world view that comes very much from their past. But at the same time, we are Americans."

Ms. Namkoong's sentiments are echoed by others in the Asian community. "We teach our children," said Dr. Sakoo Lee, President of the Korean American Association of Greater Cleveland (which boasts 5,000 members), "that their roots are in Korea but their home is in Cleveland."

Koreans did not become a visible presence here until the 1970s, when U.S. immigration quotas changed. According to Dr. Lee (and much to my surprise), one reason Koreans like Cleveland is our four-season climate, which is similar to, though slightly colder than, their homeland. But there's more to their attraction than weather.

"This city and the surrounding suburbs," said Dr. Lee, a physician with a family practice in Westlake, "are truly a multi-cultural melting pot. Every nationality group is unique with something to contribute. I've traveled in many other parts of the country, and Cleveland is one of those rare places where there's an understanding of that. Here, we can all live together, keeping what's best from our own heritage while becoming part of the community."

That receptivity and understanding was part of what helped the Japanese feel welcome in Cleveland after World War II. Forcibly removed from West Coast communities, they were encouraged to resettle here by the War Relocation Authority, and their numbers peaked in 1946. Filipinos, who settled here after 1950, make up another small subset of the Asian community. Like their Chinese and Japanese counterparts, many are professionals in the fields of medicine and technology. A large number of students from all three countries have come in recent years to take advantage of the area's colleges, medical schools and teaching hospitals, and industrial research facilities. According to Sunthorn Phetcharat, owner of the Thai Kitchen in Lakewood, there are not many people from Thailand living in Cleveland, and their stories would have to be told one by one, for they have come as individuals and not a group.

Most Cambodians and Vietnamese began to arrive in Cleveland after 1970, driven to emigrate by war and its devastating aftermath. "My family is lucky," explained Liem Nguyen, a former South Vietnamese Army captain and North Vietnamese prisoner now living on the city's West Side. "Once again we have a bright future. This is a chance to start a new life. We are willing to work very hard, night and day. We want to show our thanks and prove to Cleveland that we have much to give."

One of the things each of these ethnic groups has to give is its singular cuisine. Though influenced by geographic neighbors, each country possesses its own distinctive approach to food.

Chinese cooking represents one of the oldest continuing culinary traditions in the world. It is also the Asian cuisine most familiar to Americans. Won Kee opened Cleveland's first Chinese restaurant, on Ontario, before 1900; a second was added soon after on the west side of Public Square. Our taste for Chinese food has expanded in recent years beyond the now-familiar Cantonese and Mandarin to include the spicy styles of Szechuan and Hunan cooking. In Cleveland, diners can also sample the cuisine of the north, which unexpectedly makes use of wheat products—even bread, and the unique flavors of Taiwanese cooking, which blends a variety of Chinese regional styles with the traditional dishes of this tropical island. Chinese New Year, celebrated in February, is a great opportunity to sample a wide variety of special traditional foods.

Korean food tends to be spicy, though not necessarily fiery hot. Kimchee appears on the table at every meal. It is a peppery, piquant condiment made primarily from pickled cabbage. Chili powder, vinegar, fermented bean pastes, and sesame seeds are important ingredients in the Korean kitchen. Bounded on three sides by water, Koreans have incorporated a wide variety of fish and seafood into their diet, though they also have a national enthusiasm for beef, an appreciation said to have been left behind by the invading Mongol hordes.

Japanese cooking, too, is dominated by seafood, much of it eaten raw and accompanied by varieties of pickles and pungent condiments like momiji oroshi, made from grated white radish with red chilies, or wasabi, a horseradish paste so strong that an overly large bite can bring on tears and provide instant cleansing of the sinuses. Classical Japanese cuisine shows virtually no signs of outside influences, perhaps because the country imposed a ban on foreigners from 1640 to 1868.

The same cannot be said for the cooking styles of Vietnam, Cambodia, and the Philippines. All bear the stamp of European colonial incursions into both their territory and their traditional ways of life. So Philippine food has a decidedly Spanish twist, and one of the most characteristic dishes, a chicken-and-pork stew called adobo, is reminiscent of Mexican cookery, which shares this Spanish persuasion.

The Vietnamese got a taste from the French, who first came there in the 16th century, for sweetened milky coffee and also sausages, which they make from both meat and fish. Indian traders brought curry, used primarily by the south Vietnamese, and the Buddhist influence means there are many vegetarian dishes. Traditional cooking uses raw greens, and food is often served on crisp lettuce leaves.

Thailand, though inspired by its culinary neighbors, China, India, Burma, and Laos, was never colonized, so its food has no western leanings. Thai cooks make good use of all the tropical fruits and vegetables that grow throughout the country in abundance, and season with fresh herbs like lemon grass, green coriander, lime leaves, mint, and oriental basils. They make liberal use of coconut milk, chili peppers, peanuts, and sesame seeds. These same flavorings are used both by the Vietnamese and the Cambodians.

Soy is the salty condiment favored by the Chinese and Japanese; a similar effect is achieved by other Southeast Asian cooks through the use of a fermented fish sauce. Use of garlic, ginger, scallions, and hot capsicums (peppers) is universal, but cooks in each country, as well as in different regions, use them in quite different ways, and the results vary widely. Koreans, for example, often add the garlic at the end of cooking or eat it raw so that it keeps its bite.

Rice, of course, is an omnipresent staple. The Thai invitation to a meal translates as "Come and eat rice," while an age-old Chinese greeting is "Have you eaten rice yet?" All Asian cuisines rely on very fresh, seasonal foods and strive to retain rather than mask the natural flavors of each ingredient.

Eating styles throughout the Pacific Rim are very light and healthy. People eat few dairy products, meat in small quantities, and use only vegetable and bean oils. Rich desserts are the exception rather than the rule.

Technique and presentation are defining principles for all these Asian cuisines. Actual cooking methods tend to be quick and simple, reflecting the fact that food is eaten with chopsticks or spoons and so must be sliced and chopped into small pieces.

Delicate flavors come from painstaking preparation, with great attention to detail, and subtly seasoned sauces. The Chinese and the Japanese say that every dish must be made with four elements in mind: color, fragrance, flavor, and shape. Korean and Chinese cooks strive for balance and harmony among what they call the five basic flavors: sweet, sour, hot, tart, and salty. The equation for Thai cuisine is only slightly different: sweetness, sourness, saltiness, hotness, nuttiness, and bitterness.

We have as yet no Filipino restaurants here, though there are a couple of markets that carry ingredients for home cooking. There's only one Cambodian restaurant and a handful of Thai and Vietnamese ones. There are now a few Korean restaurants where Clevelanders can sample the food from "The Land of Morning Calm," and a few serving authentic Japanese cuisine. And although the list of Chinese restaurants is long, only a select few serve what Chinese consider to be authentic, rather than American, Chinese food.

Frances Namkoong has some advice for those who want a true Asian eating experience. "Much of the best food is not on the English language menus. But diners can ask for dishes they've heard about, enjoyed elsewhere, or things they notice other non-American people eating. A restaurant would feel honored if guests request recommendations from the kitchen."

RESTAURANTS

CAMBODIAN

PHNOM PENH RESTAURANT

Cleveland	Near West Side
13124 Lorain Ave.	Casual
☎ 251-0210	$$$$$

Owners and staff here are all natives of Cambodia, and their cuisine is a traditionally strong-flavored one that uses coconuts, peanuts, turmeric, and spices unfamiliar to Americans, such as galamga root, Asian basil, lemon grass, and lime leaves. Many dishes, usually stir-fried, are made with noodles (wheat-, rice- and potato-based) and can be ordered mild, medium, or spicy hot. Plenty of options for vegetarians. Servers speak English and will help diners find their way around the menu, which provides simple English-language explanations of each of the 111 dishes. They look similar to the Chinese cooking Ohioans are more familiar with, but the sauces and seasonings render the taste quite different. This is the only Cambodian restaurant in the region, and loyal customers come back regularly from as far away as Toledo. One enthusiast insists the Khmer shrimp and seafood rice soup is as effective as "Jewish penicillin" (chicken soup). With room for about 50 patrons, this small place does a large lunch business and caters to a late-night dinner crowd of food adventurers. It's small, with plain and simple decor, and blends in so well with the other store fronts on the street that it's easy to miss when driving by. Plenty of on-street parking in the neighborhood.

▲

Hours: Tue–Thu 11 a.m.–9:30 p.m., Fri 11 a.m.–10 p.m., Sat 11 a.m.–11 p.m., Sun 3–9 p.m.; closed Mon ■ Reservations taken, recommended on weekends for groups of 4 or more ■ Cash only ■ Bar: none ■ Takeout ■ & Full access ■ No smoking

CAMBODIAN, SEE ALSO:
Dong Duong Indochina Grocery (Pacific Rim: Asian Mix)

CHINESE

BO LOONG

Cleveland	Near East Side
3922 St. Clair Ave.	Casual
☎ 391-3113	$$$$$

This place is big, seating 400, and the first impression is of something between a cafeteria and a university dining hall with a funky red-and-gold oriental motif. But the fact that the decor lacks a slick look (part of its unique charm) does not keep this restaurant from being a hands-down favorite among Cleveland's Chinese families, and their regular, visible presence is a measure of the authentic quality of the food. Management is especially proud of the dim sum, a large selection of sweet and savory pastries, buns, and dumplings that can be ordered individually as an appetizer or in combination to create an entire meal. The number of choices is unequaled anywhere else in town. While many of the other dishes on the menu will be familiar, reflecting a variety of regional cuisines, others cater to a more Asian palate and feature such unusual ingredients as squid, chicken feet, beef tripe, and quail eggs. This is a great place, if you're feeling experimental, to put the menu aside, point to what's being eaten at another table, and have a tasting adventure by saying, "I'll have some of that." Also a great place for a late-night visit.

▲

Hours: daily 10 a.m.–2 a.m. ■ Reservations taken, recommended for 6 or more ■ MC, VS, AX, checks accepted ■ Bar: beer, wine, liquor ■ Takeout ■ 占 Full access ■ Non-smoking section

FOO DO

Cleveland   Near East Side
3101 Euclid Ave.   Casual
☎ 881-9600 $$$$$

Located next door to Channel 5, at street level, in a large office build-ing, Foo Do serves a primarily American crowd at lunch but a decid-edly Chinese one evenings and weekends. Owner David Tsang tries to accommodate both groups: daily specials are written in Chinese and posted on the walls, but he and his staff are always willing to translate for those who are unable to decipher the handsome calligraphy. The menu, which is in English, features Cantonese and Szechuan dishes. At one end of the restaurant, next to the fish tank, is a state-of-the-art large-screen TV that can be turned on for big sporting events, special shows, or Chinese-language videos. Most tables are set up for four, and there is room for about 120 diners. Metered on-street parking.

▲

Hours: daily 11 a.m.–11 p.m. ■ Reservations taken ■ MC, VS, AX, Dis accepted ■ Bar: beer, wine, liquor ■ Takeout ■ Non-smoking section

HUNAN COVENTRY

Cleveland Heights   East Side
1800 Coventry Rd.   Casual
☎ 371-0777 $$$$$

A wall of large windows lets in plenty of light and looks out onto
Coventry Road, its new multistory parking garage, and into the equally
large windows of the Food Co Op across the street. The decor is fash-
ionably elegant, though patrons—an eclectic crowd of every age—are
as likely to dress in sweaters as suits. Decor has lovely details: framed
Asian flower prints, a glass wall sandblasted in a flower motif to separate entrance from dining area, and indirect light from modern wall-
mounted sconces. Rich-looking warm-colored wood, grey carpeting,
and polished brass accent white walls and table linens. The food looks
elegant too, often garnished with flowers and butterflies beautifully
sculpted from a simple radish or wedges of tomato. The menu features
a large selection of classic dishes, both Hunan spicy and not, and there
are also some unexpected offerings tucked among the lo meins, kung
poa's, and moo shu's: mussels in spicy garlic sauce, Shanghai chicken
with honey walnuts, Mandarin noodles with sesame sauce, and lamb
Beijing-style with scallions. Plentiful options for vegetarian diners.
Portions are generous, service is attentive, and at the end of meal you
get not only a fortune cookie but a warm, individually wrapped, dis-
posable cloth for freshening hands and face. A good place to eat, visit,
and, celebrate.

▲

Hours: Tue–Thu 11:30 a.m.–9:45 p.m., Fri 11:30 a.m.–10:45 p.m., Sat noon–10:45 p.m.,
Sun 4–8:45 p.m.; closed Mon ▪ Reservations taken, for parties of 6 or more only ▪
MC, VS, AX, Dis accepted ▪ Bar: beer, wine, liquor ▪ Takeout ▪ ♿ Full access ▪
Non-smoking section

KHAN'S CUISINE

North Olmsted   West Side
23135 Lorain Rd.   Casual
☎ 777-2206 $$$$$

The exterior, complete with golden lions growling at the entrance and
brightly painted red trim, displays the elaborate and intricate Chinese-
inspired style of decoration known as chinoiserie. The interior, however, is leftover steakhouse decor. It's comfortable, if not consistent,
casual, and spacious. The real draw here is not ambience, anyway, but
food. No other place in this area prepares Mongolian barbecue. The
story goes that whenever Genghis Khan's westward moving hordes
won a battle, the soldiers celebrated by grilling hunks of beef and mutton on their heavy metal shields over huge open fires. Lacking hordes,
shields, and bonfires, the Cleveland version of this northern Chinese

specialty is tamer, but nonetheless unusual. At the rear of the dining room a large, curved buffet encircles a Mongolian firebox. Choosing from a variety of meats, seafood, and vegetables, diners create their own mix. The chef grills it to order. It's seasoned with sauces that diners can also compose themselves by combining soy, cooking wine, ginger juice, sugar water, sesame oil, minced garlic, and chili pepper. If you're bold you can experiment freely. Otherwise, follow the chef's recommendation of one spoonful of each or opt for his own special secret mix. The menu also includes a wide selection of standard Chinese dishes, including many for vegetarians, and some unusual house specialties such as triple sizzling rice (made with rice cakes, shellfish, chicken, and vegetables), hot and spicy beef with scallops, and hunan prawns with ginger. Plenty of convenient parking in a lot that surrounds this freestanding building.

▲
Hours: daily 11:30 a.m.–10 p.m. ▪ Reservations taken ▪ MC, VS, AX accepted ▪ Bar: beer, wine, liquor ▪ Takeout ▪ ♿ Full access ▪ Non-smoking section

LI WAH

Cleveland   Near East Side
2999 Payne/Asia Plaza   Dressy
☎ 696-6556 $$$$$

Chinese people eat here because they can get dishes they aren't likely to find on any other local restaurant menu: duck eggs with ginger, shredded chicken with jellyfish, pan-fried noodles with abalone, and dim sum that includes beef tripe, chicken feet, sticky rice with lotus leaf, and turnip cakes. Manager Alan Pon insists his food is the most authentic to be found between New York and Chicago. But the spacious restaurant, which can seat up to 400, attracts people of every ethnicity because, in addition to an extensive selection of flavorful Chinese dishes, the setting is attractive, comfortable, and contemporary, and service is attentive and efficient. It's a place for dining out—not just chowing down, an atmosphere that's conducive to good conversation, celebration, and gracious eating. Round tables for 10 or 12 with lazy Susans in the center are perfect for big groups. There's usually a sizable business lunch crowd. The location, in the newly renovated Asia Plaza, is convenient for folks who work downtown. Dim sum, which roughly translates as "a little bit of whatever your heart desires," is available daily until 3:00 PM, and the selection, made from carts wheeled up to your table, is sizable. On Saturday and Sunday when the clientele is mostly Chinese, there are even more choices. One small detail, noteworthy because it's so rare, important if you happen to have a baby with you, and representative of an unusual level of consideration for patrons: there's a diaper changing station in the ladies' room. (Of course, in a perfect world, there'd be one in the men's room, too). In February, when the Chinese New Year is celebrated, there is a most unusual banquet menu; tickets for this event should be purchased in advance.

▲
Hours: daily Mon–10 a.m.–2 a.m. ▪ Reservations taken, recommended for large groups of 10 or more ▪ MC, VS, AX accepted ▪ Bar: beer, wine, liquor ▪ Takeout ▪ ⅙ Full access ▪ Non-smoking section

LU CUISINE
Cleveland   Downtown
1228 Euclid, at Playhouse Square   Formal
☎ 241-8488 $$$$$

Some people rave about the singular menu, which features the traditional cuisine of China's Shandong Province, often described as the mother of all other regional styles. Others are captivated by the stunning decor—all granite, brushed stainless steel, and rosewood elegance with museum-quality artwork and artifacts displayed in illuminated showcases recessed into the walls. Still others are most impressed by the stunningly beautiful presentations of food meant to engage sight, smell, and feel, as well as taste. All elements conspire to offer a most unusual dining experience, an ideal venue for a celebration or a special event. Many Chinese families reserve the facilities for banquets and family feasts. The name of the restaurant is also the name of the cooking style, which emphasizes the use of fresh ingredients and subtle, natural flavors. No MSG is ever used, in any dish. Because wheat has long been grown in the Shandong Province, noodles and breads are an authentic part of the cuisine; flower bread (hua juan) and family cake (jiachang bing) are unique and not to be missed. The wine list is extensive and offers suggestions for matching vintages with menu selections. The restaurant is large. The long bar is designed so that no matter where you sit, you can see and talk to anyone else seated there. The main dining area can accommodate 400, but a movable wall can scale the space down as needed. There's a second, smaller dining area on another level, and rooms for private parties. Parking, which must be paid for, is available in the attached Halle Building garage, or across the street in the AMPCO lot, where it is complimentary after 5:00 p.m.

▲
Hours: Lunch Mon–Fri 11:30 a.m.–2 p.m.; Dinner Tue–Thu 5–8 p.m., Fri & Sat 5–9 p.m.; closed between Lunch & Dinner; closed Sun ▪ Reservations taken, recommended ▪ MC, VS, AX, Dis accepted ▪ Bar: beer, wine, liquor ▪ Takeout ▪ ⅙ Full access ▪ Not recommended for children ▪ Non-smoking section

SUN LUCK GARDEN

Cleveland Heights	East Side
1901 S.Taylor Rd.	Casual
☎ 397-7676	$$$$$

Let go of all preconceptions about what a Chinese restaurant is supposed to be before you walk in the door. Owner Annie Chiu has created a brilliant fusion of East and West, old and new. Daily specials highlight traditional ingredients and techniques in unlikely contemporary combinations, such as mussels in a spicy red garlic-laced broth with noodles. The decor reflects the blend. Original paintings by a local artist incorporate ancient Chinese mythological themes in a contemporary motif. Chiu serves special dishes rarely prepared in this country, never scrimping on rare or costly ingredients. Even familiar items like hot and sour soup or shan tan beef take on a new and intriguing identity here. Much of what she knows, Chiu learned by studying with master chefs in China, apprenticeships arranged by her mother's brother, who is a renowned chef and teacher there. And hers is the only Chinese restaurant around that offers extraordinary desserts. There's plum cheesecake daily and, if you're lucky, you'll visit on a day she had the urge to whip up something more unusual like pistachio mousse or chocolate pecan tarts. "People come here, before they know us," she said, "expecting the Chinese food they've eaten elsewhere. They quickly realize this is a place where they can taste something quite different than the usual." Be sure to get on Chiu's mailing list. Periodically throughout the year she hosts special events, such as a unique Chinese English High Tea. The restaurant is located at the end of a strip mall; ample parking in front.

▲

Hours: Tue–Thu 11:30 a.m.–10 p.m., Fri & Sat 11:30 a.m.–11 p.m., Sun 3–9 p.m.; closed Mon ▪ Reservations taken, recommended on weekends and at all times for groups of 5 or more ▪ MC, VS, Dis accepted ▪ Bar: beer, wine ▪ Takeout ▪ ᕦ Full access ▪ No smoking

SZECHWAN GARDEN

Lakewood	West Side
13800 Detroit Ave.	Casual
☎ 226-1987	$$$$$

Newcomers may be surprised to find that behind the unimpressive exterior of this little place located in an older neighborhood of small apartment buildings, single family homes, and storefronts, is an exceptional restaurant. Once inside, patrons encounter booths and tables (seating about 60) set with peaked cloth napkins, expert service, and authentic regional Chinese dishes. A husband-and-wife team owns the restaurant and runs the kitchen where they turn out house specialties including Hunan lobster, orange chicken, and Szechwan duck. Other interesting items on the menu are egg flower soup; a spicy pork dish with vegetables in a dark, pungent sauce; and Lake Tung Ting shrimp (made with beaten egg whites). The kitchen is willing to adjust the spiciness according to your preference for mild, medium, or hot. The atmosphere is warm and hospitable, and there's a steady flow of patrons at all hours, both for eat-in and takeout. Plenty of parking.

▲
Hours: Lunch Mon–Thu 11:30 a.m.–2:30 p.m., Fri & Sat 11:30 a.m.–2:30 p.m.; Dinner 4:30–9:30 p.m., Fri & Sat 4:30–10:30 p.m., Sun 4:30–9:30 p.m.; closed between Lunch & Dinner ■ Reservations taken, recommended on weekends ■ MC, VS, AX accepted ■ Bar: beer, wine, liquor ■ Takeout ■ ⅙ Full access ■ Non-smoking section

TAIPEI

Cleveland Heights   East Side
1946 Lee Rd.   Casual
☎ 321-6838 $$$$$

This restaurant is the only one in the Cleveland area to prepare Taiwanese cuisine—light, sweet food different from all other Asian fare and with an emphasis on shrimp and fruit. The eight-page menu also includes a large and interesting selection of spicy Szechuan and Hunan dishes, vegetarian dishes, and classic northern and southern treatments of pork, chicken, beef, and seafood. There are 12 different soups, and among the appetizers two are unique: hand-rolled temaki (cones of crisp dried seaweed filled with vegetables and the optional addition of shrimp that arrive at the table like a beautiful bouquet), and almond-crusted shrimp skewered on a piece of sugar cane. Unusual for a Chinese restaurant, Taipei has an extensive wine list, with detailed descriptions, that includes a French white specially blended to complement Asian food. The decor has a quiet elegance that incorporates traditional Chinese motifs with a contemporary look. The restaurant has its own free parking lot on the corner of Lee Road and East Overlook.

▲
Hours: Mon–Thu 11:30 a.m.–10 p.m., Fri 11:30 a.m.–11 p.m., Sat Noon–11 p.m., Sun Noon–9 p.m. ■ Reservations taken, recommended weekends ■ MC, VS, AX, checks accepted ■ Bar: beer, wine, liquor ■ Takeout ■ ⅙ Full access
■ Non-smoking section

WONG'S HUNAN CUISINE

Cleveland   Near East Side
3211 Payne Ave.   Casual
☎ 696-3811 $$$$$

This may be the only restaurant in town to offer breakfast dim sum, and most of the customers during the morning hours are Chinese—as they are again in the evening, when Chinese-language videos play on the wall-mounted TV. For this clientele, hand-lettered signs in Chinese list menu items. But at lunchtime, downtown businesspeople and college students chowing down at this small, unvarnished eatery, order from a menu printed in English. Although there's little in the way of decoration or comfort here, authentic dishes like dried fried string beans, Szechuan chicken with garlic sauce, and Hong Kong–style barbecued pork, chicken, and duck keep people coming. Wong's is hard to find because it says Che's on the outside of the building—the owner changed the name but not the sign. On-street parking.

▲
Hours: daily 9 a.m.–2 a.m. ■ Reservations not taken ■ MC, VS, Dis accepted
■ Bar: none ■ Takeout

CHINESE, SEE ALSO:
Chinese Village (Vietnamese)
Nam Hing (Vietnamese)

JAPANESE

DAISHIN
Westlake   West Side
24545 Center Ridge Rd.   Casual
☎ 899-9969 $$$$$

As you enter the vestibule, leave behind the surrounding small strip mall and nearby office park. The sound of water in a fountain, trickling over stones, welcomes you. On the other side of the second door is a huge aquarium filled with tropical fish. Beyond that is an airy, spacious, white-walled room with natural blonde wood accents. The room manages to convey both the quiet beauty of Japanese design and a sense of cosmopolitan style. To your left is a seven-seat sushi bar. Raw chunks of octopus, tuna, shrimp, and salmon, colorful as jewels, are artfully displayed in a glass case. A large photo poster shows all the different kinds of sushi. Waitresses wear kimono jackets. Some tables that offer what appears to be traditional on-the-floor seating actually make a concession to Western habits; the tables are close to the floor, but the area under them is open so diners' legs actually hang down as in a chair, and cushions are equipped with rigid backs. The menu features 19 different appetizers, and entrees, which come with miso soup and salad, represent a nice variety of seafood, chicken, and beef, with several options for vegetarians.

▲
Hours: Lunch Mon–Fri 11:30 a.m.–2 p.m.; Dinner Mon–Fri 5–10 p.m., Sat 4:30–10:30 p.m.; closed between lunch & dinner; closed Sun ■ Reservations taken, recommended
■ MC, VS, AX, Dis accepted ■ Bar: beer ■ Takeout ■ ⅙ Full access
■ Non-smoking section

OTANI

Mayfield Heights
1625 Mayfield Rd. (Golden Gate Plaza)
☎ 442-7098

East Side
Dressy
$$$$$

Two dining areas are handsomely decorated with a mixture of traditional and contemporary Japanese artwork, plants, and lantern lights. The large rooms are divided into intimate spaces by partitions and subdued lighting, and guests can choose to be seated at regular tables or on low tables surrounded by cushions. There's also counter service at the sushi bar. (Sushi is small pieces of raw fish such as tuna, shrimp, crab, octopus, or fluke on top of a spoonful of rice.) Other "raw" choices include sashimi (fish without rice) and maki (rice and fish or vegetables wrapped in seaweed); the restaurant has a large selection of all three. The presentation is a feast for the eyes. If you're not in the mood for raw fish (or never will be), you can still eat here; choose teriyaki steak, tempura vegetables (batter dipped and deep fried), or ginger chicken. For special occasions, tableside cooking is popular; Shabu Shabu is a beef and vegetable dish diners cook themselves, one bite at a time. In addition to Japanese beer, hot sake, plum wine, and sakura (a non-carbonated Japanese soft drink) are available. A nice setting for a celebration.

▲

Hours: Lunch Mon–Thu 11:30 a.m.–2 p.m., Fri & Sat 11:30 a.m.–2 p.m.; Dinner Mon–Thu 5–10 p.m., Fri & Sat 5–11 p.m., Sun 4:30–9 p.m.; closed between Lunch & Dinner
▪ Reservations taken, recommended on weekends ▪ MC, VS, AX, Dis accepted
▪ Bar: beer, wine, liquor ▪ Takeout ▪ &. Full access ▪ Non-smoking section

SHINANO JAPANESE RESTAURANT

Richmond Heights
5222 Wilson Mills Rd.
☎ 473-2345

East Side
Casual
$$$$$

Natural wood, wallpaper with a bamboo motif, and paper lanterns and screens work together to create a Japanese ambience. A 15-seat sushi bar runs the length of one wall, and behind the chefs, who work with speed and grace, is a mural of white cranes and blue water on a field of gold. The restaurant is frequented by Japanese students and business-people, which may account for the fact that tables are set not with forks but with chopsticks. Silverware is available on request. Warm wet cloths for wiping hands and face come to the table in little wooden cradles before the food. There's a lunchtime buffet that includes a wide variety of traditional dishes such as tempura, sushi, soba (buckwheat) noodles, and fried tofu. The bento box, a compartmentalized tray, offers an artful, visuallly appealing presentation plus a chance to sample a variety of meat, seafood, and vegetable dishes. There are also traditional hot pots, one-pot meals that you can cook at your table or have prepared in the kitchen. Sushi can be ordered a la carte in 44 variations, or as special combination plates. Japanese beers and a number of different brands of sake, served hot and cold, are available. The restaurant is located in the Hilltop Plaza strip, across from Richmond Mall. Packaged Japanese sweets, cookies, and crackers are for sale at the register.

▲
Hours: Lunch Mon–Fri 11:30 a.m.–2 p.m.; Dinner Mon–Thu 5:30–10 p.m., Fri & Sat 5:30–10:30 p.m., Sun (May–Sept) 5:30–10 p.m., (Oct–Apr) 4:30–9 p.m.; closed between Lunch & Dinner ▪ Reservations taken, recommended on weekends ▪ MC, VS, AX, Dis accepted ▪ Bar: beer, wine ▪ Takeout ▪ ⅚ Full access ▪ Non-smoking section

SHUHEI JAPANESE CUISINE

Beachwood
23360 Chagrin Blvd.
☎ 464-1720

East Side
Casual
$$$$$

Both atmosphere and food here are classically Japanese. The setting is serene, a calm and relaxing environment in which to sample raw fish from the sushi bar or a traditional nabe mono (a hot pot of noodles and vegetables, with optional meat or fish, in a seasoned broth). There's a menu in Japanese for those who can read it, but the English version is not intimidating for the less-experienced, with detailed descriptions of every dish. The menu is extensive: 30 appetizers, 37 entrees, plus daily specials. Portions are ample, and each dinner entree comes with a bowl of miso (a richly flavored soup made from fermented soybeans) and a choice of either a western or a Japanese salad. All the female servers are dressed in beautiful traditional costumes. They watch over diners with great care and attention, quickly removing empty plates and supplying the chopstick-challenged with silverware. Guests of all ages will be appropriately dressed in anything from jeans to a business suit. Located in the back of an office building that's not well lit after dark, the entrance, actually off Green Road, isn't easy to find.

▲
Hours: Lunch Mon–Sat 11:30 a.m.–2:30 p.m.; Dinner Mon–Thu 5:30–10 p.m., Fri & Sat 5:30–11 p.m., Sun 5–9 p.m. ▪ Reservations taken, recommended ▪ MC, VS, AX, Dis accepted ▪ Bar: beer, wine, liquor ▪ Takeout ▪ ⅚ Full access ▪ Mostly non-smoking; only 4 tables for smokers

KOREA HOUSE

Cleveland   Near East Side
3700 Superior Ave.   Casual
☎ 431-0462 $$$$$

From the outside, this place looks more like a factory than a restaurant. And in fact, it is a commercial building, surrounded by aging manufacturing and commercial spaces, that's been remodeled from within. Enter from a side door that opens into the parking lot and you'll find pristine white walls and table linens, standing rice paper and latticework screens, stylized lanterns, silk flowers, and a quiet, spare atmosphere of Asian charm. Korean food is not at all similar to Chinese food, so diners here should expect a very different eating experience. You'll encounter pot stews, ingredients like octopus, buckwheat noodles, and kim-chee (a salty, fermented side dish made of cabbage). Many dishes are spicy, but the chef is happy to adjust the heat to your taste, so feel free to order mild, medium, or hot. Two of the most popular menu items for Americans are the Korean-style barbecued chicken and bul gogi jung sik (marinated sliced beef cooked, for two or more, right at the table). The Family Style Dinners are a good way to sample a variety of dishes if you're unfamiliar with Korean cuisine.

▲

Hours: Mon–Thu, 11 a.m.–10 p.m., Fri & Sat, 11 a.m.–11 p.m., Sun, noon–8 p.m. ▪ Reservations taken, recommended for groups of more than 4 ▪ MC, VS, AX, Dis, checks accepted ▪ Bar: beer, wine ▪ Takeout ▪ ⛁ Full access ▪ Non-smoking section

KOREAN GARDENS

Fairview Park   West Side
20505 Lorain Rd.   Casual
☎ 333-4900 $$$$$

What's gray, square, and windowless on the outside, but bright, beautiful, and inviting on the inside? Hyonhee Kim's Korean restaurant. She and her chef, who is also an artist, invested five months in designing and remodeling the interior of this unlikely building, located in front of an old motel. The result is a stunning setting that echoes the lines, colors, and architectural details of a traditional Korean village home— all natural light woods, pastel colors, and latticework and rice-paper screens. Although it can seat 110, the place feels intimate because of how the space is divided. Even the tableware is noteworthy—elegant, lovely, and out of the ordinary. Though this is primarily a Korean restaurant, there is also a full, 98-dish Chinese menu (their pot stickers, for which they make their own dough, are twice the size of other restaurants') and a 10-seat Japanese sushi bar. "Most Clevelanders," said Kim, "are not familiar with Korean food, so we wanted to offer them a choice. We hope that when they come, they'll be tempted to try Korean dishes and discover how wonderful this food can be." The large handsomely designed menu is big enough to be a book, and every dish is well described. The extensive selection of Korean dishes is unique for this area: a spicy fish casserole with mussels, crab, and shrimp in a hot pepper broth; kal bee (short ribs of beef), bulgogi (marinated beef in the chef's 18-ingredient sauce), yum so tahng (goat made with sesame leaf, sesame curd, and garlic), squid and octopus stir fry; and champong noodle soup with oysters and vegetables. If you're new to Korean food, you might want to try their planned Imperial or Popular dinners, which provide an opportunity to sample a variety of dishes. Many choices here for vegetarians.

▲

Hours: Mon–Thu 11:30 a.m.–10 p.m., Fri & Sat 11:30 a.m.–11 p.m.; closed Sun ▪
Reservations taken, recommended, especially on weekends ▪ MC, VS, AX, Dis accepted ▪ Bar: beer, wine, liquor ▪ Takeout ▪ ⅋ Full access ▪ Non-smoking section

SEOUL HOT POT & DE ANGELO'S PIZZA

Cleveland   Near East Side
3709 Payne Ave.   Casual
☎ 881-1221 $$$$$

This small (seats about 40) restaurant is the only place around where one of you can get a meatball sub and the other can order jaeyook bokum (marinated pork) and twikim mandu (fried dumpling). When the owners, who came here from Korea, went into business they thought success was to be found in pizzas and subs, so they bought a downtown pizzeria, kept the name, and learned to cook Italian-style. But their Korean friends, including homesick exchange students, kept asking them to use the restaurant kitchen to make traditional Korean dishes. Ultimately, they decided the best business would be both businesses, so this restaurant menu (which does a good job of explaining what goes into all the dishes unfamiliar to Americans) features an unlikely partnership between Italian and Korean foods. But don't worry, each is prepared and served separately; your pizza won't have mung beans on it and your naeng myun (noodles) won't be served with cheese. Korean entrees are accompanied by a variety of side dishes and condiments, including pickled vegetables, rice, and hot sauce. So those with bold palates can sample gejan bekban (raw crab in hot sauce) or kimbob (a sort of eggroll made with seaweed) and others can go for the tried-and-true spaghetti and meatballs. Some tables have built-in grills for cooking your own meat, Korean-style. Don't be put off by the uninviting exterior; the inside is simple but pleasant.
Other ethnic specialties: Italian

Hours: Mon–Sat 11 a.m.–11 p.m.; closed Sun ▪ Reservations taken, recommended for large groups ▪ MC, VS accepted ▪ Bar: beer ▪ Takeout ▪ Non-smoking section

THAI

BANGKOK GOURMET

Akron   Farther South
1614 Merriman Rd.   Casual
☎ 864-5100 $$$$$

This is a family business, and family members do everything from cooking to serving. The midsized dining room, seating about 150, is decorated with Thai artwork and flowers. It's casual, pleasant, and sub-dued. Seating is mostly at booths, and ornamental partitions create a feeling of intimacy at the tables. Many Asian students studying at Akron University and Kent come here to get a little taste of home, but it's a mixed-age crowd. Even children who generally favor pizza and hot dogs love the chicken satay, the Thai version of barbecue, with bite-size pieces of meat on a stick. Everything is cooked to order, almost any dish on the menu can be prepared vegetarian style, and you can be sure the ingredients are fresh. There are curry dishes, flavorful soups, and seafood, poultry, and meat seasoned with the classic Thai blend of sweet and spicy. This is a good choice for a relaxed social get-together.

Hours: Dinner only, Mon–Thu 5 p.m.–9:30 p.m., Fri & Sat 5–10 p.m., Sun 5–9 p.m. ▪ Reservations taken ▪ MC, VS, AX, Dis accepted ▪ Bar: beer, wine, liquor ▪ Takeout ▪ ♿ Full access ▪ Non-smoking section

PAUL'S SIAM CUISINE

Cleveland Heights   East Side
1918 Lee Rd.   Casual
☎ 371-9575 $$$$$

The new owners (take note of the word "new," as the former owners earned a great deal of bad press) have kept the old chef, who is from Thailand, and his kitchen continues to turn out authentic Thai dishes like chicken coconut soup, dancing squid (it's sauteed with hot pep-pers), la rad pik (fish topped with a hot sauce of chilies and garlic), and duck choo chee (duck in a spicy curry sauce). Diners can create their own dish by choosing ingredients from a list of meats, seafood, tofu, vegetables and fruits, seasonings, and sauces. People are so enthusias-tic about those sauces—Sweet Chili, Volcano, and Peanut—that the restaurant now bottles and sells them. Not everything on the menu is fiery hot—try pad thai noodles, pineapple fried rice, chicken with pine nuts, or beef macadamia. Most entrees can be made vegetarian.

Servers, whose two weeks of training includes tasting all the food, are knowledgeable and can answer your questions. Every dish is lovely to look at and no MSG is used. Tables are wooden, chairs are upholstered and comfortable, and the work of local artists adorns the white stucco walls. Without seeming trendy, this is a popular hangout for a variety of people. On one visit I encountered a group of 13 representing three generations having a celebratory meal complete with presents; at another table a couple with British accents had their heads together; as I left, the executive director of a major museum walked in.

▲
Hours: Tue–Thu 5–10 p.m., Fri & Sat 5–11 p.m., Sun 5–9:30 p.m. ▪ Reservations taken, recommended on weekends and for parties of more than 4 ▪ MC, VS, checks accepted ▪ Bar: beer, wine, liquor ▪ Takeout ▪ Non-smoking section

THAI KITCHEN

Lakewood   West Side
12210 Madison Ave.   Casual
☎ 226-4450 $$$$$

If there's such a thing as Thai kitsch, this is it. Every available surface, including the ceiling, is festooned with the Asian version of bric-a-brac, travel posters, and paper mobiles. But the result is a charmingly tacky backdrop for very interesting and extremely healthy food. There's a good selection of rice and rice noodle dishes, soups, curries, salads, and meat, vegetable, and seafood entrees flavored with the traditional aromatic Thai seasonings of citrus, basil, lemon grass, ginger, and green coriander root. Many dishes have a spicy bite that's balanced by the use of coconut milk, honey, or crisp vegetables. Peanut and fish sauces are common. Although the names are often long and unfamiliar—Khao Bai-Gra-Pao Khai-Down (stir fried chicken with sweet basil and hot chilies on top of crispy egg) and Kaeny Choed Phug-Gard-Dong (pickled mustard vegetable soup with pork and sauteed garlic)—each exotic dish is well described on the menu and chef Sunthorn Phetcharat or his wife will happily answer all your questions. The restaurant is small, only six red-vinyl-covered tables and 14 chairs grouped around the L-shaped kitchen. Recorded popular Thai music plays in the background. In terms of the setting, eating out doesn't get much homier than this. But unless you hail from Thailand, the food will transport you to another world.

▲
Hours: Lunch Mon–Sat 11:30 a.m.–2:30 p.m.; Dinner Mon–Thu 5:30–9:30 p.m., Fri 5:30–10 p.m., Sat 5:30–11 p.m., Sun 5:30–9 p.m.; closed between Lunch & Dinner ▪ Reservations not taken ▪ Cash only ▪ Bar: none ▪ Takeout ▪ No smoking

THAI ORCHID

Lyndhurst   East Side
5136 Mayfield Rd.   Casual
☎ 461-8266 $$$$$

There's something perennially confusing about this place, but don't let
that keep you away. It was previously called Taste of Thailand. The
restaurant still looks the same but now there's a new name and a new
owner. And although the sign over the front door facing Mayfield Road
is what catches your eye, you can't enter through that door. Park in the
large lot and use the side door. They serve lunch some days but not others. But all that aside, there's nothing confusing about the fact that it's a
nice place to enjoy real Thai food. There are curries, many seafood
dishes, and full-flavored whole wheat noodles. House specials have
musical names: River and Land (a stir fry of shrimp, chicken, and beef
with mustard, cabbage,and mushrooms), Fisherman's Party (a mix of
sauteed scallops, shrimp, squid, and crab claw with vegetables, red pepper, and basil leaves), and Chicken in the Garden (chicken with vegetables in peanut sauce). A surprise is that some dishes are made with
brown rice, which is also available as a side order. Owners Payao and
Lek Sriweawnetr ran a restaurant in Boston before relocating here, but
the couple are originally from Bangkok, where Lek was sous chef for a
large hotel restaurant. Their Thai roots are reflected in the traditional
design Lek has hand-stenciled on the walls, as well as in the artwork on
display. One dining area is designated non-smoking, and a completely
separate dining room is for smokers.

▲

Hours: Lunch Thu–Sat 11:30 a.m.–3 p.m.; Dinner Sun–Wed 5–10 p.m., Fri & Sat 5–10:30
p.m. ▪ Reservations taken, recommended on weekends ▪ MC, VS, AX, Dis, checks
accepted ▪ Bar: beer, wine, liquor ▪ Takeout ▪ ♿ Full access
▪ Non-smoking section

THAI, SEE ALSO:
Siam Cafe (Vietnamese)

VIETNAMESE

CHINESE VILLAGE

Lakewood   West Side
13359 Madison Ave.   Casual
☎ 228-0110 $$$$$

More like eating in Mrs. Nguyen's dining room than in her restaurant,
dining in this spotlessly clean seven-table restaurant is so intimate you
can hear the oil sizzling in the kitchen. Yvonne Nguyen does everything
herself, cooking, managing and sometimes serving, though she looks
more like the glamorous cabaret singer she used to be in Vietnam than

chief cook and bottle washer. When she came to America, Yvonne Nguyen learned the restaurant business from her mother, who had opened the first Vietnamese eatery in Cleveland. Using her mother's traditional recipes, she prepares simple food with the tasty, nourishing feel of real home cooking, Vietnamese style. There are seven soups, and an order of any is big enough to feed two or as a meal in itself. Rice and rice noodle dishes are laced with various combinations of pork, chicken, beef, eggs, tofu, and vegetables; an unusual crepe is made with rice flour and coconut milk and stuffed with pork, shrimp, onions, and bean sprouts. Another page of the menu offers a selection of Chinese dishes that includes all the old standbys like fried rice, sweet-and-sour pork, and pepper steak, plus some less common dishes: boneless chicken Hong Kong–style, double-cooked pork, and hot and spicy Kung Po scallops. Reflecting the long-standing influence of French culture on Vietnam, French roast coffee is available to finish off the meal. On-street parking along this nicely rejuvenated section of Madison.

Other ethnic specialties: Chinese

▲

Hours: Mon–Thu 11 a.m.–9 p.m., Fri & Sat 11 a.m.–10 p.m., Sun noon–9 p.m. ▪ Reservations taken, recommended ▪ Checks accepted ▪ Bar: none ▪ Takeout ▪ ⅋ Full access

MINH ANH

Cleveland   Near West Side
5428 Detroit Ave.   Casual
☎ 961-9671 $$$$

This is a small family-style restaurant where children can feel free to get up and watch the fish in the aquarium. The walls are wood-paneled, the tables are covered in red oilcloth; there are a few green plants, and soft rock plays quietly on the radio. One waitress describes it as "a mellow little place." Vietnamese food makes use of many of the same ingredients as the cuisine of neighboring Thailand and Cambodia, so you'll find many dishes that use coconut milk, lemon grass, and peanuts. Owner Camla Wadsworth and her brother, the cook, are from Vietnam, but they use more familiar Chinese terms to help diners understand what they're ordering; so although the menu reads egg rolls, chow mein, and lo mein, you'll get the Vietnamese version. One of the most popular menu selections is a crepe, Banh Xeo, filled with beans, mushrooms, and chicken, beef, or fish. And there are some less common items as well: heo xao tuong (made with pork and spinach in a hot and sweet bean paste), tom rim (a dish of caramelized shrimp), and pho saigon (beef and rice noodle soup flavored with cinnamon). There is a decent selection of vegetarian dishes, and some surprises among the beverages: ginseng, jasmine, or sweet chrysanthemum tea, served hot or cold; mango or guava juice, soybean milk, and coconut or gin-seng soda. Parking in the rear, enter from the front.

▲

Hours: Tue–Thu 11 a.m.–9:45 p.m., Fri 11 a.m.–10:45 p.m., Sat noon–10:45 p.m., Sun 2–8:45 p.m.; closed Mon ▪ Reservations taken, recommended for large groups ▪ Cash only ▪ Bar: beer, wine ▪ Takeout

NAM HING

Cleveland	Downtown
2152 Rockwell Ave.	Relaxed
☎ 687-1618	$$$$$

This restaurant, located next to the handsome tiled entrance of the On Leong Merchants Association (a Chinese organization that has been in existence since the 1890s), is easy to spot; it is painted red with white stripes, and a lace curtain adorns the door. Opened in the spring of 1994, this family-run restaurant is small, seating about 40 at booths and tables, and modest. The floor is linoleum and the wallpaper has seen better days, but everything is immaculate and the seven-days-a-week, late-night hours make this a handy place to know about. The Chinese food is nothing unusual, mostly Cantonese, some Szechuan, and a few Americanized dishes like pepper steak and chow mein. But the Vietnamese menu is another story. There are 17 different Viet-namese soups to choose among, and each is a meal in itself. Though many dishes are unfamiliar to most Americans and the pronunciation of their names a mystery, the menu lists the ingredients in each and diners can make their selection by using the numbers to order dishes. So instead of trying to wrap your tongue around the words Hu Tieu Xao Thap Cam, you can say "Number 26, please," and expect to get a plate of seafood with soft rice noodles. Try spiking your dishes with the hot chili sauce that's on the table along with soy and fish sauces. Chi-nese and Vietnamese dishes are listed separately on the menu. Metered parking on the street.

Other ethnic specialties: Chinese

▲

Hours: Mon–Thu 11 a.m.–midnight, Fri & Sat 11 a.m.–1 a.m., Sun noon–midnight ▪ Reservations taken ▪ Checks accepted ▪ Bar: none ▪ Takeout ▪ ♿ Full access

NAM WAH

Berea	Southwest
392 W. Bagley Rd.	Casual
☎ 243-8181	$$$$$

This family owned and operated restaurant has been around for 15 years, but moved to its present location just two years ago when a fire damaged the old place. A first-time visitor may have difficulty finding this incarnation of Nam-Wah; it's in a nondescript building, in a small strip mall, behind McDonald's, near the Baldwin Wallace campus. It's a real neighborhood place, nothing fancy, with seating for about 150 people. It seems to attract working couples who want to relax over an inexpensive meal and would be a nice place for a group of friends to meet and eat. The employees are all Chinese and Vietnamese, some newly arrived in the U.S., and though their English may not always be perfect, the service they provide is friendly, without being, as one visitor put it, suffocating. The midsized menu features both Chinese and Vietnamese dishes. Some unusual dishes from the Chinese portion are bean cake with roast pork soup, Singapore style rice noodles, and wild pepper chicken. The Vietnamese food is light yet surprisingly filling. Appetizers like grilled meatballs and shrimp on sugar cane are served with rice noodles and vegetables rolled up in rice paper with a sweet vinegar dipping sauce. Two diners told me they'd never tasted Vietnamese food before eating here. One ordered bun thit nuong (pork bowl) and the other scallops in lemongrass. "We have three words to describe the food," she told me, "yum, yum, yum."

Other ethnic specialties: Chinese

▲

Hours: Mon–Thu 11:30 a.m.–10 p.m., Fri 11:30 a.m.–midnight, Sat noon–midnight, Sun Noon–10 p.m. ▪ Reservations taken ▪ MC, VS, AX, Dis, checks accepted ▪ Bar: beer, wine, liquor ▪ Takeout ▪ & Full access ▪ Non-smoking section

SIAM CAFE

Cleveland   Near East Side
3951 St. Clair Ave.   Casual
☎ 361-2323 $$$$$

Opened in 1994, this restaurant boasts a genuinely exotic, varied, and unusual menu, and eating here is an adventure. There are 18 choices of non-alcoholic hot and cold beverages, including Da Ba Mau (made with palm sugar syrup, coconut juice, and tropical fruit), and Sinh To Mang Cau Sim (a milkshake made with sour sop nectar, ginger tea, and soya bean milk). The selection of soups, appetizers, noodle dishes, and other entrees that feature roasted duck, sea scallops, grilled pork, and marinated beef is equally varied, reflecting the fact that many ingredients are common to both Thai and Vietnamese cuisines, though each is distinctive in preparation. "Vietnamese cooking," explained owner Michael Hong, "has been influenced by the French and Chinese, and tends towards the sweet and salty. Thai food, which has incorporated Malaysian and Indian flavors, is much more spicy, or sour, or a combination of both." The kitchen will adjust the hot and spicy level to suit diners' tastes, and can prepare most dishes vegetarian style. The portions are large. A host seats guests at booths or tables, and the ambience is pleasant and relaxed, a setting of light woods and polished brass with deep green accents. Smoking and non-smoking sections are well separated. Be forewarned—there's something incongruous about the place from the outside until you realize that the Siam Cafe is housed in a converted Country Kitchen restaurant. The resulting exterior is a sort of Asian barn motif with neon highlights. Plenty of parking on the east and west sides of the building.

Other ethnic specialties: Thai

▲

Hours: Mon–Fri 11 a.m.–10 p.m., Sat & Sun 11 a.m.–11 p.m. ▪ Reservations taken ▪ MC, VS, AX accepted ▪ Bar: none ▪ Takeout ▪ ᯼ Full access ▪ Non-smoking section

MARKETS

ASIAN MIX

ASIA FOODS

Cleveland   Near East Side
3216 St. Clair Ave.
☎ 621-1681

This is a family owned and operated wholesale and retail business. The owners are from Vietnam and stock food products from their native country as well as Laos, Thailand, and Korea, but the emphasis is on Chinese imports. This a small full-service neighborhood grocery, and owners describe it as typical of those you'd find in any large city in Southeast Asia.

Other ethnic specialties: Chinese, Korean, Laotian, Thai, Vietnamese

▲

Foods available: meat (fresh, frozen), fish (fresh, frozen), produce, grains, beans, flour, spices, condiments, beverages, tea, wine, prepared frozen foods, takeout meals ▪ Hours: daily 9 a.m.–7 p.m. ▪ Checks accepted

ASIA GROCERY & GIFT

Cleveland   Near West Side
4825 Pearl Rd.
☎ 459-8839

Owner John Hong is from Korea and was trained as a microbiologist. He worked in a hospital when he first came to America but soon discovered he preferred being his own boss, and for the past 16 years he's run this specialty market at the same location. He sells to restaurants as well as the general public, and 90 percent of his regular clientele is Asian. They enjoy the selection of food products, kitchenware, and gifts from China, Japan, Thailand, the Philippines, and, of course, Korea. A large parking lot is adjacent to the store.

Other ethnic specialties: Chinese, Korean, Japanese, Filipino, Thai

▲

Foods available: meat (frozen, dried), produce, grains, beans, flour, spices, condiments, tea, prepared frozen foods ▪ Hours: Mon–Sat 10 a.m.–8 p.m., Sun 10 a.m.–6 p.m. ▪ Checks accepted ▪ ♿ Full access

DONG DUONG INDOCHINA GROCERY

Cleveland   Near West Side
6406 Lorain Ave.
☎ 651-8796

Open since 1987, this is another small family-owned store that carries a variety of food products imported from Thailand, Vietnam, China, Singapore, and Cambodia. They also sell electric rice cookers and woks. Store owners Srey Trinh and husband Phung are from Cambodia but are well versed in all the products they sell and how to use them. They're happy to answer questions.

Other ethnic specialties: Cambodian, Chinese, Thai, Vietnamese

▲

Foods available: produce, grains, beans, flour, spices, condiments, tea ▪ Hours: daily 10 a.m.–6 p.m. ▪ Cash only

FAR EAST ORIENTAL MARKET

Akron   Farther South
85 Midway Plaza
☎ 630-9377

A small store with a large variety of ingredients for Chinese, Japanese, Korean, Filipino, and Thai cooking. It also does double duty as a neighborhood convenience store, so you can pick up a six-pack of your favorite soft drink and a bar of soap when you stock up on soy sauce, zuke (Japanese pickled vegetables), and kapi (fermented shrimp paste used in Thai cuisine). The Yui family has owned and operated this congenial place for eight years.

Other ethnic specialties: Chinese, Japanese, Korean, Filipino, Thai

▲

Foods available: produce, grains, beans, flour, spices, condiments, beverages, tea, wine, prepared frozen foods ▪ Hours: daily 11:30 a.m.–7 p.m. ▪ Checks accepted ▪ ♿ Full access

GLOBAL APPROACH TRADE
Cleveland   Near East Side
2999 Payne Ave.
☎ 696-1717

Located in Asia Plaza, this place has the look and feel of a modern supermarket, but you won't find peanut butter and jelly on the shelves. Reputed to be the largest Chinese grocery store in Ohio, they stock strictly Asian products. The primary focus is on Chinese foods, but they have items imported from all over Southeast Asia, including traditional cooking and serving utensils. It's easy to make your way down the wide aisles, but hard to choose from among the many different types of noodles, sauces, oils, and frozen dumplings. This is the place to find bean paste, egg roll skins, and five spice powder (a blend of anise, fennel, cinnamon, Szechuan pepper, and cloves), and tofu (a cheese-like curd made from soybeans). All sorts of fresh imported vegetables uncommon in America but typical for China are in good supply. It's no surprise that this is where many Asians shop. Ample parking in the lot that serves the entire Plaza.

Other ethnic specialties: Chinese

▲

Foods available: meat (fresh, frozen), fish (fresh, frozen), produce, grains, beans, flour, baked goods, spices, condiments, tea, prepared frozen foods ▪ Hours: Mon–Sat 9 a.m.–7 p.m., Sun 9 a.m.–6 p.m. ▪ MC, VS, Dis, checks accepted ▪ க Full access

KIM'S ORIENTAL FOOD COMPANY
Cleveland   Near West Side
4709 Pearl Rd.
☎ 741-0688

Well-stocked with products from Southeast Asia, Korea, China, and Japan, this store is enjoying increasing patronage from Americans interested in preparing real Asian specialties in their own kitchens, and in using Asian flavorings to spice up American foods. You can find seasonings in both powder and liquid form here. The cooking of each Asian country is unique and, though small, Kim's prides itself on having ingredients that reflect the full range of national and regional styles, as well as imported gifts and cookware.

Other ethnic specialties: Chinese, Korean, Japanese

▲

Foods available: produce, grains, beans, flour, spices, condiments, tea, prepared frozen foods ▪ Hours: Mon–Sat 10 a.m.–8 p.m., Sun noon–6 p.m. ▪ Checks accepted

LEE ROAD ORIENTAL TRADER

Cleveland Heights   East Side
2295 Lee Rd.
☎ 932-5353

A small well-stocked store, where shoppers can reach into open crates filled with mounds of fresh bean sprouts, ginger root, daikon radishes, pea pods, and green onions. Shelves are packed with virtually everything you need, in cans and jars, to prepare traditional Chinese, Japanese, Korean, and Thai foods. There are packages of rice flour sweets and snacks, soup mixes, and all sorts of noodles and bean threads. Big bags hold crispy, freshly made chow mein noodles, available by the pound, and dried mushrooms with beautiful names like Cloud Ears. The freezer case is stacked with frozen eggrolls and pot stickers, and many mysterious-looking things the untrained eye will find hard to identify. Although the packaging information on many products is not in English, owner and staff are always helpful. Convenient metered parking in a city lot at the rear of the store.

Other ethnic specialties: Chinese, Korean, Japanese, Thai

▲

Foods available: meat (fresh, frozen), fish (fresh, frozen), produce, grains, beans, flour, spices, condiments, beverages, tea, wine, prepared frozen foods ▪ Hours: Mon–Thu, 10 a.m.–7 p.m., Fri & Sat 10 a.m.–8 p.m.; closed Sun ▪ Checks accepted ▪ ♿ Full access

LITTLE BANGKOK GROCERY

Cleveland   Near West Side
8401 Detroit Ave.
☎ 281-0820

This is an old-fashioned little neighborhood grocery store. But mixed in with a variety of ordinary household products and convenience store items are Asian products not available in most regular markets. You'll find a good selection of Chinese teas, fresh Asian vegetables and fruits in season, unusual mushrooms, and many different types of rice.

▲

Foods available: produce, grains, beans, flour, prepared frozen foods ▪ Hours: daily 10 a.m.–7 p.m. ▪ Cash only

ORIENTAL FOOD & GIFTS

South Euclid   East Side
4271 Mayfield Rd.
☎ 291-1241

Located at the corner of Belvoir and Mayfield in a strip mall that offers ample parking, this is a large, well-stocked supermarket with products from almost all the Pacific Rim nations. You can find tubes of Japanese wasabi (horseradish), Vietnamese hot sauce, cans of pennywort and sugar cane juice for Thai recipes, five-gallon jars of Korean bean paste, and dried Chinese mushrooms. Rice can be purchased in 20- or 50-pound bags, soy sauce and sesame oil by the gallon, and exotic spices in 5-pound sacks. The selection is staggering; there are shelves and shelves of different sorts of cookies and crackers, noodles, flours, and teas of every type. In one visit I found yam noodles, acorn starch, and roasted barley tea. Freezer cases and refrigerators hold such specialties as duck and quail eggs, baby octopus and seasoned cuttlefish, fermented turnip greens and cabbage kimchee. Aisles are wide, lighting is bright, and staff are helpful. A deli-type display case features a variety of ready-to-eat noodle, fish, and vegetable dishes, and the produce section has most of the Asian vegetables you'd ever need, and some I've never seen before. You'll also find Asian-brand cosmetics, kitchen utensils, and housewares, and Asian-language videos for rent. This place qualifies as an American-style superstore with a purely Asian flavor.

▲

Foods available: meat (fresh, frozen), fish (fresh, frozen), produce, grains, beans, flour, rice, spices, condiments, beverages, tea, wine, prepared frozen foods, takeout meals ■ Hours: Mon–Sat 10 a.m.–9 p.m., Sun noon–7 p.m. ■ Cash only

SUGARLAND FOOD MART

Parma   Southwest
5408 Ridge Rd.
☎ 843-8646

The emphasis at this very small neighborhood store is on products from the Philippines, but this eight-year-old family operation also carries imported foods for all types of Asian cooking. There are many varieties of noodles, rice, and soy sauce. This is a good source for the kinds of specialized ingredients necessary for many Southeast Asian dishes: palm sugar, canned coconut, coconut and mango jellies, canned tropical fruits, and chili sauces. They even stock quail eggs. Every couple of days they have food for takeout, but the selections are varied and unpredictable. Call ahead if you're looking for a specific dish or want to request one. They also do catering.

▲

Foods available: fish (fresh, frozen), beans, baked goods, spices, condiments, tea, prepared frozen foods, takeout meals ■ Hours: Mon–Sat 9 a.m.–7:30 p.m., Sun 10 a.m.–5:30 p.m. ■ Checks accepted

CHINESE

SAN CHONG, INC.

Cleveland   Downtown
2146 Rockwell Ave.
☎ 771-0054

Located in the heart of Cleveland's Chinatown, this small store, which has been in business at the same location for 16 years, caters to a primarily Chinese clientele. They are a good source for hard-to-find green teas and also stock imported cookware and cookbooks in both English and Chinese. There's metered parking on the street and Saturday parking is free.

▲

Foods available: produce, grains, rice, spices, condiments, tea ▪ Hours: Mon–Sat 9 a.m.–4:30 p.m.; closed Sun ▪ Cash only ▪ ♿ Full access

CHINESE, SEE ALSO:
Asia Foods (Asian Mix)
Asia Grocery & Gift (Asian Mix)
Dong Duong Indochina Grocery (Asian Mix)
Far East Oriental Market (Asian Mix)
Global Approach Trade (Asian Mix)
Kim's Oriental Food (Korean)
Kim's Oriental Food Company (Asian Mix)
Lee Road Oriental Trader (Asian Mix)

FILIPINO

MANILA CHEF, THE

Cleveland   West Side
4554 W. 130th St.
☎ 671-5934

I had to bend the rules (all of my own devising of course) in order to include this place, which is not really a store or a restaurant. But since The Manila Chef is the only source of Filipino dishes around, it seemed the ends did indeed justify the means. This is essentially a catering business, begun and run by Jenny Mata, who was a doctor back in the Philippines. What makes her different from other caterers is that she will also prepare dishes, on request, in small quantities; a version of takeout plus leftovers. She won't whip up a single serving, but says many of her customers put in an order sufficient for a few meals, freezing the unused portions for later. You can get a menu by mail upon request, then order ahead by phone, and arrange a pickup time. She asks for at least a day's advance notice and prefers two. In the commercial kitchen adjacent to her home, Ms. Mata prepares such Filipino specialties as barbecue on a stick (thin slices of marinated pork charbroiled on a bamboo skewer), empanadas (buttery crusted turnovers filled with chicken, potatoes, and raisins), pancit guisado (sauteed rice stick noodles with shrimp, pork, and vegetables), okoy (batter-dipped acorn squash patties topped with shrimp and served with a garlic and vinegar sauce), and shrimp pink tails (fresh shrimp in paper-thin wrappers, seasoned with Asian spices and deep fried). For dessert, she offers cassava pie, made with coconut milk, and almond boats, which are layers of cream, roasted almonds, and meringue on a crust.

▲

Foods available: baked goods, takeout meals ■ Hours: no set hours; phone rings simultaneously in home & business, ALWAYS call in advance ■ Checks accepted ■ ♿ Full access

NIPA HUT

Parma   Southwest
5380 State Rd.
☎ 351-8818

Located in a strip mall, this small place is a cross between a convenience store and an import shop. They primarily stock ingredients for Filipino-style cooking, but since the cuisine reflects a Chinese as well as a Spanish influence, you can also find products from these countries, too. One-stop shopping for beer and candy, patis and bagoong (two types of fermented fish sauce).

▲

Foods available: meat (fresh, frozen), fish (fresh, frozen), produce, grains, beans, flour, rice, spices, condiments, beverages, tea, wine, prepared frozen foods, takeout meals ■ Hours: Mon–Sat 9 a.m.–8 p.m., Sun 12:30–6 p.m. ■ MC, VS, Dis, checks accepted ■ ♿ Full access

PHILIPPINE & ORIENTAL FOOD MART

Parma   Southwest
6170 Broadview Rd.
☎ 741-4166

With precisely the same kind of combination import and convenience store as Nipa Hut, their Parma neighbor, this market keeps a foot in both worlds. You can buy a lottery ticket, use the copy machine, and go home with a roll of toilet paper, a package of pancit (rice or bean thread noodles), and a bottle of banana ketchup. Some prepared Filipino dishes are available for takeout.

▲

Foods available: grains, beans, flour, spices, condiments, beverages, tea ■ Hours: daily 7 a.m.–midnight ■ Cash only ■ ♿ Full access

FILIPINO, SEE ALSO:
Asia Grocery & Gift (Asian Mix)
Far East Oriental Market (Asian Mix)
Kim's Oriental Food (Korean)

JAPANESE

OMURA JAPANESE FOODS

Cleveland   Near East Side
3811 Payne Ave.
☎ 881-0523

The Omura family has run this store for 30 years. Mr. Omura is now retired, and his wife is in charge and she is happy to help customers find everything they need for Japanese cooking. There's a growing interest in Japanese-style cooking, and Mrs. Omura notices that the number of Americans who come to the store is increasing. Many of them have been to Japan and developed a taste for the cuisine as it is prepared there rather than in restaurants here. She says they like her store because they know that they can find authentic-tasting quality imported ingredients.

▲

Foods available: produce, grains, beans, flour, spices, condiments, tea, prepared frozen foods ▪ Hours: Tue–Sat 9 a.m.–6 p.m., Sun noon–4 p.m.; closed Mon
▪ Checks accepted

JAPANESE, SEE ALSO:
Asia Grocery & Gift (Asian Mix)
Asian Imports (Indian, Chapter 2)Far East Oriental Market (Asian Mix)
Far East Oriental Market (Asian Mix)
Kim's Oriental Food (Korean)
Kim's Oriental Food Company (Asian Mix)
Lee Road Oriental Trader (Asian Mix)

KOREAN

KIM'S ORIENTAL FOOD

Cleveland   Near East Side
3425 Payne Ave.
☎ 391-5485

One of the largest sources for Korean foods in the area, Kim's also has a smaller selection of supplies for Chinese, Japanese, Thai, and Filipino cookery. Many varieties of rice are available in quantities ranging from 1 pound to 100 pounds. This is a place where the experienced cook can find obscure and unusual ingredients and a beginner can stock up on everything needed to get started in Asian-style cooking. The store has its own parking lot adjacent to the building.

Other ethnic specialties: Chinese, Filipino, Japanese, Thai

Foods available: meat (fresh, frozen), fish (fresh, frozen), produce, grains, beans, flour, spices, condiments, tea, prepared frozen foods ■ Hours: Mon–Sat 9 a.m.–7 p.m., Sun 10 a.m.–5 p.m. ■ Checks accepted

KOREAN, SEE ALSO:
Asia Foods (Asian Mix)
Asia Grocery & Gift (Asian Mix)
Asian Imports (Indian, Chapter 2)
Far East Oriental Market (Asian Mix)
Kim's Oriental Food Company (Asian Mix)
Lee Road Oriental Trader (Asian Mix)

Middle East, North Africa, India

THIS CHAPTER, A SORT OF PATCHWORK QUILT, pieces together an eclectic assortment of countries from two continents that share a kinship in matters of food.

Morocco, though sometimes considered part of the Mediterranean, is an Arab nation in northwest Africa. Lebanon, too, is on the Mediterranean coast of the Islamic realm. And the cuisine that has developed in both countries has been clearly influenced by French culinary practices. I included India, though it is geographically kin to China, because its way of eating is unlike the rest of Asia. The use of lentils, flat breads, butter, and other dairy products relate it more to Middle Eastern cuisine. In addition, a significant portion of India's population is Moslem, which links them spiritually as well to that part of the globe. And though Ethiopia, situated on the east coast of Africa, is literally and figuratively worlds apart from India, its traditional wats, fiery hot stews served with injera, a pancake-like bread, bear a close resemblance to spicy Indian curries eaten with roti, an unleavened round bread. As in the Middle East, the Ethiopian tradition is to eat at low tables without utensils, scooping up food with pre-washed hands and pieces of bread. And in all these countries, meatless dishes are a major part of the daily diet.

What they also have in common is that people from each of these countries have opened restaurants or markets in Greater Cleveland, which gives the rest of us a chance to be "table travelers" through these parts of the world.

There are no Ethiopian or Moroccan communities to speak of in Cleveland. The story of Ethiopian cuisine is probably best told by the one restaurant in town that serves it, for in the modern Western mind this country is profoundly linked only to images of famine and scarcity. It's difficult to imagine Ethiopia having a tasty and inviting food culture. But it does. Ethiopian food, reflecting a heritage that dates back thousands of years to the ancient Abyssinians, is especially interesting in that it has remained relatively free of European influences. It features a bread made with a form of millet called teff that grows only in Ethiopia. Berbere, a blend of ground chilies and other herbs and spices such as rue seed, ginger, cloves, bishops weed, and cinnamon, is an often-used seasoning not unlike the spice blends of Morocco. Hot and hotter is to be expected. A typical main meal consists of some type of stewed legumes, vegetables, and sometimes meat or poultry. Doro wot is made with chicken and considered a national dish.

Until very recently, Cleveland had no Moroccan restaurants. But now, one on the West Side and another new one on the East Side, near Shaker Square, offer venues for "food journeying" to what has long been considered the most exotic outpost of the Middle East. Dishes show the effects of both the French and Spanish presence there, and hint at African and Middle Eastern influences, with the use of pungent spices like cumin, ginger, nutmeg, coriander, and cardamom. A blend of 35 spices, called ras el hanout, is used to make tagines—slow-cooked stews of meat, aromatic spices, and fruit. It includes juniper, paprika, and chilies, plus all the above mentioned spices as well. Pumpkins, tomatoes, lentils, chick peas, fava beans, carrots, and eggplants are present in many dishes. Cous-cous, made from semolina (a coarsely ground, starchy form of wheat flour—also known as farina), forms the basis for most meals. It's "Moroccan spaghetti," said Khalid Arabe, owner of Taste of Morocco, in a *Free Times* restaurant review.

Currently there are approximately 100,000 Arab Americans in northeast Ohio (half that number arrived in the last 15 years) representing Christians and Moslems from 23 different homelands. Historically the Arab world has not been a cohesive one, but in Cleveland all the different nationality groups and religious sects have formed an unprecedented working relationship. "We've been able to unite as Arab Americans," said Ed Farage, founder and president of CAMEO (Cleveland American Middle East Organization), an association dedicated to helping this constituency into the political mainstream, "and concentrate on what brings us together. CAMEO, for example, is the only local group of its kind in the country. We don't define ourselves by religion or where we come from, but rather by our mutual concerns as American Arabs. Our membership is very diversified, from laborers to lawyers. Language is one thing we have in common, and another is food. We all eat the same things. The ingredients may be slightly different, but no matter where you go in the Arab world, you can get kibbee."

Lamb is the most popular meat throughout the Middle East and when mixed with bulgur, a nutty flavored cracked wheat, it becomes kibbee. It may be prepared in countless ways: eaten raw, shaped into patties and baked, or stuffed and fried. Kibbee is the national dish of Lebanon, and it is Lebanese cooking that dominates our local Middle Eastern food scene. Like much of Arab cuisine, it is characterized by subtle, rich spicing, using fennel, mint, parsley, cardamom, ginger, nutmeg, saffron, and turmeric. This is as much about history as taste and tradition: Arabs controlled the spice trade between east and west throughout the Middle Ages. Lemons, onions, and garlic also play a significant role. Beans, fruit, vegetables (especially eggplant), and cereal grains are staples. Bulgur may be steamed and eaten on its own like rice or combined with tomatoes and chick peas for tabouleh, a highly seasoned salad. Almonds and pine nuts are basic to the cuisine, and yogurt, as in Indian cuisine, is much more than the breakfast food it is in this country, used as a marinade, in sauces and dressings, and as a side dish.

Many members of Cleveland's Indian community arrived in the

1960s. A second wave, often their relatives, followed over the next two decades. Many are highly educated, taking their place in this country as doctors, professors, engineers, and research scholars. Approximately 3,000 Indian families live in Greater Cleveland, and most, according to Mukand Mehta, editor of *The Lotus*, an Indian community newspaper, try to maintain their Indian way of living. "We want very much to keep our culture intact," explained Mr. Mehta, "and contribute its richness to American life. I am delighted when I see Americans enjoying the food in Indian restaurants. The popularity of Indian cuisine among non-Indians is a wonderful thing to us."

Mehta and other members of the Indian community are justifiably proud of their cuisine. An ancient wisdom informs their cooking, and it is as much about a way of life as a way of eating. Rooted in a knowledge of how the body works, Indian cuisine is traditionally healthy, nutritious, and well-balanced. Many of the spices were first used as medicines.

Ingredients such as onions, tomatoes, lentils, yogurt, rice, cauliflower, peas, and potatoes are typical. Many vegetables are pickled. Meat plays a minor role, though the food found in restaurants gives it a more prominent place to accommodate American tastes. The characteristic heat and complex flavor of Indian cuisine—and there are distinctive regional differences—is achieved by the use of masalas, which are aromatic blends of spices such as cardamom, mace, nutmeg, cumin, and coriander, mustard seed, chilies, pepper, and cloves. Curry powder is actually only one type of masala. Cooling fruit relishes called chutney, and yogurt side dishes, are served as a counterbalance.

"We are taught from the earliest age," said Sheela Sogal, owner of The Saffron Patch restaurant, "that a cook should take no shortcuts. Care and love is the best spice of all. Everything in the kitchen should be done with heart and soul."

RESTAURANTS

ETHIOPIAN

EMPRESS TAYTU ETHIOPIAN RESTAURANT

Cleveland
6125 St. Clair Ave.
☎ 391-9400

Near East Side
Casual
$$$$$

Cleveland's only Ethiopian restaurant serves the traditional spicy cuisine of ancient Abyssinia, most of which is eaten sans silverware by scooping up stews and purees with pieces of injera, a soft flat bread that is made on the premises. Food arrives on large platters for sharing, and there are numerous combination plates on the menu that give newcomers to this cuisine a chance to sample a variety of dishes, which are primarily stews of meats, vegetables, or beans. Chicken in a sauce that resembles our barbecue is called dorowat and is made with onions, ginger, hot red peppers, rue, basil, cinnamon, cloves, and a flavoring called bishops weed. T'ibs features small chunks of beef or lamb sauteed in spiced butter with herbs and onions. There are many completely vegetarian dishes. The decor is exotic, designed to duplicate native thatched-roof huts, and you can choose to eat at a regular table or from traditional low tables and stools—made comfortable by the addition of cushions and back rests. (If you want to sit at one of these traditional basket tables be sure to let them know when you make your reservation—they are very popular.) Warm, moist cloths for cleaning your hands are served before and after the meal by women in long white dresses. Enter through the back door from the restaurant's own parking lot. You pass by the kitchen and can look inside. There's an unusually comfortable area, near the thatch-roofed bar, complete with couches and a coffee table where you can wait for your table or have a drink. Large photographs from Ethiopia are on the walls. For a very special experience, request the Ethiopian coffee ceremony. The green beans are roasted to order on the stove and brought to your table still hot; incense is lit, and the brew is made in a clay pot.

▲

Hours: Lunch Mon–Fri 11:30 a.m.–2 p.m.; Dinner Mon–Thu 5–10 p.m., Fri 5–11 p.m., Sat 4:30 p.m.–midnight, Sun 4:30–8 p.m. ▪ Reservations taken, recommended on weekends ▪ MC, VS, AX accepted ▪ Bar: beer, wine, liquor ▪ Takeout ▪ ♿ Full access ▪ No smoking

INDIAN

BOMBAY EXPRESS

North Olmsted   West Side
26703 Brookpark Rd. Extension   Casual
☎ 779-5774 $$$$$

This very small, casual, relaxed eatery attracts many Indian families as well as non-Indians. Up to 60 can be served in two rooms that are decorated with paintings featuring Indian motifs by Jyoti Patel, a female artist who is also a partner in the restaurant. A small room which can seat 15 is available for private parties. Every dish is well described on the menu, and there are numerous choices for vegetarians. Chefs Shaila Torgalkar and Jyoti Patel, who own the business with their husbands, will accommodate those who request mild spicing. They also understand that children not accustomed to Indian food are reluctant to eat many of these hot and unusual dishes, and so will go out of their way, if asked, to prepare things to please the palates of younger patrons. Some dishes offered here are rarely encountered in Cleveland. One is the famous mulligatawny soup, made with pureed lentils, chicken, and spices. It was devised by Indian cooks working in British homes during the colonial period of the 18th century; the name comes from the word mullaga meaning pepper. Other specialties are navrtna korma (a dish of vegetables and beans cooked in a creamy cardamom-flavored sauce), lamb kolhapuri (in which the meat is simmered in a very hot coconut sauce), and bhajia (a crisp fried fritter made from spinach and potatoes coated with chickpea flour batter and served with a spicy sweet-and-sour sauce). The Thali Dinners—one for vegetarians and another for meat-eaters—are sampler plates and a great way to taste two different entrees, samosa (a stuffed pastry), and a variety of side dishes and condiments. Desserts and drinks are worth a mention. They include gulab jamum (cardamom-flavored donuts in sugar syrup), kheer (a tapioca-and-rice pudding seasoned with pistachio nuts, cardamom, and saffron), tropical fruit milkshakes, sweet lassi (a rose-scented yogurt drink), and chai (real Indian tea brewed with milk, water, and spices).

▲

Hours: Sun–Thu 5:30–9 p.m., Fri & Sat 5:30–10 p.m. ▪ Reservations taken, recommended, especially on weekends and for parties of 5 or more ▪ MC, VS, AX, Dis, checks accepted ▪ Bar: beer ▪ Takeout ▪ ᕋ Full access ▪ No smoking

CAFE TANDOOR

Cleveland Heights   East Side
2096 S. Taylor Rd.   Casual
☎ 371-8500 $$$$$

Typical of Indian restaurants, the smells that greet you at the door of this attractive, well-lit restaurant are exotic. The second thing you notice upon entering is that many Indian families are eating here, a sure sign that the food is authentically prepared. Divided into two rooms, the place seats about 100 at cloth-covered tables. The menu is all Indian, but that doesn't mean you'll only find curries. And if you're not familiar with any of the dishes, the staff is knowledgeable and will graciously assist. You can order dishes made mild, medium, or spicy hot. Typical of Indian cuisine, there are many vegetarian selections, but the menu includes a large choice of chicken, lamb, and shrimp entrees, too. Traditional fried foods like pakora (batter-dipped meat or vegetables) are not at all greasy, and flavorful tandoori breads (a tandor is a type of oven) are made on the premises. Empty plates are brought warm from the kitchen, and food arrives beautifully arranged on large platters set in the middle of the table. Portions are generous, but desserts are worth saving room for. Ample parking on the street and in back.

Hours: Lunch Mon–Sun 11:30 a.m.–2 p.m.; Dinner Mon–Sat 5:30 p.m.–10 p.m., Sun 3–9 p.m. ▪ Reservations taken, recommended ▪ MC, VS, AX, Dis accepted ▪ Bar: beer, wine, liquor ▪ Takeout ▪ ⅙ Full access

SAFFRON PATCH

Shaker Heights   East Side
20600 Chagrin Blvd. (Tower E Building)   Dressy
☎ 295-0400 $$$$$

Here you'll find exotic fare, and the aroma alone is an adventure. The luncheon buffet provides a great opportunity to sample a wide variety of foods: an okra curry, saffron rice, raita (a salad of cucumbers in yogurt sauce), chicken cooked in a stovetop tandoori oven, rice and lentil crepes filled with onions and potatoes, and naan (a flat bread). Owner Sheela Sogal, who is from Indore, in central India, often greets guests herself, dressed in a stunning sari. Each region of India has its own style of food preparation; the chefs here prepare some dishes from southern India but focus primarily on the cuisine of the north—spicy, pungent dishes, many vegetarian—and make them the traditional way, from scratch. Sogul insists on using authentic ingredients, even when they are costly or hard to obtain, like mangoes or what are called curry leaves. They make their own cheese, similar to our farmer cheese (a drier, moldier version of cottage cheese), in the kitchen, too. Located in the basement of an office building, this is a large (capacity to seat about 110 diners) and surprisingly lovely place to eat, with white-walled rooms adorned with fabric borders of blue elephants. Partitions divide the space into three sections, lighting is subdued, recorded sitar music plays softly in the background, and the overall effect is one of calm, comfort, and casual sophistication. They sometimes organize special eating events around American holidays, such as a recent Mother's Day Champagne Brunch Buffet which billed itself as a way to take your mom to India for only $12.95 and featured more than 15 different traditional dishes. Ample parking.

▲
Hours: Lunch Tue–Sat 11:30 a.m.–2:30 p.m., Sun Noon–3 p.m.; Dinner Tue–Thu 5–10 p.m., Fri & Sat 5–11 p.m., Sun 5–9 p.m. ▪ Reservations taken, recommended ▪ MC, VS, AX, Dis accepted ▪ Bar: beer, wine, liquor ▪ Takeout ▪ Non-smoking dining rooms; smoking in bar only

TAJ MAHAL

Cleveland Heights   East Side
1763 Coventry Rd.   Casual
☎ 321-0511 $$$$$

Recently redecorated inside and out, the Taj Mahal has fresh carpeting and wallpaper, new stone facing on the building's exterior, and a glass-enclosed entryway. The restaurant serves primarily northern Indian cuisine, and the specialty is rogan josh (a lamb curry in which the meat is extraordinarily tender)—marinating the meat in yogurt and spices is the secret. Most dishes tend towards moderately hot, but the kitchen can turn the buzz up or down on the heat as requested. Naan (a white flour flat bread) and chapatti (a whole wheat version) are prepared fresh. Their samosa, a pastry shell stuffed with a mixture of potatoes, peas, onions, and spices, was named by *The Plain Dealer* as Cleveland's best appetizer. All dinner entrees, which run the gamut from vegetarian aloo gobi (a stir-fry curry made with cauliflower) to saag (chicken made with spinach and greens) to shrimp makhani (cooked in a tomato and cream curry sauce) are served with dal soup and aromatic basmati rice laced with almonds and raisins. Located on the corner of Coventry and Mayfield Road, the restaurant attracts many guests from the University Circle area just down the hill. They're set up to serve 50, can handle 80, and do private parties in the restaurant as well as outside catering. Customers can take advantage of the Coventry parking garage just down the block if meters are unavailable on the street in front.

▲
Hours: Mon–Thu 5–9:30 p.m., Fri & Sat 5–11 p.m., Sun 5–9 p.m. ▪ Reservations taken, recommended ▪ MC, VS, AX, Dis accepted ▪ Bar: beer, wine, liquor ▪ Takeout ▪ ♿ Full access ▪ Non-smoking section

TAJ MAHAL RESTAURANT

Cuyahoga Falls
2467 State Rd.
☎ 940-2488

Farther South
Casual
$$$$$

Formerly located in Akron's Fairlawn Town Center, this version of Mary Phelps's Taj Mahal reopened here in December, 1994. The decor is pleasant, done up in peach with floral accents, Indian prints and platters on the walls, and small, ornamental Indian trinkets on shelves. The dining area, which seats about 85, is separated from the service area by a carved wooden partition. Upon entering, you can't help but notice the good smells, and each aromatic passing plateful serves to whet the appetite. Luckily a basket of papadams (chips made from ground lentils) and chutney (a relish made of fruit and spices) to dip them in is quickly brought to your table by servers, some of whom are Indian (others are, inexplicably, Russian), wearing matching traditional jackets and pants. Phelps, married to an American, is from northern India, and her chefs are from other parts of India, so the restaurant is able to offer the cuisine of the North, which features dairy products, nut-based curries, clay oven cooking, and raised breads, as well as southern dishes, which rely more heavily on rice, intense spicing, and unleavened breads. One patron with a real taste for hot foods reported that the vindaloo here, where meat is marinated in vinegar with spices, had just the right level of heat, evoking "A slightly beaded brow but no calls to 911." The kitchen's policy is to make each dish on the mild side unless diners specifically request otherwise. The menu is extensive, with good descriptions of every listing, offering an interesting selection of vegetarian, lamb, beef, chicken, and seafood dishes prepared in many different ways. There's tandoori, where food is baked in clay ovens heated with charcoal; kadai, in which ingredients are prepared in a traditional iron frying pan; and casseroles. There's a lunch buffet Tuesday through Saturday and a Sunday buffet for lunch and dinner.

▲

Hours: Lunch Tue–Fri 11:30 a.m.–2 p.m., Sat & Sun noon–3 p.m.; Dinner Tue–Thu 5:30–9:30 p.m., Fri & Sat 5:30–10 p.m., Sun 5–9 p.m.; closed Mon ■ Reservations taken ■ MC, VS, AX accepted ■ Bar: beer, wine, liquor ■ Takeout ■ ᕕ Full access ■ Non-smoking section

TASTE OF INDIA

North Royalton
9377 Sprague Rd.
☎ 842-3555

Southwest
Casual
$$$$$

This storefront restaurant in a tiny strip mall is completely hidden from the road by a large Blockbuster Video store. But the food makes it worth the search. Owners Raj Lehal and Sunana Betra are an aunt-and-niece team. Betra is a graduate of Ohio University with a degree in journalism and philosophy, but she likes to cook. Both women are from the Punjabi region of northern India, and the menu reflects the cooking style of that area. Appetizers include samosas (pastry shells stuffed with potatoes and peas, served with mint chutney), chicken pakoras (made with a chickpea batter), and dal soup (made of lentils). Among the entrees for meat eaters there is lamb curry, ground lamb roasted on skewers over an open fire, and chicken tikka (made with a curried yogurt sauce marinade). Vegetarians will be especially pleased with the selection of meatless dishes. Mutter paneer are chunks of homemade cheese cooked in a garlic ginger sauce; bengan bhartha is a roasted eggplant stew; aloo goobi is a dish made of potatoes and cauliflower tossed with tomatoes and cooked in an aromatic ginger and cumin seed sauce. The vegan thali includes some of each of these dishes plus others you can select yourself. The two women also prepare six types of bread. The yogurt for the raita (a cross between a condiment and a side order salad) is homemade, too, and flavored with cilantro. A Taste of India is very small, seating only about 26, and not much has been done with the decor. The walls are pink and the lights are bright. But one patron said, "What it lacks in atmosphere, it more than makes up for in selection, taste, and value. This could be a fun place for a double date, with food as the focal point."

▲

Hours: Mon, Wed, Thu 11 a.m.–8:30 p.m., Fri & Sat 11 a.m.–9 p.m., Sun noon–8:30 p.m.; closed Tue ▪ Reservations taken ▪ Checks accepted ▪ Bar: none ▪ Takeout ▪ ♿ Full access ▪ No smoking

INDIAN, SEE ALSO:
Mad Greek, The (Greek)

MIDDLE EASTERN

ALADDIN'S EATERY

Cleveland Heights   East Side
12447 Cedar Rd. at Fairmount Blvd.   Casual
☎ 932-4333 $$$$$

The decor at this second, East side incarnation of Aladdin's is colorful and cheerful. Banquettes are upholstered in a tapestry-like fabric with a palm tree motif, and disks in a kaleidoscope of pastel hues hang inexplicably from the ceiling like renegade deflated balloons. Like its Lakewood predecessor, this restaurant is a comfortable, congenial, and informal setting for a meal. Tables are packed fairly close together but patrons seem to enjoy the sense of camaraderie, and many who eat here have told me they end up chatting with their neighbors, even though they have never met before. The menu duplicates some of the offerings of the Lakewood Aladdin's. Portions are generous, and vegetarians will have a field day. Some metered parking on the street and a city lot with meters, around the corner.

▲
Hours: Sun–Thu 11 a.m.–10 p.m., Fri & Sat 11 a.m.–11 p.m.; closed Mon ▪ Reservations not taken ▪ MC, VS accepted ▪ Bar: beer, wine ▪ Takeout ▪ ⅏ Full access ▪ No smoking

ALADDIN'S EATERY

Lakewood   West Side
14536 Detroit Ave.   Casual
☎ 521-4005 $$$$$

Aladdin's is bright, airy, and contemporary. It's located in a corner storefront in Lakewood, part of that city's restaurant renaissance. The decor is casual yet attractive—pale woods with teal, mauve, and beige accents. The restaurant opened in the spring of 1994 and has proved so popular that a second East Side location followed. The menu, featuring the healthy cuisine of Lebanon and the other countries of the Middle East, includes many vegetarian dishes. The kitchen prides itself on producing authentic dishes using only the freshest natural and preservative-free ingredients. There are a variety of soups, salads, and pita bread sandwiches which come stuffed or rolled. Traditional entrees include mujadara (steamed lentils and rice), sfiha (a meat pie), and shawarma (charbroiled beef and lamb). Some more contemporary variations on Middle Eastern themes can be sampled in the pita "pitzas" that make good use of tahini (sesame) sauce, feta cheese, eggplant puree, and falafel (mildly spiced chickpea and fava bean patties). The menu does a good job of explaining what goes into every dish. A small but interesting wine and beer list. A parking lot in the rear.

▲
Hours: Sun–Thu 11 a.m.–10 p.m., Fri & Sat 11 a.m.–11 p.m.; closed Mon ▪ Reservations not taken ▪ MC, VS accepted ▪ Bar: beer, wine ▪ Takeout ▪ ⅏ Full access ▪ No smoking

ALI BABA RESTAURANT

Cleveland   Near West Side
12021 Lorain Ave.   Casual
☎ 251-2040 $$$$$

This is a tiny storefront restaurant with three booths and four tables. The chairs are wood, the tablecloths are pink, and even the menu is modestly small. But even so, people are willing to travel here from across town—especially those from the Middle East who are temporarily living and working in Cleveland—for a real taste of home. This casual, low-key restaurant has now been around for more than a decade. The owner is from Lebanon, and many of the recipes come from his grandmother. In addition to the dishes we Americans have come to know well, like homoos and spinach pie, there are some other more unusual options here: labnee (a sort of cream cheese made from yogurt), moujaddara (a lentil stew), and loobi bzait (green beans simmered in a vegetable sauce and served over rice). They serve lamb and chicken shish kebabs and an interesting meat dish called soujook made from marinated ground beef. Everything is prepared without any artificial flavorings or colorings, and MSG is never used. They also offer some creative takeout options: 12- and 16-ounce containers of a variety of salads and dips, and little meat and vegetable pies and patties by the dozen. Metered on-street parking.

▲

Hours: Lunch Tue–Sat 11:30 a.m.–2 p.m.; Dinner 5 p.m.–8:30 p.m.; closed between Lunch & Dinner; closed Sun & Mon ▪ Reservations taken ▪ Cash only ▪ Bar: none ▪ Takeout

MIDDLE EAST RESTAURANT

Cleveland   Downtown
1012 Prospect Ave.   Casual
☎ 771-2647 $$$$$

I first began eating Josephine Abraham's fatiyar (meat or spinach filled turnovers), kibbee (lamb with cracked wheat and pine nuts), babaganoj (a dip of barbecued eggplant and sesame sauce), and rice pudding 25 years ago when the restaurant was located on Bolivar. My husband's mother treated us to a memorable meal there when he graduated from college. In 1974 the restaurant moved to a space in what's now called the Carter Manor and has been winning awards ever since, largely thanks to the fact that Josephine is still in the kitchen. Whenever members of the Saudi royal family visit the Cleveland Clinic, restaurant owner Ed Khouri sees to it that they get all their favorite dishes, delivered. Menu selections include lamb and chicken kebabs, stuffed eggplant or cabbage, and lima beans or string beans simmered with ground meat in a tomato sauce, plus daily specials. The Turkish coffee is always perfectly thick and sweet. A blue-and-white Arabic motif decorates the walls, and music from the jukebox, which has only Middle Eastern selections, plays softly in the background. It's easy to get comfortable, make yourself at home, and take your time here, though they are used to accommodating the more hurried pace of lunchtime diners from area office buildings. Parking is not always easy, but there are a number of nearby lots and garages.

▲

Hours: Mon–Thu 11:30 a.m.–8 p.m., Fri & Sat 11:30 a.m.–9 p.m.; closed Sun ▪ Reservations taken, recommended Fri and Sat nights ▪ MC, VS accepted ▪ Bar: beer, wine, liquor ▪ Takeout ▪ ♿ Full access ▪ Non-smoking section

NATE'S DELI & RESTAURANT

Cleveland   Near West Side
1923 W. 25th St.   Casual
☎ 696-7529 $ $ $ $ $

Primarily a lunch place, Nate's is a casual, comfortable storefront restaurant near the West Side Market. Don't let the simple, unadorned look of the place lead you to believe the food is standard luncheonette fare. The menu is a most unusual combination: lunch and dinner entrees reflect both deli favorites and Middle Eastern specialties. You can get a kosher hot dog, a good corned beef sandwich, or a hot pastrami on rye. And you'll also find authentic, subtly seasoned hommus (a dip made with chickpeas, olive oil, sesame paste, and lemons), or a tabouleh salad (parsley, tomatoes. onions, wheat, and mint). Vegetarian and Middle Eastern entrees include falafel, foul medamas (fava beans with garlic, lemon, and olive oil), shish tawook (marinated, skewered cubes of chicken), and shawarma (strips of lean beef sauteed with onions and tomatoes and served with sesame sauce). Portions are generous, and a relish plate with tomatoes, hot peppers, and turnips pickled in beet juice arrives at every table, compliments of the house. The 50-seat restaurant is often crowded at midday with business people from downtown. Breakfast offerings are strictly American. There's some metered parking on the street or use the municipal lot behind the Market.

▲

Hours: Mon–Fri 10 a.m.–6 p.m., Sat 10 a.m.–5 p.m.; closed Sun ■ Reservations taken, recommended for parties of 4 or more ■ Checks accepted ■ Bar: none ■ Takeout ■ ♿ Full access ■ Non-smoking section

PALMYRA

Cleveland   Near East Side
9491 Euclid Ave.   Casual
☎ 791-6606 $ $ $ $ $

This is a place to dine, not just eat, and the pride the management takes in the quality, freshness, and authenticity of the food is apparent. The real focus is on Middle Eastern, primarily Lebanese specialties, but the open kitchen at one end of the restaurant turns out Italian- and Mediterranean-inspired dishes, too. The cook makes pizza and pita bread in a traditional wood-burning brick baking oven. The pita, which flattens as it cools, arrives at the table warm, puffed up like a cloud, and seasoned with a flavorful blend of spices. The menu includes some dishes rarely found in this area: maklooby (rice, chicken, eggplant, and roasted almonds), saloony (mixed vegetables and lamb in a spiced broth), and karnbeit (fried cauliflower served with sesame sauce, lemon, olive oil, and fresh parsley). Also included are a sizable selection of menu items for vegetarians; sandwiches for a quick, simple lunch; and a variety of gourmet pizzas and calzone. It is often crowded at lunchtime with staff from the Cleveland Clinic and all the nearby institutions of University Circle. "One of my regular lunch customers," said owner Ashraf Yousef, "brought his wife for dinner and told me that never, in twenty years of marriage, had he seen his wife eat as much at a single sitting as she ate here." Booths and tables are comfortable, and parking is convenient, ample, and free.

Other ethnic specialties: Italian

▲

Hours: Mon–Fri 11 a.m.–9 p.m., Sat 6–10 p.m., Sun Buffet noon–8 p.m. ▪ Reservations taken, recommended at lunch, especially for large groups ▪ MC, VS, AX, Dis accepted ▪ Bar: none ▪ Takeout ▪ ♿ Full access ▪ Non-smoking section

PYRAMIDS RESTAURANT, THE

Cleveland   Near West Side
12657 Lorain Ave.   Casual
☎ 671-9300 $$$$$

It's obvious that a great deal of care went into decorating this young restaurant. The walls are done in an attractive, textured beige paper, there are many plants, and everything feels orderly, coordinated, and inviting. The 10 tables sit amidst interesting art work, tapestries, and artifacts. There are photographs from Syria labeled "Sayda, Syria where my friend Isa teaches school," or "Bedouins of the Syrian Desert." Apparently they are for sale, taken by a man named Daniel Kirk while there on a Fulbright Lectureship in the 1960s. The ambience quotient is high for such a small and inexpensive place. The menu offers a variety of Middle Eastern appetizers, sandwiches, two soups, salads, and dinner entrees featuring chicken, lamb, and beef. The Pyramids' combination plate includes shish tawook (a meat kebab), shish kafta (ground meat kebabs), shish kabob, grape leaves, fried kibbee, and hommous.

▲

Hours: daily 11 a.m.–10 p.m. ▪ Reservations not taken ▪ Checks accepted ▪ Bar: none ▪ Takeout ▪ ♿ Full access ▪ Non-smoking section

MOROCCAN

MARRAKESH EXPRESS CAFE

Lakewood   West Side
16300 Detroit Ave.   Casual
☎ 521-2244 $$$$$

When owner Lorita Green and her partner Chef Del, a Berber Moroccan, opened on Labor Day, 1994, they were the only restaurant in the state specializing in French Moroccan cuisine. (Now there's a second—see the following listing.) This 20-seat restaurant provides diners with a bit of Casablanca. Tangy smells, redolent of lemon, herbs, and exotic spices, greet you at the door. A fountain splashes in a corner and ceiling fans turn slowly. There are gold-fringed paisley tablecloths and hammered-brass-and-silver decorations. At first glance, the menu seems like an odd mix; there's pasta, Cajun roughy, and gazpacho. But don't be fooled by descriptions written to make the food seem less unfamiliar; most items are in fact prepared with a Moroccan flair and there are some truly authentic selections, including a few that blend sweet, salty, spicy, and sour flavors in a single dish in the traditional Moroccan style. A separate no-meat menu features vegetable tagines (stews), sheriya bahara (noodles with sugar and cinnamon), and a fava bean puree, the North African counterpart of hommus. On-street parking only.

▲

Hours: Mon–Thu noon–10 p.m., Fri & Sat noon–11 p.m., Sun noon–9 p.m. ▪ Reservations taken, recommended for weekdays; required for weekends ▪ MC, VS, AX, Dis accepted ▪ Bar: BYOB ▪ Takeout ▪ ♿ Full access

TASTE OF MOROCCO

Cleveland
12610 Larchmere Blvd.
☎ 421-0532

Near East Side
Casual
$$$$$

Khalid Arbabe and his wife, Laura, opened the restaurant in early 1995. The Arbabes did much of the rehab work on this old house themselves, and the result is a pleasant living-room setting with about 15 cloth-covered four-person tables. Though Berber carpets hang on the walls and some pieces of Moroccan pottery decorate the mantel of the gas-burning fireplace, they've avoided the temptation to go for the Casbah theme park look and opted instead for comfort and simplicity. Khalid Arbabe's mother, Fatima, who speaks not one word of English, came from Morocco specifically to help in this venture and brought with her a treasure chest of authentic recipes. She prepares a classic soup known as harira (made with lentils, chickpeas, and tomatoes), couscous (exotically seasoned steamed semolina served with chicken, lamb, or vegetables), a fish tagine that changes daily, shish kebab, and a vegetable charmoula (a Moroccan version of the French eggplant and tomato dish called ratatouille). The menu may be small by American restaurant standards, but everything on it delivers what the name of the place promises—a taste of Morocco, which is a unique blend, as the menu explains, of African, Middle Eastern, and European influences. Baskets of freshly baked sesame rolls accompany entrees, which are also served with the house salad or soup. The restaurant has its own parking lot, and its location, among galleries and antique stores, continues Larchmere's trend towards revitalization and renewal.

▲

Hours: Lunch Tue–Fri 11 a.m.–3 p.m.; Dinner Tue–Thu 5–10 p.m., Fri 5–11 p.m., Sun 5–9 p.m.; closed between Lunch & Dinner; open Sat 11 a.m.–11 p.m.; closed Mon
- Reservations taken, recommended ▪ MC, VS, AX, Dis accepted ▪ Bar: BYOB
- Takeout ▪ No smoking

MOROCCAN, SEE ALSO:
Sans Souci (Mediterranean Mix, Chapter 3)

MARKETS

INDIAN

ASIAN IMPORTS
North Olmsted   West Side
26885 Brookpark Rd. Ext.
☎ 777-8101

Asian Imports offer their mostly American clientele a selection of imported foods from India, with a smattering of products from Japan, Korea, and the Caribbean. The unlikely combination mirrors the overlap of cultures and cuisines; many of the ingredients essential to Indian cooking, for example, are used in equal measure in Caribbean dishes. A good source of rare spices, rice in 40-pound bags, and tropical juices like guava and papaya. Rich Indian sweets redolent with rose water and cardamom are also available.

Other ethnic specialties: Caribbean, Japanese, Korean, Pakistani

▲

Foods available: produce, grains, beans, flour, baked goods, spices, condiments, beverages, tea, coffee, prepared frozen foods, takeout meals ▪ Hours: Tue–Sat noon–8 p.m., Sun noon–5 p.m.; closed Mon ▪ MC, VS, AX, Dis, checks accepted
- ♿ Full access

INDIA FOOD EMPORIUM
Willowick   East Side
1217 E. 305th St.
☎ 585-1835

An emporium carries a wide variety and a large selection, and this place is aptly named. They've got frozen Indian-style heat-and-serve meals, pigeon peas, red and yellow lentils, pappadum (a cracker made from bean flour), and mango ice cream. Spices like cloves, coriander, and cumin are inexpensive, and dudhi (a large light green squash), chili peppers, ginger root, and bitter melon are generally available. They stock basmati rice, a flavorful white rice that smells like popcorn when it's cooking.

▲
Foods available: produce, grains, beans, flour, baked goods, spices, condiments, beverages, tea, prepared frozen foods ■ Hours: Tue–Sat 1–7 p.m., Sun 2–6 p.m.; closed Mon ■ Checks accepted ■ ঙ Full access

INDIA FOOD & SPICES

Parma   Southwest
5500 Pearl Rd.
☎ 845-0000

Owner Bhavna Patel takes pride in the fact that although this store is small it can supply customers with virtually any spice they ask for. He carries fruits and vegetables basic to Indian style dishes including bitter melon, okra, eggplant, long beans, mangoes, and guavas. A good selection of chutneys, Indian pickles (mango, gooseberry, ginger, lime), and flours made from ground beans—adoo besan, moong, dhokla, urad, and bajari. For an inexpensive weekend of armchair travel, you can stop in, buy some Indian ice cream and pastries, and rent an Indian video. There are a few basic, non-Indian grocery and household items available.

▲
Foods available: meat (frozen), produce, grains, beans, flour, baked goods, spices, condiments, beverages, tea, prepared frozen foods ■ Hours: Tue–Fri 1–7:30 p.m., Sat noon–7 p.m.; closed Mon ■ Checks accepted

INDO-AMERICAN FOODS

Maple Heights   Southeast
5131 Warrensville Center Rd.
☎ 662-0072

A small convenience store that's best described as the Indian version of a 7-11. Dried, canned, and packaged staples include rice and spices, mango juice, and movies to rent (Indian and Pakistani with subtitles). Some seasonal produce. This is where local Indian families run when they need a jar of ghee (clarified butter), a can of ginger pickles, or a bottle of coconut oil.

▲
Foods available: meat (frozen), produce, spices, condiments, beverages, tea, prepared frozen foods ■ Hours: Mon–Sat 11 a.m.–8 p.m., Sun noon–6 p.m. ■ Checks accepted

PATEL BROTHERS

Middleburg Heights   Southwest
6876 Pearl Rd.
☎ 885-4440

Tucked among the larger stores that are part of Southland Shopping Center is this small, family-owned shop offering Indian and Pakistani foods. Some basic household staples are shelved with the pickled mangoes, chutney, and chili paste. You'll find fresh items like bitter melon, squash, long beans, Chinese okra, eggplant, guava, and mango, rotis (bread) and Indian pastries. A wide selection of masala (spice mixtures) and sambal (spicy condiments).

▲

Foods available: produce, grains, beans, flour, baked goods, spices, condiments, tea, coffee, prepared frozen foods ▪ Hours: Tue–Sat 11 a.m.–8 p.m., Sun 11 a.m.–6 p.m.; closed Mon ▪ Checks accepted ▪ よ Full access

SPICE CORNER

Akron   Farther South
3779 Spicer St.
☎ 535-1033

As its name suggests this store specializes in spices and is a good source for hard-to-find flavorings essential to many traditional Indian, Pakistani, and Malaysian dishes. Their aroma mingles with the smell of incense, the only non-food item available here, and the air is thick with the exotic scents. Produce available in season includes bitter melon, long squash, guavas, and Asian vegetables. There are jars of relishes and pickles from India, a variety of lentils and rice, and flour specially ground for making chapati (Indian flat bread) as well as already-made frozen chapati. As so much Indian cuisine is meatless, this is a great source of food ideas and products for vegetarians.

Other ethnic specialties: Malaysian, Pakistani

▲

Foods available: produce, grains, beans, flour, spices, condiments, beverages, tea ▪ Hours: Weekends only, Sat & Sun 11 a.m.–6 p.m. ▪ Checks accepted ▪ よ Full access

MIDDLE EASTERN

ALADDIN'S BAKING COMPANY

Cleveland   Downtown
1301 Carnegie Ave.
☎ 861-0317

Freshly baked pita, a traditional flat bread made without sugar, oil, or fat, is the specialty here. A selection of Middle Eastern dishes is available daily, and you can purchase a full meal, already prepared. There's fatiyar (spinach and meat pies), beef or chicken shawarma (meat formed into a loaf around a skewer and cooked by rotisserie), kafta (meatballs), and shish kabob. You can get containers of tabouli (a salad made with bulgur wheat, onions, mint, tomatoes, olive oil, and lemon juice), hummus (chick pea spread), and baba ghannouj (eggplant spread). For dessert, choose from Middle Eastern and Mediterranean-style pastries, including Beirut-style baklava and pick up Turkish or Lebanese coffee. For use in your own recipes, they stock feta cheese, a wide variety of olives, olive oils, spices, and condiments.

▲
Foods available: baked goods, spices, condiments, coffee, prepared frozen foods, takeout meals ■ Hours: Mon–Fri 6:30 a.m.–6 p.m., Sat 7 a.m.–5:30 p.m., Sun 8 a.m.–2 p.m. ■ MC, VS, Dis, checks accepted

ASSAD BAKERY

Cleveland   West Side
12719 Lorain Ave.
☎ 251-5777

Don't be misled by the name—this is much more than a bakery. Brothers Mike and Fred Assad founded the business in 1990 and employ almost all their extended family. They bake fresh pita on the premises and prepare meat and spinach pies as well as Middle Eastern pastries. Exotic fruits and vegetables such as raw dates, fresh figs, loquats, and cactus pears are available seasonally. There's an interesting selection of cheeses, olives, nuts, spices, and olive oils. They also stock some unusual cookware, Middle Eastern drums, and Arabic clothing. Mike describes his clientele, many regulars who enjoy the friendly, personal service, as "like a United Nations."

▲
Foods available: produce, grains, beans, flour, baked goods, spices, coffee, prepared frozen foods, takeout meals ■ Hours: Mon–Sat 9 a.m.–9 p.m., Sun 9 a.m.–8 p.m. ■ MC, VS, AX, checks accepted ■ ♿ Full access

HALAL PRODUCTS

Cleveland   Near West Side
4164 Lorain Ave.
☎ 651-2448

The chicken, goat, lamb, beef, and fish available here comply with Muslim dietary laws. The store also carries a selection of food products imported from the various countries of the Middle East, including dates, raisins, and figs. Shoppers will also find a health food corner and a selection of Islamic books and clothing. Some non-ethnic food products are available, such as cheese, juices, cookies, flour, and rice.

▲

Foods available: meat (fresh), fish (fresh), produce, grains, beans, flour, spices, condiments, beverages, tea ■ Hours: Mon–Sat 9 a.m.–8 p.m.; closed between 1–3 p.m. Fri, Sun 11 a.m.–5 p.m. ■ Checks accepted ■ ⏺ Full access

CHAPTER 3

Mediterranean

THE TERM "MEDITERRANEAN" generally refers to the coastal regions of the countries surrounding the sea of that name. I've used it here rather cavalierly to provide a collective heading for a diverse group of countries and areas in Southern Europe. What ties them together in my mind is the robust, earthy flavors of their foods. Mediterranean cooking is characterized by its reliance on olives and olive oil, garlic, onions, lemons, grapes and the wines that can be made from them, capers (the pickled flower bud of a shrub that grows in the region), tomatoes, and green herbs like thyme, parsley, rosemary, basil, fennel, and bay leaves. Good bread and fresh fruit are seen as essential parts of every meal. With its emphasis on seafood and fresh garden vegetables, Mediterranean cuisine is considered to be one of the healthiest diets in the world. Both the tastes and simple techniques are well-suited to a contemporary American lifestyle, and this approach to food has grown increasingly popular in recent years. In Cleveland, restaurants provide diners with a chance to explore Mediterranean cuisine as it is prepared in Greece, Italy, and southern France.

Between 1890 and 1920, 5,000 Greeks settled in Cleveland. They were mostly males intending to stay only long enough to make their fortunes and then return home. These protporoi (pioneers) took low-paying, menial jobs at first, but once they decided to remain and establish roots in the community many started their own small businesses. They sent for their wives or returned home to find a bride to bring back to Cleveland. By 1922 there were at least 137 Greek-owned businesses in town, among them coffeehouses, candy stores, and restaurants.

Much of Greek cultural and social life, even for second-, third-, and fourth-generation Greek Americans, centers around the city's four Greek Orthodox churches. "I have to travel far to get to church", said Debbie Alexandrou who was born on the island of Samos, but has lived here since her marriage 32 years ago, "but I love it there because it's just like being in Greece. I can pretend that I am back home."

Small in number and close-knit, the Greek community of Cleveland is very dedicated not only to preserving their cultural heritage but to sharing it, and they sponsor many festivals around town. Food is always an important element. "All our events include food," said Penny Sikoutris, born here to Greek immigrant parents. "When Greeks get together, they eat. Years ago, the general public was not so familiar with our cuisine. Now that they've grown accustomed to it, they seem to like it as much as we do!"

Beyond its commonalities with all Mediterranean cooking, some ingredients are particular to Greek cuisine. Dill, sage (which seems to flourish in the sea air), oregano, and mint are used often. Lamb is the favored meat, and cheeses are made from goat's milk. Phyllo, thin sheets of pastry dough, goes into a variety of dishes. Honey is used with abandon in pastries.

Recently I attended a festival held at the Church of the Annunciation, the oldest Greek Orthodox church in the city. It was built on a parcel of land on West 14th, just across the river from "Greek Town," that was purchased in 1912. The array of food made by members of the congregation was staggering, as it always is at this annual celebration: there was pastitsio, moussaka, dolmathes, tiropeta, and spanakopeta, lamb shanks, baked fish, and souvlakia.

And tray after tray of desserts, almost floating in a sea of golden sweetness: baklava, galaktoboureko, and kataife. To no one in particular I said, "What would Greeks do without honey?" The man behind me replied, "Not have a reason to live."

Italians have long been one of the largest ethnic groups in Cleveland. The earliest immigrants came after the Civil War from northern Italy, followed in the years just preceding World War I by people from the central and southern regions. Between 1889 and 1924, 25,000 Italians came to settle here. They were stone masons, bootmakers, quarrymen, and produce sellers. They tended to live in close proximity to one another, build their own churches, and attend to all their needs through hometown societies. Big Italy, which no longer exists, was a downtown area that stretched from Ontario to East 40th Street. Little Italy was, and is, perched on Murray Hill along Mayfield Road, much like a little hill town in the old country. By 1911, 96 percent of the people who lived there were Italian born and most were from the Abruzzi region.

In 1919 an Italian immigrant named Vitantonio began making pasta machines in his Little Italy garage. He expanded, making the kinds of cookware Italians needed in their kitchens: tomato strainers, cavatelli and pizelli makers. His grandson, Louis, continues to run this local company under the family name, and it has become a large manufacturer and distributor of old-world kitchen tools. "Yesterday's ethnic customers," said Louis Vitantonio with obvious pride, "have been replaced by today's gourmet cooks. In spite of the trend towards convenience, there are still people who want food produced the traditional way."

Americans of Italian descent are for the most part fully absorbed into the mainstream of American life. Though Little Italy continues to be a densely populated Italian enclave and home to some of the city's best-known Italian restaurants and stores, Italian Americans are spread throughout Greater Cleveland now. But for many, no matter where they live, Italian-American clubs that promote cultural awareness and pride provide a link with their heritage. Local cookbook author Maria Volpe Paganini says much of this cultural legacy is expressed through food and family, the two basic and essential elements of the Italian soul.

"To Italians, family is what matters most and food is at the center of day-to-day family life. Food is more important to us than politics or money and we think about it a great deal. We gather around the table, and while we eat good food, we talk."

Italian cuisine has profoundly influenced how Americans eat, though the Italian dishes we're most accustomed to bear little resemblance to the real thing. Even the term Italian food is misleading. There are approximately twenty regions in that country, and every one has its own culinary heritage. In each, the unique foods produced there represent the area's distinctive style: Modena is the one true source for balsamic vinegar, Parma for prosciutto ham, and Emilia-Romagna for genuine parmigiano-reggiano cheese.

Pasta, however (and there are over 200 different types and shapes), is common to all. Cooks throughout the country also appreciate the qualities of Italian varieties of rice (Arborio, Vialone Nano, Carnaroli); polenta (a cornmeal mush); cannellini and other beans; and anchovies. And they do wondrous things with veal.

Though the cooks of southern France are a breed unto themselves, their culinary traditions are inextricably linked to their Italian neighbors. But as a group they have no real Cleveland history to speak of, for, as someone from Provence once said to me, "Why would they leave?" Which leaves me with only their cuisine to write about.

It's been described as full gusto, passion, and vitality, imbued with the warm sunshine of their climate and the peasant's appreciation for nature's bounty. Their soups are said to have distinctive personality, and their lamb, which grazes on wild herbs, is like no other. In addition to the ingredients favored by all Mediterranean cooks, the kitchens of southern France are stocked with mushrooms, potatoes, shallots, and leeks. But it is not the type of ingredients so much as their freshness and the way in which they are combined to let the flavor of each shine through that characterizes this style of cooking. Ably practiced in Cleveland by chef Paul Rodier and his staff at Stouffer's Sans Souci, it is ultimately the art of beautiful and savory simplicity.

RESTAURANTS

GREEK

GREEK EXPRESS, THE

Cleveland
The Arcade, 401 Euclid Ave.
☎ 589-0534

Downtown
Casual
$$$$$

This small eatery in the Old Arcade caters to a busy business crowd. At first glance the cafeteria-style service, plastic tableware, and styrofoam plates give the impression that this is just another fast food joint. But the quality, freshness, and authentic Greek taste convey a different message. You wouldn't choose this spot for a romantic tete-a-tete (though the charm of the landmark Arcade creates its own special atmosphere) or a leisurely meeting over lunch. But it is a good spot to stop for a quick, interesting meal. The menu offers an eclectic selection including traditional Greek dishes like gyros, avgolemono (egg lemon) soup, and chicken kebobs plus curries, salads, and rice pilaf. The restaurant itself seats about 25, but there are additional tables available along the walkways of the Arcade. Phone orders accepted for takeout.

▲

Hours: Mon–Sat 9 a.m.–4 p.m. ▪ Reservations not taken ▪ Cash only ▪ Bar: none ▪ Takeout ▪ ᴦ Full access ▪ Non-smoking section

GREEK ISLES, THE

Cleveland
500 W. St. Clair Ave.
☎ 861-1919

Downtown
Casual
$$$$$

Owners Dr. Nick Stavridis and George Servetas have created a restaurant that evokes the flavor and feel of Greece. Recorded Greek music plays quietly in the background of this open, airy space with bright white walls. Big windows let in lots of natural light that sets off the blue cloth napkins and crisp white tablecloths. An extensive wine list includes a selection of Greek imports. There are some traditional hot and cold appetizers that cannot be found anywhere else in town, such as taramosalata (a sort of whipped caviar), and a spicy sausage called loukaniko. The menu includes both classic Greek specialties like moussaka (layers of eggplant and ground beef in a bechamel-type sauce) and dolmathes (stuffed grape leaves), and some more unusual offerings, such as Kokinisto arni (braised lamb in a tomato sauce), baccalao and kalamarakia (pan fried cod or squid), and ortykia (grilled quail). There are numerous choices for vegetarians including spanakotipopita (layers of filo dough, spinach and feta cheese) and a meatless pastitsio (a macaroni and cheese dish), as well as simple beef and chicken dishes to satisfy the less adventurous palate. Parking can be an effort during the day—if you're lucky you'll find an on-street space, otherwise pay for a place in nearby lots.

Hours: Mon–Thu 11 a.m.–11 p.m., Fri 11 a.m.–midnight, Sat noon–midnight, Sun noon–11 p.m. ■ Reservations taken, recommended Friday & Saturday ■ MC, VS, AX, Dis, checks accepted ■ Bar: beer, wine, liquor ■ Takeout ■ ⚬ Full access ■ Not recommended for children ■ Non-smoking room

MAD GREEK, THE

Cleveland Heights   East Side
2466 Fairmount Blvd.   Casual
☎ 421-3333 $$$$$

The Mad Greek is well-known for serving a unique combination of Greek and Indian foods with a few Middle Eastern specialties like hoomis and baba ghanouj thrown in for good measure. Owner Loki Chopra's mother came from Bombay to help them create the Indian dishes on the menu, and his former wife supplied the Greek recipes, which she was taught by her mother. On the Greek side, entrees include gyros, shish kebob, moussaka, dolmades, and a sampler plate called mezedakia. The Indian half offers chicken marinated in yogurt sauce, lamb and spinach curry, and vegetable goa made with a creamy coconut sauce. Over the years, cooking techniques have been adjusted to reflect the current interest in reducing salt and fat consumption, and the portions have gotten noticeably smaller (which you may view as either a plus or a minus). There are also burgers, for the less adventurous palate. The original dining room is done with a classic Med decor—white walls accented with colorful ceramic tiles and lots of green plants. The newer bar and additional dining area feature more unusual, black and silver accents with an art deco motif. A touch of European alfresco dining is provided here when the warm weather arrives; huge windows open to create a streetside cafe.

Other ethnic specialties: Indian

Hours: Lunch Mon–Sat 11 a.m.–4:30 p.m.; Dinner Mon–Thu 4:30–11 p.m., Fri & Sat, 4:30 p.m.–1 a.m., Sun, 4:30–11 p.m. ■ Reservations taken, recommended, Friday and Saturday ■ MC, VS, AX, Dis, checks accepted ■ Bar: beer, wine, liquor ■ Takeout ■ Non-smoking section

MARDI GRAS LOUNGE & GRILL

Cleveland
1423 E. 21st St.
☎ 566-9094

Downtown
Casual
$$$$$

You might come here for the food; the menu is peppered with Greek specialties such as pastitsio and mousaka, plus a few spicy Cajun dishes like shrimp Creole and blackened chicken. It's the only place in town you can get saganaki (flaming Greek kasseri cheese) or a souvlaki (marinated broiled lamb) at 3:00 a.m. on a Thursday. But this is no typical ethnic restaurant, and people are just as likely to find their way here because the bar is open late and the music is hot. A favorite lunchtime hangout for *Plain Dealer* employees, with a standard selection of salads and sandwiches, it also attracts enthusiastic jazz hounds three nights a week. Any time of the day or night, the clientele is a mix of white- and blue-collar folks, and the ambience is dark and funky. There's a parking lot across the street.

Hours: Mon–Wed 11 a.m.–2:30 a.m., Thu–Sat 11 a.m.–4:30 a.m.; closed Sun. Breakfast served 1 a.m.–4:30 a.m. ▪ Reservations taken ▪ MC, VS, AX, Dis, checks accepted ▪ Bar: beer, wine, liquor ▪ Takeout ▪ ♿ Full access ▪ Not recommended for children

PLAKA, THE

Cleveland
11633 Clifton Blvd.
☎ 221-2333

Near West Side
Casual
$$$$$

Attached to Cliff Hangers Bar and Grill, this small restaurant seats between 40 and 50 diners in a separate dining room. There are no printed menus. Owner and chef George Koropolis, who describes his place as an authentic Greek taverna, decides daily what he'll prepare and chalks up the specials on a board that's never the same twice. There's always a mix of 10 to 12 Greek, Italian, and American dishes, very reasonably priced. "When people come here for the first time and read my menu board," said Mr. Koropolis, "they're afraid the food won't be any good because the prices are inexpensive. After they taste, they're very surprised, and very happy." On a given night, patrons might find broiled lamb, veal stuffed with spinach and feta cheese, quail, and five different chicken dishes. Although the kitchen officially closes, Koropolis says that as long as there are people in the restaurant who want to eat, he'll keep cooking.

Hours: Tue–Sun, 5–11 p.m.; closed Sun & Mon ▪ Reservations taken, recommended ▪ MC, VS, checks accepted ▪ Bar: beer, wine, liquor ▪ Takeout ▪ ♿ Full access ▪ Non-smoking section

THEO'S RESTAURAUNT

Cleveland   Near West Side
4250 Pearl Rd.   Casual
☎ 459-1555 $$$$$

Housed in a bank built in the early part of this century, this restaurant has been owned and operated by the same family since 1978. The Loizos preserved many of the building's unique architectural details (like the high, carved ceilings) in their renovation, and the result is an elegant and unusual place to dine. The large dining area, with hand-painted tables, is an ideal setting for big groups and special celebrations. There are non-Greek dishes on the menu, but the house specialties are traditional Greek favorites and the portions are generous. All the appetizers are made by owner John Loizas' wife Tula; her tyropites (a flaky pastry dough filled with a mix of cheeses) and keftedakia (a spiced, baked meatball) are outstanding. The service is attentive and friendly. The restaurant is easy to find, located directly across from Deaconess Hospital, and there is ample off-street parking in back
▲
Hours: Mon–Sat 11 a.m.–9 p.m.; closed Sun & holidays ■ Reservations taken ■ MC, VS, AX accepted ■ Bar: beer, wine, liquor ■ Takeout ■ Non-smoking section

GREEK, SEE ALSO:
Georgio's (Mediterranean Mix)
Sans Souci (Mediterranean Mix)

ITALIAN

ALDO'S

Brooklyn   Near West Side
8459 Memphis Ave.   Casual
☎ 749-7060 $$$$$

The question is, how can Aldo's still be considered one of Cleveland's best kept secrets when the restaurant has been enthusiastically reviewed by *Cleveland Magazine, The Plain Dealer, The Akron Beacon Journal, Northern Ohio Live,* and *Currents*? But that's how folks at nearby American Greetings corporate headquarters and food aficionados from all over (some of whom say they come three or four times a month) describe this intimate little place. Tucked inconspicuously behind a nondescript facade in a six-store strip mall (part of the Memphis/Ridge business district), Aldo's serves traditional, but never standard, Italian fare. Each forkful is to be savored and every meal is really a celebration of the joys of good food. On any given night, specials could include brushetta with roasted peppers and boccancini, pasta fagiole, spezzatino di vitelle (veal stew), crepes stuffed with veal in basil sauce with escarole, and tripe in fresh tomato sauce. The decor is modern-looking, bold in turquoise and black, but the Zappa family photos on the wall lend a homey touch. It's painfully small, seating just 35, and not the best choice for large parties. If you have to wait for a table, your only option is to stand in the narrow entryway, but no one seems to mind, and newcomers chat with Aldo regulars. Customers, some in sweatshirts, some in suits and silk, call out greetings to Aldo, who often stops and visits, and everyone ends up feeling like a guest in his home rather than a customer. Service is impeccable and at the same time friendly. This is a place you'll want to remember. More than likely, they'll remember you, too.

▲

Hours: Tue 4 p.m.–9:30 p.m., Wed 4–10 p.m., Thu 11:30 a.m.–10 p.m., Fri 11:30 a.m.–11 p.m., Sun 4–9 p.m.; closed Mon ■ Reservations not taken ■ Checks accepted ■ Bar: beer, wine, liquor ■ Takeout ■ &. Full access ■ Not recommended for children ■ Non-smoking section

AMICI'S ITALIAN RESTAURANT

Lakewood   West Side
18405 Detroit Ave.   Casual
☎ 221-1150 $$$$$

Described by one veteran East Side diner as "Well worth the trip", Amici's is like a bit of New York City's Little Italy transplanted to Lakewood. It's a small, friendly, inviting space, narrow and deep, with lots of wood, green plants, and wine racks on the front walls. Tables have paper cloths over linen. The feeling here is comfortable without frills, the servers' pace is efficient without being too fast, and it's the sort of spot you might like to come after work to relax, order a bottle of good wine from the extensive list, and meander through a meal. There's food from all regions of Italy, but the kitchen definitely has a Northern bent; seafood and veal are considered house specialties. They're justifiably proud of the fact that, unlike most restaurants, they don't buy their veal precut—Amici's purchases a whole leg and they cut it themselves. Fresh bread with herbed garlic butter is brought to the table soon after you're seated. Entree servings are generous without being overwhelming.

▲

Hours: Lunch Mon–Fri 11:30 a.m.–2 p.m.; Dinner Mon–Thu 4:30–10 p.m., Fri 4:30–11 p.m., Sat 4:30–11 p.m., Sun 4:30–9 p.m.; closed between Lunch & Dinner; Sat & Sun Dinner only ■ Reservations taken, recommended on weekends ■ MC, VS, AX, Dis, checks accepted ■ Bar: beer, wine, liquor ■ Takeout ■ &. Full access ■ Not recommended for children

BOVALINO'S ITALIAN RISTORANTE

Westlake   West Side
27828 Center Ridge Rd.   Casual
☎ 892-9300 $$$$$

A red, white, and green awning helps you identify this free-standing brick building on a residential stretch of road as a restaurant and not a home. It is an utterly sweet little place, and driving up I had the same feeling I remember from years ago, in Italy, when we'd unexpectedly stumbled upon a delightful restaurant in the middle of nowhere. Inside, green plants hang in leafy profusion from latticework suspended from the ceiling and it's as though you've come into a garden, an outdoor trattoria perhaps, somewhere in southern Italy. The town of Bovalino, for which the restaurant was named, is in Calabria, at the southern tip of Italy, and that's where owner Rus Lentini's grandparents came from. Using some of his family recipes, the kitchen turns out more than 60 different Italian dishes that reflect southern and northern cuisine; two additional daily specials might be anything from Chicken Milanese to lobster-filled ravioli. Rus himself is in there every morning at five, starting the sauces that will simmer all day, and he won't let anyone else prepare them. He also makes fresh pizza dough daily. Portions are huge, enough for the next day's lunch if you have an average appetite. The menu offers Rus's hand-picked selection of imported and domestic wines, red and white, and an Italian beer. There's room for 40 diners and in the warm weather, additional seating outside in a small fenced-in courtyard adjacent to the parking lot.

▲

Hours: Mon–Fri 11:30 a.m.–10 p.m.; Dinner only Sat 4:30–10 p.m.; closed Sun ■
Reservations taken, for Friday and Saturday until 7 p.m.; open seating thereafter ■
Cash only ■ Bar: beer, wine ■ Takeout ■ &. Full access

BUCCI'S

Berea   Southwest
One Berea Commons   Dressy
☎ 826-4500 $$$$$

Some of the windows of this comfortable, pleasant restaurant overlook the entrance to the Metroparks' Mill Stream Run Reservation. Others look out onto Berea's historic downtown triangle. Wherever the maitre d' seats you, you'll quickly realize that this is the sort of place where you settle back into the quiet, intimate reading-room atmosphere and enjoy the view. Shortly after you're seated, good bread and rolls and flavored butter will arrive at the table. The kitchen consistently turns out a good selection of Italian favorites. The ravioli, cavatelli, and gnocchi are homemade. Some of their more unusual offerings include angel hair pasta with baby squid and tri-colored peppers, and chicken sauteed with capers and fresh herbs in a balsamic vinegar, lemon, and brown sauce. This second Bucci's is more formal than the original. Think of eating here as an occasion, even if you don't have anything special to celebrate. Dress up a bit, let the subdued lighting set the mood, and take your time, because this is a place you choose when you want to appreciate a well-served, well-prepared meal eaten in good company.

▲

Hours: Mon–Sat 11:30 a.m.–11 p.m., Sun 3–8 p.m. ▪ Reservations taken, recommended on weekends ▪ MC, VS, AX, Dis accepted ▪ Bar: beer, wine, liquor ▪ Takeout ▪ ⅙ Full access ▪ Not recommended for children ▪ Non-smoking section

BUCCI'S

Rocky River West Side
19373 Hilliard Rd. Casual
☎ 331-5157 $$$$$

This is the original Bucci's, opened 25 years ago. It was so successful that the family eventually started a second restaurant in Berea (see next listing for more information). A small, homey, intimate restaurant seating between 50 and 60 people, Bucci's specializes in central and southern Italian food. The ceiling has exposed beams, there are hanging plants, and the pastel-toned wallpaper features classic scenes of Italian peasant life: vineyards, farms, and villages. The lighting is pleasantly soft, candles glow on each table, and linens are cloth. The bread basket brought to the table by servers who are both friendly and fast includes regular Italian bread, fat-free ciabatta bread, and freshly made garlic butter. Entrees, which are large, are served on oven-warmed plates and come to the table piping hot. There's always a homemade soup of the day, stuffed eggplant, pasta primavera made with angel hair and a light blush sauce, and beef funghetto (tenderloin in wine sauce). They also do pizza, all the classic pasta dishes (with smaller side orders available for children under 12), plus steak, chicken, veal, and seafood. And if you still have room, there's spumoni, homemade cannoli, and tiramasu.

▲

Hours: Lunch Tue–Fri 11:30 a.m.–2 p.m.; Dinner Tue–Thu 4–10 p.m., Fri 4–11 p.m., Sat 4–11 p.m., Sun 4–9 p.m.; closed between Lunch & Dinner; closed Mon ▪ Reservations taken, for groups of 7 or more only ▪ MC, VS, AX, Dis accepted ▪ Bar: beer, wine ▪ Takeout ▪ ⅙ Full access

D'AGNESE'S ITALIAN RESTAURANT

Seven Hills Southwest
7531 Broadview Rd. Dressy
☎ 328-1740 $$$$$

The owners pride themselves on offering fine Italian cuisine from all regions. Many of the recipes come from partner Franko Boffice's father Luigi, born in Italy and a professional chef for 40 years. Boffice and Ricardo Sandoval opened D'Agnese's (the 'G' is silent, pronounce the name dan-YEAH-sass) five years ago in a small single room that held only 20. The restaurant's popularity grew to such proportions that they expanded. The larger version, which still has the small intimate feel of a New York supper club, seats 70 amidst an old-world–style decor, and it's often crowded with diners rubbing elbows. "We're busy," said Sandoval, " because of the food, not the decor. People know the food they eat here is authentic." They offer hearty portions of richly flavored, earthy Italian food, the kind that begs for bread to wipe the plate clean. The chicken cacciatore is simmered in a garlic marinara sauce thick with onions, peppers, and mushrooms. Zuppa Di Pesce features shrimp, calamari (squid), clams, whitefish, and mussels. Linguini Arrabiata is made with olives, onions, and hot cherry peppers. Veal Pizzaiola is cooked with mushrooms and black olives in a homemade marinara sauce that's prepared fresh each day. They also have some dishes not often offered on restaurant menus in this area such as scungilli (conch) salad and Chicken Contadino, a peasant specialty made with peas, pimentos, broccoli, romano cheese, and wine butter.

▲

Hours: Lunch Mon–Fri 11:30 a.m.–2 p.m.; Dinner Mon–Thu 4:30–10 p.m., Fri 4:30–11 p.m., Sat 4:30–11 p.m.; closed between Lunch & Dinner; closed Sun ■ Reservations taken, but only a limited number accepted ■ MC, VS, AX, Dis, checks accepted ■ Bar: beer, wine, liquor ■ Takeout ■ ♿ Full access ■ Not recommended for children

FRANKIE'S ITALIAN CUISINE

North Olmsted   West Side
4641 Great Northern Blvd.   Casual
☎ 734-8646 $$$$$

Established in 1967, Frankie's is a midsized restaurant that families flock to because the atmosphere is casual and the food, served in generous quantities, is the kind almost nobody can resist: veal parmesan, lasagna, spaghetti with marinara sauce, meatball and sausage sandwiches, and hand-tossed pizza. The garlic bread is worth a special mention. The dishes on this menu are meant to satisfy rather than surprise, and food is prepared and presented "mamma's kitchen–style" without flash or nouveau anything. But the sauce is so popular they sell it by the quart, meatballs by the dozen, lasagna by the tray, and pizzas by the sheet for takeout. The restaurant seats about 95 in a pleasant, modern setting, and the kitchen will cook for private parties in the restaurant in a room that can easily accommodate 10-30. They do off-site catering as well. Jeans are acceptable here, but you wouldn't feel out of place if you dressed up a bit to make your own out-to-eat occasion special. A three-item kids' menu for the under-10 set, and some entrees, like chicken piccata and veal à la Frankie, are geared to those who'd rather eat light.

▲
Hours: Mon–Thu 11 a.m.–11 p.m., Fri & Sat 11 a.m.–midnight, Sun 4–10 p.m. ▪
Reservations taken, for groups of 6 or more only ▪ MC, VS, AX accepted
▪ Bar: beer, wine, liquor ▪ Takeout ▪ ఈ Full access ▪ Non-smoking section

FRANKIE'S ITALIAN CUISINE

Westlake   West Side
25939 Detroit Rd.   Casual
☎ 892-0064 $$$$$

The first Frankie's, in North Olmsted, was so successful that in 1986 this second incarnation opened in Westlake's Williamsburg Square Center (a strip mall, so parking is never a problem). Easy to reach via I-90 (Columbia Road exit), this Frankie's is a bit larger than the other, comfortably seating up to 150 in a pleasant, well-lit dining room decorated in a contemporary style with plants and wooden ceiling fans. (For more information, see the previous entry for the original Frankie's, North Olmsted.)

▲
Hours: Mon–Thu 11 a.m.–11 p.m., Fri & Sat 11 a.m.–midnight, Sun 4–10 p.m. ▪
Reservations taken, for groups of 6 or more only ▪ MC, VS, AX accepted
▪ Bar: beer, wine, liquor ▪ Takeout ▪ ఈ Full access ▪ Non-smoking section

GUARINO'S RESTAURANT

Cleveland   Near East Side
12309 Mayfield Rd.   Dressy
☎ 231-3100 $$$$$

According to Marilyn Guarino, the restaurant established in 1918 by her father-in-law, Vincent Guarino, now claims the honor of being the oldest continuously operating Italian restaurant in town. It's not unusual for tour buses to stop here. The family used to live above the restaurant; now one floor has become a bed and breakfast and another is a series of Victorian-style parlors where dinner is served to private parties of 2 to 50 people. Downstairs, the restaurant, which seats between 75 and 90 people, also has an antique Victorian motif. The food is primarily southern Italian with some northern influence. In addition to the standard selection of pasta dishes with a variety of sauces, the menu includes wedding soup, lumache (snails), saltimbocca (veal with prosciutto ham and cheese), and brasciole (a thin steak stuffed and rolled). The wine list offers both California and Italian varieties. In warm weather, there's outdoor dining amidst the grape and trumpet flower vines that Vincenczo Guarino originally brought with him from Sicily. Valet parking available on weekends; otherwise use their lot adjacent to the restaurant.

▲

Hours: Mon–Wed 11:30 a.m.–10 p.m., Thu 11:30 a.m.–11 p.m., Fri 11:30 a.m.–11:30 p.m., Sat 12:30–11:30 p.m., Sun 1–8 p.m. ▪ Reservations taken, recommended on weekends ▪ MC, VS, AX, Dis accepted ▪ Bar: beer, wine, liquor ▪ Takeout ▪ Ġ. Full access ▪ Non-smoking section

JOHNNY'S BAR

Cleveland   Downtown
3164 Fulton Rd.   Formal
☎ 281-0055 $$$$$

The latest Zagat survey describes Johnny's, a sumptuous, upscale restaurant that sits inconspicuously on a corner in an aging blue-collar neighborhood, as "outstanding in every way." Cleveland's own food experts and cookbook authors Fred and Linda Griffith rank it among the best in town. The place has a genial, private-club ambience, a unique and stunning decor, and unforgettable northern Italian food prepared with an innovative, continental flair by up-and-coming chef Vid Lutz and his staff. When the three Santusso brothers took over the restaurant from their parents, they decided to re-create a bygone era; entering their restaurant is like going back to the 1930s. "We wanted a restaurant that looked like a real restaurant from the old days," said Joe Santusso, "when food service was at its height and eating out was an experience. The look is post-Deco, pre-streamline, the same as New York's Radio City Music Hall, and we reproduced everything exactly, down to the last detail of aging the color of the wood." Those details include faux-leopardskin carpeting, crisp linens, fine china, wood paneling, original murals painted on the walls, black leather banquettes, and a mahogany bar. There is both a sense of humor and an elegance in it all. The food, however, is serious business, made for people who appreciate and understand fine dining. The menu is large, and there are a number of specials each day featuring fish, veal, and pasta. The potato gnocchi is made according to Mamma Santusso's original recipe by Joe's aunt, and all the other pasta is made fresh on the premises, too. In their book, *The Best of the Midwest*, the Griffiths describe these pastas as "light-as-air" and name the pasta puttanesca, the angel hair with escargot, the mussels marinara, the baked calamari, and the veal tenderloin as standouts. In true old-world style, fresh herbs are grown in the garden out back.

▲

Hours: Lunch Mon–Fri 11:30 a.m.–3 p.m.; Dinner Mon–Thu 5–10 p.m., Fri 5–11 p.m., Sat 5–11 p.m.; closed between Lunch & Dinner; closed Sun ▪ Reservations taken, for parties of 4 or more on Fri & Sat ▪ MC, VS, AX accepted ▪ Bar: beer, wine, liquor ▪ Takeout ▪ Not recommended for children ▪ Non-smoking section

JOHNNY'S DOWNTOWN

Cleveland   Downtown
1406 W. 6th St.   Dressy
☎ 623-0055 $$$$$

The menu at this second Johnny's, opened in 1993, is close to that at the original Johnny's on Fulton Avenue (see previous description), featuring pasta, veal, and fish. The main difference here is that preparation is less refined, more reminiscent of the rustic cuisine of Tuscany. The setting, however, is not a duplicate of the old place, though it is equally special, evoking images of the once famous and stately Oak Room in New York's Plaza Hotel. There's plenty of highly polished mahogany; leather, heavy, high-backed, upholstered chairs; and snowy table linens. The handsome barroom, which is often crowded and lively, is separate from the dining room, and meals are served there too. The dining area is lighter, brighter, and more spacious, offering panoramic views of downtown. The entire setting is sophisticated and chic, and attracts a very urbane sort of clientele who come to see and be seen, enjoy the food, and listen to the music. A great place to bring out-of-towners and suburban visitors to give them a taste of just how suave this city can be.

▲
Hours: Lunch Mon–Fri 11:30 a.m.–3 p.m.; Dinner Sun–Thu 5–10:30 p.m., Fri & Sat 5–11:30 p.m.; closed between Lunch & Dinner ▪ Reservations taken, for parties of 4 or more; required for parties of 4 or more on Fri & Sat ▪ MC, VS, AX accepted ▪ Bar: beer, wine, liquor ▪ Takeout ▪ ♿ Full access ▪ Not recommended for children ▪ Non-smoking section

MAMMA SANTA'S

Cleveland   Near East Side
12305 Mayfield Rd.   Casual
☎ 231-9567 $$$$$

My husband and I have been eating here since 1971, when we were students down the hill at CWRU and the restaurant was only 10 years old. We liked the casual, friendly, relaxed atmosphere, affordable prices, good taste, and plentiful portions. Twenty years later, Mamma Santa's still offers all those some qualities and now we take our kids there. The restaurant attracts a steady crowd of students, couples, families, and workers whose collars come white, blue, pink, and just about every other color, too—many from the institutions of nearby University Circle. Many have been eating here for years. When it's full, and it often is, the restaurant can serve pizza and pasta to about 120 at booths and tables spread among three rooms. The cooking is Sicilian-style, and the noodles are all homemade. When you want to try something different from spaghetti with meatballs, order noodles with faggioli (beans), lenticchie (lentils), or ceci (chickpeas). Pizzas are baked to order, so it can take 20 minutes, but you can get an antipasto plate and garlic toast or a side of fried green peppers to hold you. Lights are low, and old wine bottles and pictures of Italy are all the decor you'll find. Seniors get a discount. A limited number of parking spaces in the rear, otherwise you're on your own, on the street.

▲

Hours: Mon–Thu 11 a.m.–11:45 p.m., Fri & Sat 11 a.m.–12:45 p.m.; closed Sun ■ Reservations taken, only for large groups ■ MC, VS accepted ■ Bar: beer, wine ■ Takeout ■ ᕕ Full access ■ Non-smoking section

MARIA'S

Lakewood   West Side
11822 Detroit Ave.   Casual
☎ 226-5875 $$$$$

Maria's has been around more than 35 years, by owner Maria Bastuli's reckoning, but the restaurant has undergone a facelift in recent years and now has a more up-to-date look. It's easy to spot—they've installed a neon version of their logo, a fork and spaghetti filled pasta bowl, that can be seen from two blocks away. Inside, there's a pleasant bar and three dining rooms, two handsomely decorated with a flower motif on curtains and wallpaper, one featuring a red, white, and green parachute stretched across the ceiling. Lots of framed photographs of Italy on the walls, with booths and tables for up to 150. Dressings, sauces, and pasta are all made on the premises. The pasta is available by the pound to go. Servings are generous, and when the menu says clam sauce it means *clam* sauce: huge meaty chunks plus some still in the shell grace an order here. They serve their own tasty version of garlic bread called cucina bread, toasted with parmesan cheese. Pizza, calzone, lasagna, and ravioli are available in addition to classic veal and chicken dishes. There's a three-item children's menu. Try to leave room for Maria's signature confections, which include chocolate fettuccine served with vanilla ice cream and raspberry sauce and chocolate salami made with pistachios—voted one of Cleveland's best chocolate desserts by *The Plain Dealer*.

▲

Hours: Mon–Thu 11 a.m.–10 p.m., Fri 11 a.m.–11:30 p.m., Sat 5–11:30 p.m., Sun 4–9 p.m. ■ Reservations taken, for groups of 6 or more only ■ MC, VS, AX accepted ■ Bar: beer, wine, liquor ■ Takeout ■ Non-smoking section

MASSIMO DA MILANO

Cleveland
1400 W. 25th St.
☎ 696-2323

Near West Side
Dressy
$$$$$

After you leave your car for free valet parking, you enter the restaurant through an impressive glass-enclosed granite and marble foyer. This was once the Forest City Bank Building, a grand old Neo-Classical edifice that went up in 1903. Echoes of its former glory still resonate in the main dining room, a large space distinguished by huge columns, large windows, and a high ornate ceiling. But everything else is très trendy and chic, from the granite tables and contemporary chrome chairs to the black napery. Another adjoining dining area is all skylights, exposed brick, and modern art, with a long sleek bar at one end. The food, too, reflects this blend of old and new. Traditional recipes from Tuscany, Piedemonte, and other regions of northern Italy have been updated. So you'll find fettucine made with field mushrooms and Marsala cream sauce, scallops of veal finished with red wine and sundried tomato pesto, and chicken stuffed with Fontina cheese and served with a marinara fresca. Foccacia bread is baked on the premises and is served with herbed olive oil for dipping. The lunch buffet, all you can eat for a fixed price, is very popular, offering a large selection, no-wait, and the same attentive service from the staff. It includes at least two soups, four hot pasta dishes, nine or ten antipasto salads, fresh-baked pizza, Italian cheeses and cold cuts, and a variety of other dishes. A bakery, open to the public, sells bread, rolls, and Italian pastries. A more casual cafe located behind the bakery counter at the front of the restaurant serves breakfast (Italian or American style) plus quick lunches. The combination of the very casual cafe, the upscale bar area, and the elegant main dining room means diners have a real choice.

▲
Hours: Mon–Thu 11:30 a.m.–10 p.m., Fri & Sat 11:30 a.m.–11:30 p.m., Sun 4–9 p.m.;
Breakfast available in the Cafe Massimo only, 7–10 a.m. ▪ Reservations taken, recommended ▪ MC, VS, AX accepted ▪ Bar: beer, wine, liquor ▪ Takeout
▪ ♿ Full access ▪ Not recommended for children ▪ Non-smoking section

MOLINARI'S FOOD & WINE

Mentor
8900 Mentor Ave.
☎ 269-1230

Farther East
Casual
$$$$$

Molinari's is a small (50 seat) restaurant and wine bar in the midst of a specialty food store. The look is sophisticated New York contemporary, and the view into the kitchen from the dining room is a source of entertainment and interest. The menu, which changes seasonally, is northern Italian and northern California. The wine list is not only extensive but full of great values, reflecting retail rather than restaurant pricing. The chef specializes in bold flavors and unique, creative presentations, so diners might be able to order calamari with three-pepper butter, fettuccine pomodoro, an egg pasta tossed with sun-dried tomatoes, red and yellow baby tomatoes, garlic, herbs, and shaved parmigianno regianno, or a gourmet pizza that's topped with fresh crabmeat, scallions, peppers, white cheddar, and chevre (goat cheese). On Mondays, when the restaurant itself is closed, Molinari's hosts special events, open to the public, such as wine and beer tastings. Their newsletter, which comes out four times a year, includes announcements for these events along with the season's new menu and a list of upcoming cooking classes. Call to get on their mailing list or pick up a copy at the restaurant.

▲

Hours: Lunch Tue–Sat 11:30 a.m.–2 p.m.; Dinner Tue–Thu 5:30–10 p.m., Fri & Sat 5:30–11 p.m.; closed Mon ▪ Reservations taken, recommended ▪ MC, VS, AX, Dis, checks accepted ▪ Bar: beer, wine, liquor ▪ Takeout ▪ & Full access ▪ Non-smoking section

MR. Z'S

Cleveland   Near West Side
3312 W. 117th St.   Casual
☎ 941-2504 $$$$$

This is not merely a restaurant but a Cleveland tradition. The Zappones have been serving Italian food to their customers for three generations, and one room in this huge restaurant (seats 250 in four separate dining areas plus the bar) is the historic streetcar that was once Tony Zappone's diner. The walls feature an unparalleled photo history of the city and lots of Cleveland memorabilia. The menu is classic Italian, with Sicilian accents; there are all the pasta dishes you'd expect, like lasagna, rigatoni, and linguine, wood-fired brick oven pizzas and roasted chicken, calzone and strombolino (the Italian version of a sandwich), and daily specials that run the gamut from veal picata (sauteed with lemon and capers), cannelloni (a crepe stuffed with meat, spinach in a cheese sauce), and fettucine alla pascatore (flat pasta noodles with mussels and squid in a marinara sauce). The entire wine list is made up of wines produced in Ohio. This is a great place for special occasions; they can accommodate large groups, the kitchen offers family-style dinners for parties of four or more, and there is a banquet and party menu. Z's has something for almost everyone: the after-work crowd, music enthusiasts, couples, groups of friends, and families with children of all ages. The place is often packed with regulars, but newcomers feel welcome, too. Happy hour buffet daily from 4:30 PM-7 PM; appetizers are free with drinks.

▲
Hours: Mon–Thu 11 a.m.–11 p.m., Fri & Sat 11 a.m.–1 a.m.; closed Sun ▪ Reservations
taken, required on weekends ▪ MC, VS, AX, Dis, checks accepted
▪ Bar: beer, wine, liquor ▪ Takeout ▪ ♿ Full access ▪ Non-smoking section

PLAYERS ON LARCHMERE

Cleveland	Near East Side
13114 Larchmere Blvd.	Dressy
☎ 283-7529	$$$$$

After nearly a decade of success on the West Side, Players set up shop
on the East Side, too, in 1993. Serving regional Italian (especially
northern) specialties with a California flair, this Players is housed in a
completely renovated, handsome dining area that manages to be both
hip and inviting. The kitchen is open to view through a window
wreathed in strands of garlic, long red chilies, and bunches of dried
herbs. Before they open each evening, all the servers taste each of the
chef's specials, so they speak from experience when they answer your
questions about each dish. Every plate leaves the kitchen looking like a
piece of abstract art, and combinations are unexpected and intriguing:
thinly sliced duck breast olivade (served over sauteed escarole with
pine nuts, amifissa olive sauce, and roasted sweet potato puree); clams
and mussels in brodo seasoned with fennel, garlic, and saffron; or a
designer pizza rustica topped with roasted seasonal vegetables, herbs,
and extra virgin olive oil. There's a spontaneously created and ever-
changing feast, listed on the menu as Chef Michael's Four Course Dinner. For a smaller appetite and simpler fare, there's a create-your-own
pasta or pizza option, and a varied selection of salads, soups, and appetizers. They have their own small parking lot at the side of the building.

▲
Hours: Sun & Mon 5–9 p.m., Tue–Thu 5–10 p.m., Fri & Sat 5–11 p.m. ▪ Reservations
taken, recommended ▪ MC, VS, AX, Dis accepted ▪ Bar: beer, wine, liquor ▪ Takeout
▪ ♿ Full access ▪ Non-smoking section

PLAYERS ON MADISON

Lakewood	West Side
14527 Madison Ave. (at Belle)	Dressy
☎ 226-5200	$$$$$

The building's old pressed-tin ceiling, painted white, is still in evidence, and the old wood floors have been sanded to gleaming perfec-
tion, but everything else about Players is sleek and contemporary, that
uncanny blend of minimal and glamorous. The most interesting lights
I've ever seen in a restaurant, odd little bits of glimmering shape, hang
clothesline-style across the two dining areas. Tables are white cloth
under glass; handpainted ceramic plates and beautiful bottles of herb

vinegars produced locally by Christopher Layne decorate the walls. The menu reflects that same panache. Traditional Italian dishes are updated: calamari are stuffed with spinach and pine nuts and served over sauteed smoked tomatoes and leeks; ravioli are made with saffron and are filled with a blend of roasted acorn squash, pine nuts, and ricotta and served over caramelized onion in a sage butter sauce; gnocchi, made on the premises, come with sun-dried tomatoes, peas, and four-cheese sauce; and pizza can be ordered with roasted garlic, arugula, herbed chicken, smoked mussels, or shitake mushrooms. But lest you think it's all just too trendy, on one visit I saw two kids happily tucking into platefuls of spaghetti with tomato sauce with milk chasers.

▲

Hours: Sun & Mon 5–9 p.m., Tue–Thu 5–10 p.m., Fri & Sat 5 p.m.–midnight ▪ Reservations not taken ▪ MC, VS, AX, Dis accepted ▪ Bar: beer, wine, liquor ▪ Takeout ▪ ♿ Full access ▪ Non-smoking section

PORCELLI'S

Cleveland   Near East Side
12022 Mayfield Rd.   Dressy
☎ 791-9900 $$$$$

This once very small restaurant has expanded next door and now has two dining rooms—but the larger size has not changed the intimate feel of the place. The decor has a chic, understated artistic elegance. Owner Robert Porcelli, who studied painting in Rome, hangs his own works on the walls, and even the black plates with a beautiful border design make a gorgeous backdrop for the food. The overall effect of the crisp, snowy table linens, candle glow, and servers dressed in classic black and white is reminiscent of the fine little restaurants that abound in Rome and Florence. Most diners look like they're on their way to the symphony or coming from the theater, and just being here makes you feel a bit glamorous and oh-so-interesting. You won't find the familiar American renditions of Italian food here, so don't come with an appetite for meatballs. What you can sample is fresh pasta in light cream sauces that are laced with brandy and garlic or infused with fresh green herbs. Dishes on this menu and five daily specials make optimal use of veal and seafood, fresh tomatoes, exotic mushrooms, imported full-flavored cheeses like bocconcino and reggiano, and smoked meats such as pancetta and prosciutto. The cappuccino, espresso, and desserts made from family recipes are a perfect ending.

▲

Hours: Sun 4–10 p.m., Mon–Thu 5:30–10 p.m., Fri & Sat 5–11 p.m. ▪ Reservations taken, recommended on weekends ▪ MC, VS, Dis accepted ▪ Bar: beer, wine, liquor ▪ Takeout ▪ Not rec. for children ▪ Non-smoking in dining rooms; smoking in bar only

PORTOFINO RISTORANTE

Strongsville
12214 Pearl Rd.
☎ 572-3466

Southwest
Formal
$$$$$

The restaurant, located in a small, fairly new shopping plaza, has a formal air. The waiters, well dressed in white shirts and colorful ties, are professionals: they know how to use their crumb combs, pronounce the Italian names of each dish correctly, and pay meticulous attention to the details of fine service. Tables are dressed in purple and white linens with fresh flowers on each. This is definitely not a place for the kids when they're still in the throes of the terrible twos (or threes, fours, and fives). Decor, in this intimate 75-seat restaurant, is contemporary, with black marble accents, and even the faucets in the restrooms are stylish. While waiting for your table you can relax on plush couches and leaf through *Wine Spectator* or sit at the five-seat bar in the back. Once you are seated, your waiter will bring bread and mix a dipping dish of extra virgin olive oil and balsamic vinegar tableside for you. Food preparation and presentation are definitely artistic. The cuisine is a blend of northern and southern influences; dishes are classic but in no way ordinary. Fusilli pasta is dressed in a rose cream sauce with pancetta (Italian bacon), onions, and vodka; capelli puttanesca is made with angel hair pasta, anchovies, capers, olives, and chili peppers; and the manicotti, stuffed with ricotta and spinach, comes in a tomato sauce bechamel. There's an interesting selection of antipasto and salads, chicken, and veal dishes, and a fabulous-looking dessert tray. For lunch, there's a two-pasta chef's sampler, Bis Della Casa (at dinner it includes three different pastas).

▲
Hours: Lunch Mon–Fri 11:30 a.m.–2:30 p.m.; Dinner Mon–Fri 5:30–9:30 p.m., Sat 5:30–10 p.m.; closed between Lunch & Dinner; closed Sun ▪ Reservations taken, recommended ▪ MC, VS, AX accepted ▪ Bar: beer, wine, liquor ▪ ⅙ Full access ▪ Not recommended for children ▪ Non-smoking section

RISTORANTE GIOVANNI'S

Beachwood
25550 Chagrin Blvd.
☎ 831-8625

East Side
Formal
$$$$$

Established in 1976, Giovanni's specializes in fine northern Italian cuisine and has earned a reputation as one of northeast Ohio's best restaurants. The wall of the lobby is peppered with awards; the Chefs of America named it one of the nation's finest, *Cleveland Magazine* gave it Silver Spoons for both best Italian and best service, the American Automobile Association honored it with four diamonds for exceptional cuisine and service, and *Wine Spectator* called its wine list one of the most outstanding in the world. Located in a stark, modern concrete office building that gives no hint of the plush and sparkling elegance inside, this is a place to enjoy leisurely, sumptuous five-course meals, an appropriate setting for celebrations and special occasions. The dining area is roomy, seating about 120, and the appointments are luxurious; wood gleams, linens are crisp, crystal chandeliers sparkle, waiters wear tuxedos, the copper and brass espresso machine is polished to a high shine, and champagne buckets are ready and waiting. The menu is a blend of traditional cuisine prepared with a contemporary sensibility; river mussels in roasted tomato broth, fusilli pasta with braised veal, swordfish and calamari diavolo, or a parmesan crusted veal chop with tomato concaisse.

▲
Hours: Mon–Fri, Lunch 11:30 a.m.–2:30 p.m.; Dinner Mon–Fri 5:30–9:30 p.m. (lounge open between lunch & dinner), Sat 5:30–10:30 p.m.; closed Sun ▪ Reservations taken, recommended ▪ MC, VS, AX, Dis accepted ▪ Bar: beer, wine, liquor ▪ Takeout ▪ ♿ Full access ▪ Not recommended for children ▪ Non-smoking section

SFORZO'S FAMILY RESTAURANT

Cleveland   Near West Side
5517 Memphis Ave.   Casual
☎ 351-3703 $$$$$

The Sforzo's 15-year-old business caters to families, and the restaurant is usually crowded during the dinner hour with patrons of all ages. A different crowd, without children, fills the place in a second wave, after 8:30. Its unpretentious appearance in a working class neighborhood may not attract strangers, but people who know about their friendly atmosphere, good service, and homestyle Italian food come from all parts of Cleveland to eat Sforzo's pasta, veal, and chicken dinners. The regular menu has a sizable selection of all the most popular northern Italian standards, and daily specials might include linguine carbonera, bay scallops diablo over angel hair pasta, chicken marsala, and a sauteed escarole in garlic and oil. Half-orders are available for many dishes, and the menu also includes American-style entrees and sandwiches. There's pizza too. A private party room can handle groups up to 60. Parking is plentiful and convenient.

▲
Hours: Mon & Tue 11 a.m.–9 p.m., Wed 11 a.m.–10 p.m., Thu–Sat 11 a.m.–11 p.m.; closed Sun ▪ Reservations taken, recommended on weekends ▪ MC, VS, AX, Dis accepted ▪ Bar: beer, wine ▪ Takeout ▪ ♿ Full access ▪ Non-smoking section

'STINO DA NAPOLI

Rocky River   West Side
19070 Detroit Rd.   Casual
☎ 331-3944 $$$$$

This very tiny eatery with cosmopolitan big city panache is primarily
a takeout place, and a very popular one judged by the size of crowd that
lines up at the counter to pick up their orders of Augustino (Stino) Iac-
ullo's Neopolitan specialties. Whether you choose to take out or eat
there at one of the eight small, marble-topped tables, it's an opportunity to sample the fresh, flavorful cuisine of southern Italy, dishes like
spaghetti al fumo del vesuvio (featuring a tomato sauce smoothed by
cream and studded with smoked bacon and onions), penne all arrabiata (tube-shaped pasta in a spicy tomato sauce) or gnocchi alla Napo-
letana (hand-rolled potato dumplings baked with mozzarella, ricotta,
and parmigiano cheese). Patrons get so into the food that the servers
even have some special stuff on hand for spot-cleaning olive oil and
tomato sauce from shirtfronts and cuffs. Cappuccino and espresso are
available, as well as Italian desserts like tiramasu and cannoli. Toddlers
are as comfortable here as their well-dressed parents, and although it's
literally elbow to elbow, with knees touching under the table, everyone
seems to manage to make themselves at home. But this is not a place for
parties larger than four. Then again, you can always order a full pan of
lasagna alla meridionale 24 hours in advance and serve it at home.

▲
Hours: Tue–Sat noon–9 p.m. ▪ Reservations taken, recommended ▪ Checks accepted
▪ Bar: none ▪ Takeout ▪ ઇ. Full access ▪ No smoking

TRATTORIA ON THE HILL

Cleveland   Near East Side
12207 Mayfield Rd.   Casual
☎ 421-2700 $$$$$

A host will seat you, and shortly thereafter you'll be presented with a
basket of fresh, crusty Italian bread. Then you can order from the a la
carte menu featuring such classic entrees as veal marsala, chicken
picata, lamb chops calabrian, cavatelli, ravioli, and gnocchi. Or you can
try the house set menu, a fixed-price four-course meal that includes
their antipasto buffet, soup, linguine with a choice of one of four
sauces, and sorbet. There are also pan pizzas on the menu and a fair
number of choices for vegetarians. Sauces are homemade, as are all the
pastas except for the linguine, which is imported from Italy. Cappuccino and espresso are available. The decor is simple but sophisticated:
black-and-white checkerboard floor tiles, white walls, white table
linens, wood accents, muted lighting, and potted plants. Unspoken
convention keeps attire to the casual side of dressy, the ambience is

subdued, and the impression is that this would be a good spot for a romantic dinner. At lunchtime, the restaurant attracts businesspeople and hospital staff from University Circle, and the atmosphere is a bit louder and livelier. Although there's a nonsmoking section, most of the tables are in a single room and the separation is not really effective. A bar in front has a few additional tables where food is also served. The restaurant has its own parking lot around back.

▲
Hours: Mon–Thu 11:30 a.m.–10 p.m., Fri 11:30 a.m.–11 p.m., Sat 4–11 p.m., Sun 4 p.m.–10 p.m. ▪ Reservations taken, recommended ▪ MC, VS, AX accepted ▪ Bar: beer, wine, liquor ▪ Takeout ▪ Non-smoking section

TUSCANY
Woodmere Village   East Side
28601 Chagrin Blvd.   Casual
☎ 464-6220 $$$$$

Like the Eton Collection shopping center where it is located, this place radiates trendiness. Everything is chic, from the moms who wheel their babies in strollers directly up to the tables, to the dapper, silk-tied business types who do lunch here, to the requisite black-and-white decor. There are only 16 close-together tables to seat the serious regional Italian food lovers who flock here. Pasta is made on the premises, and pizzas are baked in a brick oven. Breakfast is self-serve: a classic continental offering of bagels, muffins, and pastry; a vegetable frittata (an Italian omelet); a calzone stuffed with eggs, bacon, cheese, and tomatoes; or a foccacia bread topped with caramelized onions, smoked salmon, and cream cheese. Lunch and dinner menus feature a large selection of traditional chicken, veal, and pasta dishes, and soups, salads, and desserts. Tuscany also does catering and is as much a gourmet grocery and bakery as a trattoria. (See their market listing in this chapter for more information.)

▲
Hours: Breakfast Mon–Sat 9:30 a.m.–11 a.m.; Lunch 11:30 a.m.–4 p.m.; Dinner 5–10 p.m. ▪ Reservations not taken ▪ MC, VS, AX, Dis, checks accepted ▪ Bar: none ▪ Takeout ▪ No smoking

MEDITERRANEAN MIX
GEORGIO'S
Lakewood   West Side
11709 Detroit Ave.   Dressy
☎ 226-6333 $$$$$

Chef Donna Oakin, who created the menu for this recently opened restaurant with her husband Brian, has woven together the authentic flavors and presentations of the Mediterranean region to create a unique menu reflecting the food traditions of Greece, southern France, Spain, and Italy. Pasta dishes, pizza, veal, lamb, and numerous seafood entrees are accented with pan sauces and a contemporary palette of seasonings. Bread is baked daily in a wood-burning brick oven visible from the dining area, and a basketful comes to the table before diners even order. Use it to soak up the herbed olive oil laced with balsamic vinegar and freshly grated parmesan cheese that arrives with it. Dinner plates arrive looking like they've passed through a New Year's Eve party, decorated with a colorful confetti-like sprinkling of shredded greens and purple cabbage. A Mediterranean garden terrace motif is achieved with wall murals; faux windows give a glimpse of seascapes. Lighting is soft and candles glow on each table. The restored pressed-tin ceiling and marble-topped bar add to the feeling of understated polish. Ample parking on the street, in a lot at the back, and in a public lot across the street.

Other ethnic specialties: French, Greek, Italian, Spanish

▲

Hours: Mon–Thu 5–11 p.m., Fri & Sat 5 p.m.–midnight, Sun 4–10 p.m. ▪ Reservations taken, required weekends ▪ MC, VS, AX accepted ▪ Bar: beer, wine, liquor ▪ Takeout ▪ ♿ Full access ▪ Not recommended for children ▪ Non-smoking section

SANS SOUCI

Cleveland	Downtown
Stouffer Tower City Plaza Hotel, 24 Public Square	Dressy
☎ 696-5600	$$$$$

Diners feel like pampered hotel guests here, with attentive service in an elegant yet relaxed atmosphere; a meal can feel like a short vacation. The menu, which changes often, bears the stamp of the many different national cuisines found in the Mediterranean region, including southern France, Italy, Spain, Morocco, and Greece. Special events throughout the year feature unique fare from each of these countries. French-trained Chef de Cuisine Claude Rodier draws on traditional ingredients and recipes for his daily menus but transforms every dish with his own distinctive culinary flair. Diners might encounter a goat cheese and eggplant terrine (the name comes from the dish in which this layered pate is prepared); chicken spiced with saffron; a sauce made of crushed fresh tomatoes, citrus, and capers; a side of roasted red-pepper couscous; or vegetables in a vermouth cream sauce. Count yourself especially lucky when his bouillabaisse is available. A selection of freshly baked breads is served with olive tapenade (a flavorful spread with the consistency of soft butter)—a meal in itself. The kitchen draws much of its inspiration from the foods of Provence, often called the "cuisine of the sun," and the decor echoes that bent. The place glows with the sunny warmth of southern France, and stunning, panoramic, handpainted wall murals depicting flower-filled country landscapes are so vivid you can almost hear the bees buzzing. Like the French country style it emulates, it is both homey and opulent; all at once charming, comfortable, and gracious. The plaster walls with earth-tone wash, oak floors, rough-hewn exposed beams, and large hearth accented with copper pots, bunches of dried herbs, and baskets enhance the effect. Yet in other areas, there's no shortage of carpeting, marble, and tapestry fabrics. All conspire to create a wonderful setting for celebrating a special event or doing business. The selection of wines is extensive, and a panelled wine room which can be used for private parties of up to 10 is located at the front of the restaurant. Just a few words about the dessert cart: don't let it pass you by. The fruit tarts, chocolate confections, and other sweets taste as wonderful as they look. Hotel parking is complimentary for patrons.

Other ethnic specialties: French, Italian, Spanish, Moroccan, Greek

▲

Hours: Lunch Mon–Fri 11:30 a.m.–2:30 p.m.; Dinner Mon–Thu 5:30–10 p.m., Fri–Sat 5:30–11 p.m., Sun 5:30–10 p.m.; special hours for holidays ▪ Reservations taken, recommended ▪ MC, VS, AX, Dis, checks accepted ▪ Bar: beer, wine, liquor ▪ &. Full access ▪ Not recommended for children ▪ Non-smoking section

MARKETS

GREEK

ATHENS PASTRIES & IMPORTED FOODS

Cleveland   Near West Side
2545 Lorain Ave.
☎ 861-8149

Recorded Greek music is almost always playing softly in the background. Dark roasted coffee beans, spices, and golden baklava pastry dripping honey syrup give off a heady and decidedly non-midwestern scent. The overall effect upon entering the store is to feel as though you've left Cleveland far behind. You'll find every sort of Greek delicacy imaginable here—feta cheese, many different kinds of olives, fresh filo dough, pastries, and spinach and meat pies. You'll also find toiletries imported from Greece, kitchenware, religious icons, music tapes, and Greek greeting cards. There are many brands of olive oil and a variety of the nuts, seeds, and seasonings used in Mediterranean cooking. A candy counter, like one once found at the neighborhood corner store, has a mix of Greek and American treats and sweets. On-street parking.

▲
Foods available: meat (fresh, frozen), fish (fresh, frozen), grains, beans, flour, baked
goods, spices, condiments, beverages, tea, wine, prepared frozen foods, takeout meals ▪
Hours: Mon–Thu 8:30 a.m.–5:30 p.m., Fri & Sat 8 a.m.–6 p.m.; closed Sun
▪ Checks accepted

ITALIAN

ALESCI'S OF SOUTH EUCLID

South Euclid   East Side
4333 Mayfield Rd.
☎ 382-5100

This is a 7,000-square-foot gourmet Italian food superstore. Alesci's
opened in 1943 and has been at this location since 1957. The selection
of prepared foods is just this side of awesome: Italian meatballs,
lasagna, subs (one favorite is the "Grinder" made of hard-crust Italian
bread, salami, cappicola, provolone, and roasted pimientos), and more
than 15 different types of pizza sold by the slice, ranging from standard
pepperoni to exotic ones like crabmeat pizza, broccoli pizza, spinach
pizza, and pizza bianco (white pizza). There are more than 30 types of
salads in the deli, including pasta salads and olive salads, and fresh Italian sausage is available at the deli counter, too. They prepare 13 varieties of homemade pasta sauces, sold fresh and frozen by the pint or
quart. They are famous for their Italian bread and also bake pepperoni
bread, strawberry whipped cream cakes, sfogiatelli, and breadsticks.
Spices, grated romano cheese, and coffee (38 kinds) are available in
bulk. Many brands of olive oils and balsamic vinegar are available in
either quart or gallon sizes. They also carry imported pastas, pignoli
nuts, confetti candy, polenta, semolina, and couscous. Delivery service
and catering. Nonfood items include pasta machines, pizza stones,
ravioli plates, and kitchen accessories. Parking lot.

▲
Foods available: grains, beans, flour, baked goods, spices, condiments, beverages, tea,
coffee, wine, prepared frozen foods, takeout meals ▪ Hours: Mon–Thu 9 a.m.–6 p.m.,
Fri 9 a.m.–6:30 p.m., Sat 9 a.m.–6 p.m., Sun 9 a.m.–2 p.m.
▪ MC, VS, AX, Dis, checks accepted ▪ ♿ Full access

BARONA'S BAKERY

Maple Heights   Southeast
15842 Libby Rd.
☎ 662-8383

Family owned and operated since 1949, Barona's has built a solid reputation that reaches all the way to Mentor and Brunswick on spumoni,
gelati, and lemon ice homemade the old-world way and large, beauti-

fully decorated cakes, including casata, for all occasions. They bake a variety of cookies that include both Italian and other ethnic specialties like kolache. No bread.

▲

Foods available: baked goods ■ Hours: Mon 8 a.m.–4 p.m., Tue–Fri 8 a.m.–5:30 p.m., Sat 8 a.m.–5 p.m., Sun 8 a.m.–1 p.m. ■ Cash only ■ ♿ Full access

BRAMATE'S IMPORTED FOODS

Parma Southwest
6863 W. 130th St.
☎ 845-2700

The Brammates, who came here from Italy in the 1950s, have been in business for 40 years and their four sons have joined them. Primarily a bakery, the store offers a large selection of Italian-style cakes, cookies, and breads. Two of their specialties are cannoli, a cream-filled pastry, and fogliatelli, 15 layers of thin, flaky dough layered with cream. They also have a well-stocked deli counter, make their own fresh pasta, and offer a selection of packaged brands from Italy, too. There are some food products from other countries of the Mediterranean region.

▲

Foods available: meat (fresh, deli), grains, beans, flour, baked goods, spices, condiments, wine, beer, takeout meals ■ Hours: Mon–Sat 9 a.m.–6 p.m., Sun 9 a.m.–2 p.m. ■ MC, VS, AX, checks accepted ■ ♿ Full access

COLOZZA'S CAKES & PASTRIES

Parma Southwest
5880 Ridge Rd.
☎ 885-0453

Because Angelo Colozza bakes every day, Clevelanders can take home some very special Italian desserts. There's Santa Lorenzo, alternating layers of puff pastry, raspberry filling, amaretto-soaked sponge cake, and whipped cream topped with shaved chocolate; three-layer glazed fruit tortes; and rum-babas. His traditional cassata cake is rum-soaked, ricotta-filled, and studded with chocolate chips and diced fruit. He also makes what he refers to as "American" cassata cake with strawberries and whipped cream, cannoli, and sfogiatelle, a sweet ricotta-filled pastry that looks like a clam shell. Colozza will decorate any of his 30 varieties of tortes (some of which he'll sell by the slice) and cakes to suit any occasion.

▲

Foods available: baked goods, coffee ■ Hours: Wed–Fri 7 a.m.–6 p.m., Sat 7 a.m.–5:30 p.m., Sun 7 a.m.–3 p.m.; closed Mon & Tue ■ Checks accepted ■ ♿ Full access

CORBO'S DOLCERIA

Cleveland   Near East Side
12200 Mayfield Rd.
☎ 421-8181

Family owned and operated for over 30 years, this is a landmark in Little Italy. Though every day brings in regular customers from the neighborhood, people from all over the state stop in to buy one of their famous casata cakes (a strawberry-and-cream-filled yellow layer cake) and cannoli. They bake Italian-style cookies, breads, and sheet pizzas as well. Spumoni (Italian ice cream) and Italian ices are available, too.

▲

Foods available: baked goods, takeout meals ▪ Hours: Tue–Sat 8 a.m.–6 p.m., Sun 8 a.m.–1 p.m.; closed Mon ▪ Checks accepted ▪ ♿ Full access

DISTEFANO'S HIGHLAND DELI & BAKERY

Highland Heights   East Side
5600 Highland Rd.
☎ 442-7775

This is what most grocery stores were like just a generation ago: a family-owned, friendly neighborhood place, not too big or too small, with a regular and familiar clientele. Shoppers will find homemade sausage, meatballs, lasagna, and chicken cutlets prepared for takeout or heat-at-home, and freshly baked breads, pastries, and cookies. There's a large selection of olive oils, spices, imported and domestic wines, and packaged pasta plus a few basic household items.

▲

Foods available: flour, baked goods, spices, condiments, beverages, tea, wine, prepared frozen foods, takeout meals ▪ Hours: Mon–Fri 9 a.m.–8 p.m., Sat 9 a.m.–6 p.m., Sun 9 a.m.–1 p.m. ▪ Checks accepted ▪ ♿ Full access

FRAGAPANE BAKERY & DELI

North Olmsted   West Side
28625 Lorain
☎ 779-6050

This is a bakery, an Italian deli, and an import store. They make the usual Italian-style breads, cakes, cookies, and pastries; pans of lasagna and sheets of pizza; frozen homemade sauces, garlic bread, sausage, and pasta. They also stock a selection of wines, sauces, peppers, and pasta from Italy. Large variety of non-Italian baked goods, too, from croissants to strudel. They have two other locations:, in Bay Village and Olmsted Falls (see separate listings for details).

▲

Foods available: meat (fresh, deli), baked goods, condiments, beverages, tea, coffee, wine, prepared frozen foods, takeout meals ▪ Hours: Tue–Thu 6 a.m.–6:30 p.m., Fri &

Sat 6 a.m.–7 p.m., Sun 6 a.m.–3 p.m.; closed Mon ■ MC, VS, checks accepted
■ ৬ Full access

FRAGAPANE BAKERY & DELI

Bay Village   West Side
650 Dover Center Rd.
☎ 871-6340
See North Olmsted store entry for details.

▲
Foods available: meat (fresh, deli), baked goods, condiments, beverages, tea, coffee, wine, prepared frozen foods, takeout meals ■ Hours: Tue-Sat 6 a.m.-6 p.m., Sun 6 a.m.-2 p.m., closed Mon ■ MC, VS, checks accepted

FRAGAPANE BAKERY & DELI

Olmsted Falls   West Side
8161 Columbia Rd.
☎ 235-1444
See North Olmsted store entry for details.

▲
Foods available: meat (fresh, deli), baked goods, condiments, beverages, tea, coffee, wine, prepared frozen foods, takeout meals ■ Hours: Tue-Sat 6 a.m.-6 p.m., Sun 6 a.m.-2 p.m., closed Mon ■ MC, VS, checks accepted

FRATELLI IMPORTED FOODS

Mayfield Heights   East Side
1627 Golden Gate Plaza
☎ 473-0848

A number of Fratelli family members are working partners and they like to say they've built their ten-year-old business on service and smiles. They prepare standard Italian fare including cavatelli, calzone (a less common variation is filled with artichokes and fontina cheese), stuffed manicotti, pizza, and a variety of pastas and sauces. They also experiment with other dishes and recipes, and the chef says "We're always trying something new. If people like it, I make it again." They bake Italian cookies, breads, and rolls, too, and shelves are stocked with a large selection of imported soups. They also carry pizzelle makers, pasta machines, espresso pots, and bocci balls. With 24 hours' notice, they'll put together a party tray or a complete dinner. They also carry some ingredients for Greek and Middle Eastern cooking, including tahini (sesame paste) and grape leaves.

▲
Foods available: beans, flour, baked goods, spices, condiments, beverages, tea, coffee,

wine, prepared frozen foods, takeout meals ■ Hours: Mon–Sat 9 a.m.–6 p.m., Sun 9 a.m.–2 p.m. ■ MC, VS, AX, Dis, checks accepted ■ & Full access

GALLUCCI ITALIAN FOOD

Cleveland   Near East Side
6610 Euclid Ave.
☎ 881-0045

The Gallucci family has been selling Clevelanders Italian specialty foods since 1912. Current manager Ray Gallucci, the third generation to be involved in this importing and retailing business, goes "shopping" in Italy every year. Because they buy directly from producers themselves, they're able to pass the cost savings on to their customers, a loyal and devoted breed. It's not uncommon for customers to be the second and third generation of their family to frequent Gallucci's, following them from the old downtown location to their fine new Euclid Avenue store. The space is large, modern, and convenient, and the selection of everything Italian is huge. I've never seen so many different kinds of canned and jarred roasted red peppers in one place. Some of the pasta and olive oils are packaged so attractively that I buy them to give as gifts. Gallucci's offers customers a number of unique products: a grilled artichoke that comes from Italy in a large vacuum-sealed tray; mascarpone, a thick sweet cream used in traditional desserts like tiramasu; polenta prepared in a refrigerated roll; and a ham from Parma, only recently allowed into this country, called Parmacotto, that is cooked instead of cured like the famous prosciutto from the same region. They have their own baker on staff who makes a very special and hard-to-find little clamshell-shaped pastry filled with sweet ricotta cheese, called sfogliatelle. The store is often packed on Saturdays with many shoppers driving in from the distant suburbs, but it's a congenial kind of crowd. You might have to take a number and wait in line at the counter if you want a hunk of parmigiano-reggiano, antipasto salad, or some pancetta (an herb-flavored smoked bacon). They have their own parking lot, and staff will even help shoppers get their purchases packed in the car.

▲

Foods available: meat (fresh, frozen), grains, beans, flour, baked goods, spices, condiments, beverages, tea, wine, prepared frozen foods, takeout meals ■ Hours: Mon–Fri 8 a.m.–6 p.m., Sat 8 a.m.–5 p.m.; closed Sun ■ MC, VS, Dis, checks accepted ■ & Full access

GIGANTI'S IMPORTED FOODS

Maple Heights   Southeast
15800 Broadway Ave.
☎ 475-5252

The Gigantis family bakes bread seven days a week as well as Italian-style pastries. The store features a very large selection of olive oils and vinegars. The shelves are filled with a variety of canned imports, including tuna, sardines, olives, and peppers. They have coffee from Italy, too. Specialty takeout items available daily include Italian subs, cavatelli, and rigatoni. They will gladly prepare party trays and order spices in bulk.

▲
Foods available: meat (fresh, deli), grains, beans, flour, baked goods, spices, condiments, wine, takeout meals ■ Hours: Mon–Thu 9 a.m.–6 p.m., Fri & Sat, 8 a.m.–6 p.m., Sun 9 a.m.–1 p.m. ■ Checks accepted ■ ♿ Full access

LAPUMA FINE PASTRIES

Mayfield Heights   East Side
5732 Mayfield Rd.
☎ 461-7117

This bakery is now in its fifth generation of family ownership, and the business is 100 years old. They make 100 different kinds of cookies, and a variety of breads, cakes, and pastries using classic recipes rooted in the kitchen traditions of Calabria, Sicily, and Naples. Choose from fig-filled cookies to macaroons with pignoli (pine nuts); a layered pastry filled with custard, sweet ricotta cheese, and candied fruits; and rum cake, scalatti bread, or a Sicilian twist. They also offer a large selection of European-style breads, pastries, and cakes (French, Hungarian), and non-ethnic doughnuts, muffins, and brownies. There's a small cafe where you can get a calzone or a piece of pepperoni bread for lunch (or to go), or cappuccino and a treat.

▲
Foods available: baked goods, beverages, tea, coffee ■ Hours: Tue–Thu 7:30 a.m.–6:30 p.m., Fri & Sat 7:30 a.m.–4 p.m.; closed Mon ■ MC, VS, checks accepted ■ ♿ Full access

MAYFIELD ITALIAN IMPORTS

Cleveland   Near East Side
12018 Mayfield Rd.
☎ 791-0700

I've shopped at this Italian food market in the heart of Little Italy for 25 years. When my husband and I lived in University Circle, with no car and a few dollars, this was where we went when we wanted to treat ourselves well. I always felt I was getting more than my money's worth in atmosphere, friendly personal service, and foods not available in most ordinary supermarkets that turned our meals into Italian feasts. I loved the big open bags of nuts, dried mushrooms, and beans, and now that I'm feeding three hungry sons I like the extra-large restaurant-size jars and cans. Shelves are stocked with a nice selection of pastas, sauces, olive oils, and some imported kitchenware like pasta bowls and pizzelli makers. There are packaged baked goods as well as fresh pastries, cookies, and cakes. Behind the counter is a stock of fresh Italian sausage, domestic and imported prosciutto, Genoa salami, and bocconcini, (the sweet, fresh version of mozzarella cheese), plus a large selection of other deli meats and cheeses, sliced to order. There are many types of olives and antipasto salads. They specialize in takeout, and at the back are steaming trays of meatballs, lasagna, and manicotti. They also do catering and have added a few small tables where you can sip a freshly made espresso and nibble a cannoli or inhale a slice of pizza. Parking is always tricky in this old and densely populated neighborhood.

▲

Foods available: baked goods, spices, condiments, wine, beer, prepared frozen foods, takeout meals ▪ Hours: Mon–Fri 9:30 a.m.–6 p.m., Sat 9 a.m.–5 p.m.; closed Sun ▪ MC, VS, AX, Dis, checks accepted ▪ ♿ Full access

MOLISANA ITALIAN FOODS

Broadview Heights   Southwest
8037 Broadview Rd.
☎ 526-4141

The two women who started this business took its name (though they feminized it) from the Molisan region of Italy on the Adriatic coast. They aim to offer traditional Italian foods in a modern, upscale European-style setting, complete with marble countertops, custom-made cabinetry, and ceramic floor tiles. There's a varied and interesting selection of deli meats and cheeses, which they use for made-to-order sandwiches on their freshly baked breads and authentic crusty little bread rolls called panni. They prepare gourmet pizzas, party trays, and offer a complete catering service. Lots of interesting imports available, and they'll assemble unusual food gift baskets, incorporating some of the kitchenware they carry. Use their cookware catalog to special-order products, too. And while you're trying to decide what to buy, you can sample a cup of their espresso or cappuccino from the coffee bar.

▲

Foods available: meat (deli), beans, flour, baked goods, spices, condiments, beverages, tea, coffee, wine, prepared frozen foods, takeout meals ▪ Hours: Mon–Fri 10 a.m.–6 p.m., Sat 10 a.m.–5 p.m.; closed Sun ▪ Cash only ▪ ♿ Full access

PRESTI BAKERY

Cleveland — Near East Side
12111 Mayfield Rd.
☎ 421-3060

In its third generation as a family business, this is another Little Italy fixture. Though they carry some non-Italian baked goods like doughnuts, danish, and brownies, they are best known for their crusty preservative-free Italian breads, baked fresh daily. They come in many shapes—some are even still molded by hand, rather than machine. They also offer pepperoni bread, spinach bread, foccacia, and pizza, which you can buy ready-to-eat or for heat-and-eat at home. The freezer case holds homemade soups and marinara sauce, there's milk and soda in the cooler, and hot coffee and tea to go.

▲
Foods available: baked goods, beverages, tea, coffee, takeout meals ■ Hours: Mon–Sat 6 a.m.–7 p.m. Sun 6 a.m.–6 p.m. ■ Checks accepted

RITO'S ITALIAN BAKERY

Parma — Southwest
10551 W. Pleasant Valley Rd.
☎ 845-9414

A family business for 27 years, they specialize in Sicilian- and Neapolitan-style foods and are especially proud of their almond paste cookies and sfogliatteli, a cheese-filled pastry. They prepare lasagna and eggplant parmesan, sheet pizzas, and homemade breads and rolls. The deli counter maintains a nice selection of meats and cheeses, and sandwiches are made to order. They also carry a selection of non-Italian cookies and doughnuts, and bake cakes for all occasions. A second and similar Rito's is located at 4053 W.130th St. (see next listing).

▲
Foods available: baked goods, coffee, wine, prepared frozen foods, takeout meals ■ Hours: Mon–Sat 7 a.m.–7 p.m., Sun 7 a.m.–3 p.m. ■ MC, VS, checks accepted ■ ♿ Full access

RITO'S ITALIAN BAKERY

Cleveland — West Side
4053 W.130th St.
☎ 671-3424

See other Rito's listing for details.

▲
Foods available: baked goods, coffee, wine, prepared frozen foods, takeout meals ■ Hours: Mon & Tue 7 a.m.–4 p.m., Wed–Sat 7 a.m.–7 p.m., Sun 7 a.m.–3 p.m. ■ MC, VS, checks accepted

STONE OVEN BAKERY CAFE, THE

Cleveland Heights   East Side
2245 Lee Rd.
☎ 932-3003

Opened in January, 1995, in a converted bank, Stone Oven is the brain-child of Tatyana Rehn, a Russian immigrant and former engineer. But it's traditional Italian, not Russian breads, that she hand shapes and bakes in small batches in stone-lined ovens that give the place its name and the bread its distinctive crust. It all began when she tasted bread, freshly made by an Italian chef, at her brother-in-law's New York restaurant. It was, she recalls, the first good bread she'd had since leaving Russia, and she decided to perfect her own baking skills at home. At her new bakery, where the only piece of kitchen machinery she'll allow is a mixer, she and her staff prepare traditional focaccia loaves, Siciliano and Pugliese bread, and others scented with rosemary or flavored with olives, cheese, or nuts. She does a large wholesale business, supplying many area restaurants and grocery stores. Italian desserts like tiramasu and clafuttis (apple and prune custard) are also available along with bread pudding, scones, muffins, and cookies. There are about 10 tables in this spacious cafe, and you can order a sandwich made, of course, on their own great bread, or a cup of cappuccino. On-street parking and additional parking in a city lot at the back.

▲
Foods available: baked goods, beverages, tea, coffee, takeout meals ■ Hours: Mon–Thu 7 a.m.–10 p.m., Fri & Sat 7 a.m.–midnight, Sun 9 a.m.–6 p.m. ■ Checks accepted ■ ᕷ Full access

TUSCANY GOURMET FOODS

Woodmere Village   East Side
28601 Chagrin Blvd.
☎ 464-6220

Located in the upscale Eton Collection shopping center, this is both a sophisticated gourmet shop and a small, urbane cafe. Whether you're sitting down or stocking up, this place is all about eating, and food is even used to decorate. Salted hams, dried peppers, and strands of garlic hang over sleek glass cases filled with a huge variety of pasta and vegetable salads, take-home veal and chicken entrees, and hunks of prosciutto, mortadella, and genoa salmai. Another case displays a large and mouthwatering array of traditional pastries, cakes, and cookies. Fresh breads are stacked on shelves suspended from the ceiling. The food looks so tempting you might just decide to just buy all you need for a meal ready-made. But if you still are inspired to cook, there's an extensive selection of imported Italian flavored vinegars, olive oils, sauces, and pasta, plus candies, tins of biscuits, and bottled waters. Staff will assemble gift baskets.

▲

Foods available: meat (fresh, deli), grains, beans, flour, baked goods, spices, condiments, beverages, tea, coffee, wine, takeout meals ▪ Hours: Mon–Sat 9:30 a.m.–10 p.m. ▪ MC, VS, AX, Dis, checks accepted ▪ ♿ Full access

CHAPTER 4

Europe East of the Danube

EUROPE EAST OF THE DANUBE RIVER includes newly emerging and re-emerging nations, groups engaged in fierce struggles to redefine both their borders and their identities. Some of the countries whose names I learned in grade school no longer exist, and places I never knew existed now proclaim themselves nations, long lost in the no-man's-land of the Soviet bloc. So it is problematical even to begin with a simple list of countries whose heritage is reflected in this chapter. Perhaps it is more accurate to focus on the people rather than the place, for it is through their lives that traditions endure. Czech, Slovak, Lithuanian, Croation, Polish, Slovenian, Serb, Hungarian, Byelorussian and Ukrainian immigrants all left the land they knew for a new start in Cleveland, transplanting their cultural and food traditions in the process.

A local newspaper editorial written in 1851 urged immigrants to immediately become "Americanized" by "casting off" their Euro-

pean "skins." It was advice few could really follow, needing that
sense of national identity to see them through the hardships of
being strangers in a strange land, often engaged in grueling, mind-
numbing labor. Most stuck close to their own kind, finding both
comfort and protection in the proximity of their countrymen.

This was especially true for those of Eastern European descent,
and they formed distinct ethnic corridors throughout the city, with
nationality neighborhoods growing around the various industries
and factories where the men earned their hourly wage.

Ed Miggins, Cleveland State professor and co-editor of *The Birth
of Modern Cleveland*, has written that these sections of the city grew
up "between spires and stacks," neighborhoods demarcated by ethnic churches and industrial chimneys.

As the century came to an end, each of the various Slavic groups
had formed its own self-help societies, social clubs, schools, and
religious congregations based on ethnic affiliations. Singing societies, sports clubs, and dance groups created a sense of solidarity
that has endured, even as following generations left the old neighborhoods, moved to the suburbs, and became fully assimilated into
an American lifestyle.

These are heritages difficult for an outsider to fully understand,
and I admit my shortcomings here. There are at least 12 different
so-called Slavic nationality groups. "Historically, as well as in the
present," explains Algis Ruksenas, Executive Director of Cleveland's
International Services Center, "there has been a tendency to
homogenize the various Eastern European peoples, to bunch them
together and see them as a single entity. Immigration officials used
to mistakenly log newcomers in as Russians when in fact they may
have been from Poland, Lithuania, Latvia, or Estonia. Each nationality is a distinct cultural group, as different as an Italian from a
Frenchman though both are from what's called western Europe."

Czechoslovakia as a state was a modern political entity representing an affiliation of Czechs and Slovaks. Cleveland's Czech
community is one of its oldest and largest. The Slovaks are a separate immigrant group, and in the early 1900s the Cleveland area was
home to the largest number of Slovaks in the world. Poles, too, came
in great numbers. The Association of Polish Women in the USA
chose Cleveland as the site for their first annual convention in February, 1913. In a 1930 census, 32,688 people named Poland as their
country of origin.

At one time, only Hungary itself had more Hungarians than

Cleveland, and we still rank fourth in this country in the number of Croations living here. There are approximately 16,000 Lithuanians here, and they are one of the most active Lithuanian communities outside of Lithuania itself. It's hard to identify the numbers of Russians who have come here because there has always been a question about what the word actually means. Under that umbrella might be included Byelorussians, Carpatho-Russians, Great Russians, and Ukrainians. And Jews from all these Eastern European homelands formed yet another separate, distinctive subset of immigrant Americans (see Chapter 7, American Regional).

What all this really means is that, collectively, the people of Eastern Europe have had a profound effect on the development of Cleveland, significantly impacting who and what this city has become. Ruksenas, himself an immigrant from Lithuania, calls them "the quiet influence," for they interacted with the city from the bottom up. They were the muscle that provided the infrastructure for a growing Cleveland.

Years ago there were countless restaurants and boarding houses all around the city where the foods beloved by these Slavic groups could be had. Now there are relatively few. But there remains a surprisingly large number of shops, bakeries, and butchers that cater to these ethnic groups—tangible evidence of their longstanding presence and deep roots in the community. Many of the stores have been run by one family for generations or have been in the same location for half a century or more. There a visitor today will encounter the timeless aroma of pickles and paprika, kielbasa and kraut. The sight of mounds of potato-filled pierogies, slices of liver sausage, and strips of flaky strudel tell a story of day-to-day life that perennially unfolds around the table. In their own way, these stores are windows looking back into the lives of all those Eastern European immigrant families. Though culturally diverse, they have always shared a taste for many foods and a common style of preparing them.

Eastern and Central European cooks traditionally make hearty, filling food rich with the taste of butter, cottage cheese, and sour cream. The cuisine depends upon potatoes, cabbage, beets, mushrooms, peppers, noodles, and dumplings seasoned with dill, caraway seeds, onions, garlic, and parsley as well as paprika.

All varieties of meat and poultry are used in soups and stews laced with root vegetables. Pickling is the favored way to handle garden produce. Sausage-making is an art, and the variety is almost endless; the same could be said of their traditional pastries, cakes, and cookies, many made with fruit such as apples, cherries, and plums.

"People who have Americanized," said Ruksenas, who was seven when he arrived in Cleveland with his parents as a World War II refugee, "can recapture their heritage with a recipe, which is literally and figuratively palatable. Often that's all that remains of their cultural legacy. While I think it's terribly important to understand that the sum and substance of each of these old-world cultures is much more than sausage and sauerkraut, food is without a doubt a basic, concrete connection to one's own history, and menus harken back to a deeper, more abstract cultural wealth."

Every Clevelander with Eastern European roots I've ever spoken with insists that nobody makes dishes as good as their own grandmother's, but nonetheless they can all be depended upon to do justice to a plateful of stuffed cabbage or a brimming bowl of goulash, no matter who prepared it. "For Eastern Europeans," explained Chris Jagelewski, whose grandparents came from Poland, "eating is a social occasion, and social occasions always include eating. When I was growing up, friends and relatives regularly gathered around the kitchen table to eat, talk, and laugh. My mother and my grandmother always had something extra ready to serve to unexpected guests. There's an old Polish housewives' saying that goes, "If you have no leftovers, tomorrow will be a beautiful day." I think it means that when people come together and enjoy your food, it's a good thing."

 **RESTAURANTS**

CROATIAN

DUBROVNIK GARDEN RESTAURANT

Eastlake   Farther East
34900 Lakeshore Blvd.   Casual
☎ 946-3366 $$$$$

Coming here is more than going out to eat—it's a cultural event. That's because this restaurant is located inside the American Croatian Lodge, which also houses the Croatian Heritage Museum, Library, and Gift Shop (usually open on Friday and Saturday nights, Sunday afternoons, and by appointment). The lobby, too, always has some interesting historical or craft exhibits on display. The restaurant itself feels like a private club, but all are welcome. You step up into the dining room which has tables down the center and booths on the sides, and step down to the bar. The walls feature paintings of Croatian cities done by a local artist as well as carved wooden plates and other pieces of folk art and craft. The back of the menu is a full-page history of the ancient seaside town of Dubrovnik. There are four traditional Croatian entrees: the Dubrovnik Grill, which includes raznici (pork and veal kebabs) and cevapcici (a blend of beef, pork, and veal); the Croatian Dish, made with raznici, cevapcici, pork chops, and chicken; Veal Ljubljana (a slice of veal rolled around pieces of ham and cheese, batter-dipped and fried); and the Chef's Specialty of sauerkraut, sausage, smoked pork chop, and bratwurst. The rest of the menu is pure Ohio, an eclectic mix of spaghetti, steak, and a dish called Chicken American. Whatever you choose to eat for your main course, try to leave room for their palacinke, a light and delicate dessert.

▲

Hours: Lunch daily 11 a.m.–2:30 p.m.; Dinner daily 4:30–10 p.m.; closed between Lunch & Dinner ■ Reservations taken, recommended ■ MC, VS, AX, checks accepted ■ Bar: beer, wine, liquor ■ Takeout ■ ♿ Full access

CROATIAN, SEE ALSO:
Marie's Restaurant (Eastern European Mix)

CZECH

CZECH INN

Garfield Heights — Southeast
9729 Granger Rd. — Casual
☎ 587-1158 — $$$$$

This restaurant is easy to find, located in a freestanding building with a sign out front on the top of Granger Road hill at East 98th. But its neighborhood bar exterior gives no clue to what's inside. On the other side of the bar is a pretty, light-filled room with lace curtains at the windows, natural-toned maple wood floors, and fresh flowers on every table. Czech travel posters and woodcuts of Prague dot the walls. Recorded Czech music plays softly in the background. The aim is to create a comfortable, casual place to relax and eat. And when it comes to eating, there's a clear choice: either tried-and-true American fare or Czech classics like tripe soup, roast duck and dumplings, roast pork with sauerkraut, goulash, veal paprikash, and a version of sauerbraten that features marinated beef braised and served in creamy root vegetable sauce. There are also potato pancakes and pierogi. Take note: the kitchen reserves the right to close early when business is slow, so if you're planning to arrive towards the end of the evening it might be wise to call ahead.

▲
Hours: Mon 11 a.m.–8 p.m., Tue–Thu 11 a.m.–9 p.m., Fri 11 a.m.–10 p.m., Sat noon–10 p.m., Sun noon–8 p.m. ■ Reservations taken, required for parties of 4 or more ■ MC, VS, AX, Dis accepted ■ Bar: beer, wine, liquor ■ Takeout ■ Non-smoking section

GENEVA FAMILY RESTAURANT

Cleveland   Near West Side
14039 Lorain Ave.   Relaxed
☎ 941-9121 $$$$$

Martin and Dawn Pokorny opened their little restaurant in 1994, and their portrait hangs on one wall over a carved wooden plaque that thanks you for coming. Although their pride in their Czech heritage is clearly in evidence—there's a "Proud To Be Czech" bumper sticker on the register and another sign proclaiming "Czech Power"—there are just a handful of Eastern European items on an otherwise ordinary eggs-and-burger menu. But once you've tasted the chicken paprikash, with a gravy so flavorful and abundant that it made me want to spoon it up like soup, you're likely to decide this is a place to know about. In addition to the chicken, they regularly have stuffed cabbage and peppers, and halushky, sauteed cabbage and onions with potato dumplings. On Sundays they do roast pork, dumplings, and sauerkraut and sometimes Martin, whose family originally came from Prague, will prepare something special like Bohemian beef "birds" (round steak rolled around a pickle) with soft bread dumplings. The building, which looks like it was once home to a national food franchise, sits in an asphalt wasteland, but inside the Pokornys have made it homey and pleasant with a teal color scheme and flowered wallpaper. There are booths and tables, a four-stool counter, and paper placemats. They also do private party catering.

▲
Hours: Tue–Fri 7 a.m.–8 p.m., Sat 7 a.m.–4 p.m., Sun 8 a.m.–4 p.m.; closed Mon ■ Reservations taken ■ Checks accepted ■ Bar: none ■ Takeout ■ Non-smoking section

JOHN'S CAFE

Cleveland   Near East Side
3658 E. 52nd St.   Casual
☎ 641-3671 $$$$$

The unimposing two-story wood-frame building that has housed John's for 20 years blends right in with the surrounding neighborhood.

You won't even see it until you're right in front of it. Inside, it looks like almost any tavern; the only clue that this place has ties to the Old Country are the accent of owner George Radler, the Czech beers available at the bar (which takes up half the space), and recorded Czech music playing softly in the background. Everything looks old and well-used, from the wood paneled walls to the eight plastic-covered tables to the nine bar stools. The waitress *cum* barmaid, who's been here since 1976, says John's is the first place she ate when she came to America, and she stayed. Ordering here is simple; there's always Czech beef or liver dumpling soup, roast pork and roast duck, and one special entree each day, like ptacky (rolled beef), chicken paprikash, goulash, svickova (pickled beef), and wiener schnitzel. I've been told by quite a few folks that the duck made with caraway seeds is just this side of heaven. The dumplings are unusual—they look like slices from a loaf of soft bread, and like the sauerkraut, have an intriguing sweetness. Roast goose is available on request, by ordering in advance. There seem to be a lot of regulars, folks from the neighborhood who come to relax, and I've spoken with people from all over Cleveland who think of this as their own little secret find. Depending on business, the bar sometimes stays open after the kitchen closes.

▲

Hours: Tue–Sat 11:30 a.m.–7 p.m., Sun Noon–6 p.m.; bar open longer; closed Mon ▪
Reservations taken, recommended ▪ Cash only ▪ Bar: beer, wine, liquor ▪ Takeout ▪
& Full access ▪ Non-smoking section

OLD PRAGUE RESTAURANT

Vermilion   Farther West
5586 Liberty Ave.   Casual
☎ 967-7182 $$$$$

Set in the heart of Vermilion's historic harbor district, the place looks like a European mountain chalet. Definitely a "destination restaurant," patrons consider it well worth the 45-minute trip from downtown Cleveland, a drive many of the area's Czech Americans make regularly. The cook is from Czechoslovakia, as are the two women, both named Vera, who own and operate the restaurant, which has been in Vera Kalousek's family for 23 years. Del Donahoo has visited here, and Dick Feagler's a regular. The most popular dishes are roast duck with sauerkraut and dumplings, roast pork—a close second, and Moravian beef. They make shishki, a meat-on-a-stick appetizer, goulash, paprikash, and schnitzel. It's the kind of food you keep on eating even when you know you're full. They bake all their own pastries, including melt-in-your-mouth strudel. There are also some simple American items on the menu, like steak and ham and catch of the day. The only options for vegetarians are salad and a meatless paprikash. They carry wines and beers made in Czechoslovakia, including the famous Pilsner Urquell. The size of the place is modest, the ambience warm and comfortable in the old-world style, with Czech folk art on display.

▲

Hours: Sun–Thu noon–9 p.m., Fri & Sat noon–10 p.m.; closed Mon; open Fri, Sat, Sun only November–February ▪ Reservations taken, recommended on weekends ▪ MC, VS accepted ▪ Bar: beer, wine ▪ Takeout ▪ ⴠ Full access ▪ No smoking

EASTERN EUROPEAN MIX

MARIE'S RESTAURANT

Cleveland   Near East Side
4502 St. Clair Ave.   Casual
☎ 361-1816 $$$$$

Marie's is definitely the sort of place you'd have to know about before choosing it. A storefront amidst mostly commercial buildings, it offers little to attract a passerby (the area would never be mistaken for a restaurant row). But once you do know about it, there's every reason to get yourself there because of the made-from-scratch food Mila Sabljic prepares each day. Only recently arrived from the former Yugoslavia four years ago, Mila makes stuffed cabbage, chicken paprikash, stuffed peppers, beef goulash, schnitzel, and dumplings the old-world way. She also prepares cevapi (a grilled Croatian sausage), and if you call a few days in advance she'll make roast lamb or pork for a large group. The effort here is on the food and not the atmosphere. There are two small rooms; the front section handles the takeout business. The rooms have high, old-fashioned ceilings of pressed tin, wood paneling, and plastic runners on the floor. One patron described the place as 15 degrees shy of comfortable, but nonetheless a good place to eat. I'd have to agree, and so would my three sons who found the hefty portions and informal, friendly atmosphere much to their liking. The prices make it possible for a family like mine to eat well without having to take out a second mortgage on the house. The place is often busy at lunch with a downtown business crowd, but the dinner hour seems to draw fewer people, mostly folks from the neighborhood.

Other ethnic specialties: Croatian

▲

Hours: Mon–Sat 11 a.m.–9 p.m.; closed Sun ▪ Reservations taken, recommended ▪ Checks accepted ▪ Bar: beer, wine, liquor ▪ Takeout ▪ ⴠ Full access ▪ Non-smoking section

HUNGARIAN

BALATON RESTAURANT

Cleveland
12523 Buckeye Rd.
☎ 921-9691

Near East Side
Casual
$$$$$

This diamond-in-the-rough, a few blocks from Shaker Square, hasn't changed much in the past 30 years—which means the fake wood paneling is still on the walls and the tables feature red paper placemats. It also means the food is as good as ever; classic entrees like Becsi-Szelet (a thin boneless breaded veal cutlet), goulash, and stuffed cabbage are served in huge portions (half portions are available) for a moderate price. Everything is homemade, from scratch, by owner Louis Olah's mother. Leave room for a traditional dessert: strudel, palacsinta (crepe), or Dobos Torte (an eight-layer cake). People who enjoy good food in a come-as-you-are atmosphere rave about this place. Cleveland's oldest Hungarian restaurant, it has received praise from *Cleveland Magazine*, the *Cincinnati Enquirer*, and out-of-state newspapers as far afield as Florida, New Jersey, and Kansas. Parking is on-street but rarely a problem.

▲

Hours: Tue & Wed 11:30 a.m.–8 p.m., Thu–Sat 11:30 a.m.–9 p.m.; closed Sun & Mon ■ Reservations not taken ■ Cash only ■ Bar: none ■ Takeout

MARINKO'S FIREHOUSE

Willoughby Hills
2768 Stark Dr.
☎ 943-4983

East Side
Casual
$$$$$

Here you can enjoy Hungarian specialties in a restored fire station. The building is the former Willoughby Hills firehouse, and it's decorated with firehouse memorabilia, firefighting equipment, and antiques. There are six separate dining areas, including the room with the bar, a banquet room, and a 60-seat outdoor patio with vine-covered gazebo and fountain. The way the space is broken up, even when the place is busy it doesn't feel too large or crowded. Although the menu is weighted towards standard American fare, the szekely goulash, chicken paprikash, potato pancakes, sausage with cabbage and noodles, and stuffed peppers insure that the restaurant keeps one foot firmly planted on the side of ethnic cooking. Traditional dumplings called spaetzle are available with all the Hungarian entrees. The chef creates an ever-changing Hungarian combination plate daily for those who want to try grazing Eastern European style. They draw clientele of all ages, including family groups, from the surrounding counties. Some come for the food, others for the casual, friendly tavern-like atmosphere, and still others for fun of the nostalgic setting. Plenty of convenient parking.

▲

Hours: Mon–Thu 11:30 a.m.–10 p.m., Fri & Sat 11:30 a.m.–midnight, Sun 1–7 p.m.
- Reservations taken, required on weekends and for large groups
- MC, VS, AX, Dis accepted ■ Bar: beer, wine, liquor ■ Takeout ■ ら Full access

LITHUANIAN

GINTARAS DINING ROOM

Cleveland   East Side
877 E. 185th St.   Casual
☎ 531-2131 $$$$$

This was once a private restaurant, reserved for the members of Lithuanian American Club, but it is now open to the public. The entrance is at the back of the building. There's not much to look at outside, but inside it's pleasant, with wood paneling and details carved in the old-world tradition—much as a living and dining room might be in a home in the Lithuanian countryside. Eating here was described by one patron as "The Total Lithuanian Dining Experience." Here's a place to taste bulvinai blynai (potato pancakes), koldunai (another version of pierogi), naliesnikai (crepes), and balandeliai (stuffed cabbage), with the possibility of falling into conversation with some Clevelanders of Lithuanian descent, and learning a bit of their history, too. Owner Vito Jacubaitus can talk you from about A.D. 1100 to the present, if you have the time. There are many American items on the menu, too, from shrimp cocktail to charbroiled chicken, and the selection of desserts includes both traditional treats like homemade strudel and tortes, and American-style carrot cake. Rooms are available for private parties, banquets, and meetings.

▲

Hours: Tue & Wed Lunch only 11:30 a.m.–3 p.m., Thu & Fri 11:30 a.m.–8 p.m., Sat Dinner only 4–8 p.m., Sun Lunch only 11 a.m.–3 p.m.; closed Mon ■ Reservations taken, recommended on weekends ■ MC, VS, Dis, checks accepted ■ Bar: beer, wine, liquor
- Takeout ■ ら Full access ■ Non-smoking section

POLISH

PARMA PIEROGIES

Lyndhurst   East Side
5445 Mayfield Rd.   Casual
☎ 449-2000 $$$$$

Parma Pierogies, as the name suggest, began as a West Side operation, when Mary Poldruhi decided to quit corporate Cleveland and go into business for herself. The concept grew out of her experience waiting in long lines at a local smoke-filled tavern with her family every Friday night just to get a plateful of authentic pierogies. There had to be an alternative, and she decided to create it. The first Parma Pierogies opened in 1991 and a second, on the East Side, in 1994. Now even the old, traditional grandmas take the trouble to thank her, because the pierogies she sells have such homemade, handmade taste that they no longer need to spend long hours preparing them in their own kitchens. (For more information about the food and the restaurant, see the following description.)

▲
Hours: Mon–Thu 11 a.m.–9 p.m., Fri & Sat 11 a.m.–10 p.m., Sun 1–7 p.m.
■ Reservations taken, but not needed ■ Cash only ■ Bar: beer, wine ■ Takeout
■ ♿ Full access ■ No smoking

PARMA PIEROGIES

Parma   Southwest
Parmatown Plaza, 7707 W. Ridgewood Dr.   Casual
☎ 888-1200 $$$$$

You walk in past the restaurant's large pink stuffed flamingo mascot (which wears white socks and sneakers), order and pay fast-food-style at the counter, and then carry a tray filled with plastic and styrofoam to your table. But there the resemblance to the national eat-and-run chains ends. Nothing sits under heat lamps waiting to be claimed. The pierogies, prepared fresh each day, actually taste homemade and are cooked to order. The stuffed cabbage, potato pancakes, and kielbasa are the real thing, too. Traditional potato- and kraut-filled versions of what some call "Polish ravioli" are augmented with some modern variations including broccoli and cheddar, spinach and mozzarella, and mushrooms and Swiss. They can be had boiled or deep fried, with butter and onions, sour cream, or tomato sauce. And when your order is ready, staff will bring it to your table. And though they'll check back later to see if everything's okay or if your coffee cup needs refilling, tipping is not allowed. There are also dessert pierogies filled with fruit, served a la mode if you choose, and cheese-, nut-, and apricot-filled kolachki (cream cheese pastry). The decor is cheerful and bright, done in shades of pink and green with paisley print wallpaper and plenty of space between tables. Everything seems organized for convenience and there are plenty of booster seats and high chairs on hand. This is an excellent choice if you're in a hurry, want good-for-you food at a good-for-your-wallet price, or are looking for an easy, simple meal out with the kids—even those who still have a great deal to learn about table manners.

▲
Hours: Mon–Thu 11 a.m.–10 p.m., Fri & Sat 11 a.m.–11 p.m., Sun 1–7 p.m. ■ Reservations taken, but not needed ■ Cash only ■ Bar: beer, wine ■ Takeout ■ ♿ Full access ■ No smoking

SOKOLOWSKI'S UNIVERSITY INN

Cleveland   Near West Side
1201 University Rd.   Casual
☎ 771-9236 $$$$$

This cafeteria, popular with the downtown business crowd for lunch, began as a tavern that Mike Sokolowski's grandfather opened in 1923. In the 1950s, Mike's parents turned it into a restaurant and Mom Sokolowski cooked hearty meals for the men who worked at the nearby steel mills. Now the restaurant has expanded and serves a group that includes judges, truckers, and everybody in between. It fills three rooms and a kitchen, added on in 1979. The original wood-paneled bar is in the back. The next room has a wood-burning fireplace, old trestle tables, and gorgeous copper pots that were once used at Cleveland's Leisy Brewery. The latest expansion was to connect and convert the garage next door, a huge place where dragsters were once built. The food line offers homestyle Ohio cooking plus the same Polish specialties they've been serving up for more than 40 years: stuffed cabbage with mashed potatoes, stuffed peppers, pierogi, fresh bratwurst, and smoked kielbasa.

▲

Hours: Lunch Mon–Fri 11 a.m.–3 p.m.; Dinner Mon–Fri 5–9 p.m.; closed between Lunch & Dinner; open for private parties & catering on Sat & Sun ▪ Reservations taken, for large parties only ▪ MC, VS, checks accepted ▪ Bar: beer, wine, liquor ▪ Takeout ▪ ♿ Full access ▪ Non-smoking section

RUSSIAN

RUSSIAN HOUSE RESTAURANT

University Heights   East Side
13968 Cedar Rd.   Dressy
☎ 371-6177 $$$$$

This is the only Russian restaurant in the area, and it's become a social gathering place for many of the city's 14,000 Russian immigrants. Dining doesn't get much more authentic than this. Patrons get a taste here not only of genuine Russian foods like blintzes, borscht, sturgeon, and pelmeni (a meat dumpling), but of a real Russian dining experience. Once inside on a busy night, it's hard to believe that Cedar Road and a strip mall are just on the other side of the door. Tables look festive with wine-colored cloth napkins that fan out of sparkling, long-stemmed water goblets. On weekends the atmosphere is boisterous and lively; it's crowded, the band plays for hours, and the dance floor is filled. People spend long hours here talking, drinking, smoking (no political correctness here), and, of course, eating. Owner Vadim Arutyunov, a chemical engineer in his former life, describes the food as simple (except for the caviar, an American favorite), the kind real people like to eat in the regions of Georgia, the Ukraine, and the Caspian Sea. My Russian acquaintances tell me it reminds them of home.

▲

Hours: Tue–Thu 11 a.m.–9 p.m., Fri–Sun noon–midnight; closed Mon ▪ Reservations taken, recommended, especially on weekends ▪ MC, VS, Dis, checks accepted ▪ Bar: beer, wine, liquor ▪ Takeout ▪ ♿ Full access

SLOVENIAN

ANNIE'S

Chester Township	Farther East
8430 Mayfield Rd.	Dressy
☎ 729-4540	$$$$$

Owner Ana Leben advises patrons to "Come hungry," and even then the portions are likely to be too much for most diners. This may be classified as simple meat and potatoes food, but it's the kind of meat and potatoes few can resist—smooth-as-velvet paprikash, crispy schnitzel, and hearty Slovenian sausage; real mashed potatoes and perfect homefries. Leben ran Cleveland's Slovenian Village for eight years and moved out to Chester Township in 1993 because she wanted to expand. Her new restaurant seats 115 comfortably in what was once a spacious home; in addition to the main dining area, there's one small room with only four tables for privacy, another that's a converted porch, a delightful space full of windows, and a separate room for smokers. Growing up on the border of Austria and Hungary, Ana has a rich bank of European food memories to draw upon for her menu, which features such specialties as stuffed cabbage, goulash, and roast pork. There's also roast pheasant with mushroom stuffing, some Italian-inspired dishes, and nightly specials. A new chef is currently working to design some vegetarian items to add to the menu. There are options for children and seniors, and a Sunday brunch, all served up in a friendly, relaxed atmosphere.

▲

Hours: Tue–Thu 11 a.m.–9 p.m., Fri & Sat 11 a.m.–11 p.m., Sun Brunch 9 a.m.–3 p.m.; Sun Dinner 4–9 p.m.; closed Mon ▪ Reservations taken, recommended at all times; required Thu–Sat ▪ MC, VS, AX, Dis, checks accepted ▪ Bar: beer, wine, liquor ▪ Takeout ▪ Non-smoking section

DONNA'S

Euclid	East Side
689 E. 105th St.	Relaxed
☎ 486-3838	$$$$$

This is a frayed-at-the-edges luncheonette in the Old World Plaza commercial district. The place has neither style nor flair (10 plastic-covered tables and a counter with 10 stools in a storefront space), but if you want to eat real Slovenian food, then that's reason enough to come here. Donna Pirc makes stuffed cabbage, tripe, kidney stew, goulash, chicken paprikash, roast pork, wiener schnitzel, and Slovenian sausage with sauerkraut, and she's been doing it for 18 years. There's also apple, cherry, and cheese strudel, and palacinka (a dessert crepe). The rest of the menu is a simple sandwich to spaghetti mix. Most of the customers are regulars, from the neighborhood, and they like the big portions as well as the familiar, affable feel of the place, where grandmas and grandbabies alike make themselves at home. When you come looking for Donna's don't be confused by the sign out front—it says Donna & Rose's. On street parking.

▲

Hours: Mon–Sat 9 a.m.–8 p.m.; closed Sun ■ Reservations not taken ■ Checks accepted ■ Bar: none ■ Takeout ■ ♿ Full access

FANNY'S

Cleveland	East Side
3539 E. 156th St.	Casual
☎ 531-1231	$$$$$

This friendly place has been a neighborhood fixture for almost 50 years. Started by the current owners' mother and grandmother, its menu still features Slovenian specialties like imuk (a stew), beef goulash served over spaetzles, ajmont soup (chicken soup made Slovenian-style with a dash of vinegar), and pork and kraut goulash. "Our customers don't want us to change," said Shirley Davido who owns and operates the restaurant with her brother Terry Kollar. Many items on the menu are not ethnic at all, just simple, home-cooked food like liver and onions or roast chicken. You can't miss this big blue building with brown-and-red trim located in an old residential neighborhood, not far from Raddell's Slovenian Sausage Shop (see market listings for more information). Inside, it feels like walking into someone's home; dining areas are a series of small, cozy rooms with flowered wallpaper. Patrons dress up or down, depending on how they feel, what occasion brings them out to eat, and whether they went home after work or not. This is the kind of place to bring children, knowing they'll find foods they like in low-key, family-oriented surroundings. There's a large enclosed porch where you can wait for a table or wait for friends, and plenty of parking in the restaurant's own lot.

▲

Hours: Mon–Sat 7 a.m.–8 p.m., Sun 11:30 a.m.–7 p.m. ■ Reservations not taken ■ Cash only ■ Bar: none ■ Takeout ■ Non-smoking section

FRANK STERLE'S SLOVENIAN COUNTRY HOUSE

Cleveland | Near East Side
1401 E. 55th St. | Casual
☎ 881-4181 | $$$$$

Sterle's began life as the Bonner Cafe, a bar with some food, that opened for business 40 years ago. When Frank Sterle bought the place it was just one small room, but like Topsy, it just grew and grew. Now, the huge space which can handle as many as 300 people, is a tourist destination, attracting suburban visitors and out-of-town guests who want to get a taste of Cleveland's ethnic past. It begins at the parking lot, a large enclosed area that you enter through an impressive, decorative gateway, like the entrance to a castle. The leitmotif, inside and out, is a European mountain chalet, with all the accompanying old-world warmth and hospitality. Waitresses wear a version of Slovenian traditional dress, much like a German dirndl, and many have worked here for years. And they're adept at managing the heaping platefuls of roast pork, stuffed cabbage, and paprikash. There's always a selection of American standbys, like meat loaf and roast chicken, and some so-called European favorites (mostly Italian-style), but the really interesting part of the menu is Slovenian: kidney or tripe stew, jeterca (liver with onions), klobase and zelje (sausage and sauerkraut), and segedin goulash. There's a large bar in front and a separate room for meetings and private parties.

▲

Hours: Tue–Sat 11:30 a.m.–9 p.m., Sun 11:30 a.m.–8 p.m.; Mon Lunch only 11:30 a.m.–3 p.m. ■ Reservations taken, recommended for parties of five or more ■ MC, VS, AX, checks accepted ■ Bar: beer, wine, liquor ■ Takeout ■ ♿ Full access

UKRAINIAN

UKRAINIAN KITCHEN RESTAURANT

Parma | Southwest
5392 State Rd. | Casual
☎ 351-1125 | $$$$$

In the words of one visitor, this is an "unpretentious, undiscovered hideaway with comfort food we can all be comfortable with." It's a place, she added, that's more like your aunt's house than a restaurant, where you go not to dine but to have supper. It's simple and small, with seating for only about 25. Owner Taras Broustourniak, who also does some of the cooking as well as hosting and waiting tables, does not advertise his young restaurant, relying on word of mouth and the patronage of his fellow Ukrainians. He's justifiably proud of his food, made from authentic old recipes. His kitchen uses only fresh ingredients and prepares such hearty and heart-warming dishes as borscht, vushka (savory little meat-filled dumplings), nalysnyky (chicken and onions wrapped in a pancake), and kapusta (sauerkraut with sausage and potato dumplings). Stuffed cabbage, potato pancakes, and perets (stuffed peppers in a grilled-mushroom-and-sour-cream gravy) are also everyday standbys, and there are daily specials like roast pork with all the trimmings. Every entree comes with a carrot slaw and a beet-and-sour-cream salad. While this might not be the spot for a romantic interlude, it's a good choice for families and old friends looking to spend some relaxed, enjoyable time around the table. It's easy to drive right past if you've never been here before. The restaurant shares the building with a tanning salon and is directly across the street from a Sunoco gas station. There's a small parking lot in front.

▲

Hours: Tue–Thu 11 a.m.–8 p.m., Fri & Sat 11 a.m.–9 p.m., Sun 11 a.m.–8 p.m.; closed Mon ■ Reservations taken ■ Cash only ■ Bar: none ■ Takeout ■ ও Full access ■ No smoking

MARKETS

CZECH

BOHEMIAN HALL

Cleveland   Near East Side
4939 Broadway Ave.
☎ 641-9777

The elderly female members of the Sokol Greater Cleveland (a Czech athletic club) raise money by preparing traditional Czech dumplings, which they sell frozen year-round on Wednesdays and Saturdays. They also hold a Christmas bake sale featuring homemade strudel and raisin-and-almond bread, and another at Easter when they offer raisin-filled sweet breads. Prices are always reasonable. On the third Friday of every month, which is Bohemian Hall's Fish Fry, caraway seed, barley, Czech mushrooms, and imported gifts are available for purchase by the general public. They also have a cookbook of tried-and-true Czech recipes that includes breads, soups, dumplings, and main course dishes. They have a few copies left and are currently work-ing on a new one. Call for information, and be sure to let the phone ring a long time. You can ask to be put on their mailing list.

▲

Foods available: baked goods, prepared frozen foods ■ Hours: n/a ■ Checks accepted ■ ও Full access

VACLAV SOREJS HOMEMADE SAUSAGE

Cleveland   East Side
3935 E. 131st St.
☎ 561-7266

Vaclav Sorejs has been in business for 30 years at the same location. Born into a family of butchers, he is skilled at making head cheese, garlic and prazsky sausage, cottage hams, and rice and liver rings just like his forbears. His is primarily a wholesale business. The one day a week that he's open for retail sales, it's mostly an older generation of Bohemians, Poles, and Slavs who come to buy. "Most younger people," says Sorejs, "won't come here just for meat. They'd rather get everything from the supermarket or eat fast food." But according to one of the regular customers, a man who likes to live close to his Czech roots, "They have no idea what they're missing." The name's on the front of the building—it's easy to find.

▲
Foods available: meat (fresh) ▪ Hours: Thu only 8 a.m.–1 p.m. ▪ Cash only
▪ & Full access

EASTERN EUROPEAN MIX

BUETTNER'S BAKERY

Cleveland   Near East Side
704 E. 185th St.
☎ 531-0650

There's been a family-owned bakery at this spot for 70 years or so, according to the current manager, who has been there 31 years herself. They still use old-fashioned gas ovens with rotating shelves and the products they turn out are not quite like their counterparts made in more modern stoves. In fact, in a tradition that hearkens back to a time when the baker's oven was used by the entire community, Buettner's makes these special ovens available to the public at holidays and roasts whole pigs and lambs for various ethnic celebrations. Swedish limpa bread is available at Christmastime and Irish soda bread around St. Patrick's Day. The rest of the year they make a variety of Polish, Slovenian, Hungarian, and Croatian specialties, including kuchens, strudels, nut and poppyseed rolls, and kolachy plus a variety of non-ethnic breads, danish, pies, and donuts.

Other ethnic specialties: Croatian, Hungarian, Polish
▲
Foods available: baked goods ▪ Hours: Tue–Fri 8 a.m.–4:30 p.m., Sat 8:30 a.m.–4:30 p.m., Sun 9 a.m.–12:30 p.m.; closed Mon ▪ Checks accepted ▪ & Full access

GERTRUDE HOME BAKERY

Cleveland   Near East Side
6506 Gertrude Ave.
☎ 641-7582

This bakery's been in existence for 75 years, but the present owner has been there only three years. The change in management has not meant a change in product or process. The bakery continues to turn out homemade Eastern European specialties like Polish sweet breads, punczke, strudel, and kolacke. They also bake loaves of rye, Vienna, and pumpernickel bread daily, as well as cookies and cakes.

▲
Foods available: baked goods ▪ Hours: Wed–Sun 7:30 a.m.–6 p.m.; closed Mon & Tue ▪ Checks accepted

INTERNATIONAL FOODS

Cleveland Heights   East Side
2078 S. Taylor Rd.
☎ 932-5000

This small store is part deli, part grocery, and the best of what they have to offer is in the glass case filled with one of the biggest selections of smoked fish anywhere in town, including sable and lox, and Eastern European specialties like pierogies and pelmeni (a Russian dumpling stuffed with meat, potato, or cheese). They also stock 20 varieties of herring, 60 different kinds of old-world prepackaged cakes and cookies, and 25 different types of chocolate candy. Beer, wine, and mineral water available.

Other ethnic specialties: Polish, Russian

▲
Foods available: baked goods, beverages, tea, wine, prepared frozen foods, takeout meals ▪ Hours: Thu 10 a.m.–8 p.m., Fri 10 a.m.–5 p.m., Sat 10 a.m.–7 p.m., Sun 9 a.m.–2 p.m.; closed Mon–Wed ▪ Checks accepted

K & K MEAT SHOPPE

Maple Heights   Southeast
6172 Dunham Rd.
☎ 662-2644

The claim to ethnic fame at this full-service meat market is their homemade fresh and smoked sausages, including Polish-style hurka (with rice) and Slovenian links. They also offer various types and cuts of meats, a deli counter that prepares sandwiches to order, and a selection of imported items that complement their meats such as pickles and mustards.

Other ethnic specialties: Polish, Slovenian, Western European

Foods available: meat (fresh), baked goods, condiments, beverages, tea, takeout meals
■ Hours: Mon–Fri 9 a.m.–6 p.m., Sat 8 a.m.–5 p.m., Sun 9 a.m.–2 p.m.
■ MC, VS, Dis, checks accepted ■ ₺ Full access

KATHY'S KOLACKE & PASTRY SHOP

Westlake   West Side
25076 Center Ridge Rd.
☎ 835-6570

Located in King James Plaza, this bakery is best known for its kolacke. The Polish version of this traditional pastry is light, flaky, and filled with fruit and nuts. The Czech form is soft, sweet, and stuffed with meat. Kathy Schreiner runs this one-woman business that was named "Best Ethnic Bakery" in the Cleveland Sweet Revenge contest. She also makes Hungarian nut and poppyseed rolls, a cheesecake that's been featured on Del Donahue's TV show, and a large variety of non-ethnic cookies, cakes and cupcakes, brownies, and muffins.

Other ethnic specialties: Hungarian, Polish

Foods available: baked goods, beverages, coffee ■ Hours: Tue, Thu, Fri 10 a.m.–5 p.m., Wed 10 a.m.–4 p.m., Sat 9 a.m.–4 p.m.; closed Sun & Mon ■ Checks accepted ■ ₺ Full access

RADDELL'S SAUSAGE SHOP, INC.

Cleveland   East Side
478 E. 152nd St.
☎ 486-1944

Specializing in the traditional foods of Slovenia, Lithuania, and Germany, Raddell's is in its third generation of family ownership, though it operated under the name John Czech's until 1980. It's best known for the large variety and old-world quality of its meats and sausages. "People come from all over just to buy our sausage," said partner Mark Tichar. "The homemade rice and blood sausage and the Slovenian smoked sausage are among our best sellers, and customers even ask us to UPS our ethnic specialties out of state." They also offer imported chocolates, noodles, jams and jellies, pickles, cookies, and European mineral waters. Located in a freestanding building with its own parking area.

Other ethnic specialties: German, Lithuanian, Slovenian

Foods available: meat (fresh), grains, baked goods, spices, condiments, tea, coffee ■ Hours: Mon–Sat 8 a.m.–5 p.m.; closed Sun ■ Checks accepted ■ ₺ Full access

FARKAS PASTRY

Cleveland   Near West Side
2718 Lorain Ave.
☎ 281-6200

Atila Farkas and his wife have been baking and selling Hungarian pastry in this tiny shop near the West Side Market for 30 years, and the only advertising they've ever needed is the reputation of their products. The word "shop," in this case, is a euphemism. The store is in fact the kitchen itself, and on the two days they're open for retail sales, the line spills out onto the sidewalk and the doorway is almost always crowded with people. Hungarians, Germans, Serbians, and Slovaks as well as generic Clevelanders gossip in a babble of languages while patiently waiting to buy some of whatever is still left. Farkas bakes traditional dobos, hazelnut, and chocolate tortes; nut, poppyseed, and fruit rolls; Napoleons; and zserbo. Get there early if you want to have a selection, or call to place an order in advance. And leave enough time to engage Farkas in conversation; it's always an interesting experience.

▲
Foods available: baked goods, ■ Hours: Fri 9 a.m.–4 p.m., Sat 9 a.m.–2 p.m. ■ Cash only

LAURINDA'S

Middleburg Heights   Southwest
(see description)
☎ 566-1700

Laurinda's is not really a store at all. They bake to order only and deliver your goodies right to your door. While they specialize in Hungarian strudel, kolackes, nut horns, and a cheesecake made from a closely guarded and very old family recipe, they're unique in that they'll also custom bake items using your own recipes. Since everything is made to order, there are no shortcuts taken or commercial techniques used; everything is made from scratch, with no preservatives, using only the freshest and best ingredients. Place orders by phone during business hours.

▲
Foods available: baked goods ■ Hours: daily 8 a.m.–5 p.m. ■ Cash only

LUCILLE'S STRUDEL SHOPPE

Cleveland   Near West Side
5303 Detroit Ave.
☎ 961-1410

A specialist in hand-stretched strudel, owner Herman Belohlavek Jr.

learned the authentic old-world technique from his father. He prepares apple, cheese, nut, poppyseed, cherry and cheese, and blueberry strudel, and everything is made from scratch, fresh each day. And that day starts at 6:30 a.m., when Belohlavek arrives at the shop to get the 36 strips of strudel started. He also bakes traditional Hungarian pastries, including nut and poppyseed rolls, almond crescents, "pull-apart" kuchen, and linzer cookies. Fresh-from-the-oven breads available on Saturdays.

▲

Foods available: baked goods, coffee ■ Hours: Wed & Thu 10 a.m.–5 p.m., Fri 9 a.m.–6 p.m., Sat 9 a.m.–5 p.m.; closed Sun–Tue ■ Checks accepted ■ ♿ Full access

LUCY'S SWEET SURRENDER

Cleveland   Near East Side
12516 Buckeye Rd.
☎ 752-0828

The new owners of this 40-year-old bakery (formerly known as Lucy's Hungarian Strudel) continue and expand the tradition of making unique, authentic Eastern European specialties. The woman who prepares the strudel dough has been stretching it the old-fashioned way for more than 35 years, and this is still a cut-no-corners, everything-from-scratch operation. They even buy the apples they use for strudels and pies fresh from local growers. This is one of the few places that still bakes zserbo, layers of crisp dough alternating with raspberry preserves, hazelnuts, and chocolate, and grillazs, a "lace" cookie soaked in rum and cream. Lucy's also offers kolach, a braided yeast bread with golden raisins, Dobos Torte, cream cheese and sour cream cookies filled with fruit, and nut and poppyseed rolls. Also available are other types of European-style cakes and pastries, muffins, bread, doughnuts, and pies, and some Hungarian imports like letcho (a pickled salad) and paprika. An informal, impromptu gathering place for Hungarians from all around town. Parking lot adjacent to the store.

▲

Foods available: baked goods, spices, condiments, coffee ■ Hours: Wed–Fri 7 a.m.–4 p.m., Sat 7 a.m.–3 p.m., also open by appointment. ■ Checks accepted

LYDIA'S HUNGARIAN STRUDEL SHOP

Parma Heights   Southwest
6230 Stumph Rd.
☎ 885-2600

Best known for their strudel, here they prepare not only five or six classic varieties but also an unusual vegetable strudel. All are sold either freshly baked or frozen for home baking. A small family-owned bakery in business for 20 years, Lydia's has a good selection of other Hungarian pastries like fruit horns, linzer tarts, and ladyfingers.

▲
Foods available: baked goods, coffee ▪ Hours: Mon–Sat 8 a.m.–5:30 p.m.; closed Sun ▪ Checks accepted

MARY'S HUNGARIAN PASTRY SHOP
Lakewood   West Side
12701 Madison Ave.
☎ 228-0088

Yes, there is a Mary, and she bakes everything herself using authentic Hungarian recipes. This one-woman business does a seven-day-a-week trade in dobos, nut, and mocha tortes; cherry, cheese, apple, and pineapple strudel; zserbo; nut and poppyseed rolls, and an assortment of Hungarian yeast breads. Mary also keeps busy baking a variety of cookies, birthday cakes to order, donuts, and danish.

▲
Foods available: baked goods, coffee ▪ Hours: Mon–Sat 9 a.m.–5 p.m., Sun 11 a.m.–2 p.m. ▪ Checks accepted ▪ ᕕ Full access

MERTIE'S HUNGARIAN STRUDEL SHOP
Middleburg Heights   Southwest
6606 Smith Rd.
☎ 362-0012

Mertie Rakosi has done all the baking herself, from scratch, for 14 years—and for many more before that for a bakery on Buckeye. The variety of strudels is almost endless: apple, cherry, cheese, apricot, blueberry, poppyseed, lemon, raspberry, and peach. She also prepares a sugar-free version of her apple strudel. Ethnic goodie seekers will also find dobos, double chocolate, Black Forest, strawberry, and lemon tortes here, as well as ladylocks and homemade noodles.

▲
Foods available: baked goods ▪ Hours: Tue–Fri 8 a.m.–5 p.m., Sat 8 a.m.–4 p.m.; closed Sun & Mon ▪ Checks accepted

HUNGARIAN, SEE ALSO:
Buettner's Bakery (Eastern European Mix)
Kathy's Kolacke & Pastry Shop (Eastern European Mix)
Puritan Bakery (Western European Mix, Chapter 5)

POLISH

CHAMBERS BAKERY

Cleveland   Near East Side
3696 E. 69th St.
☎ 271-6080

This small Slavic Village bakery has a regular clientele and solid, 70-year-old reputation. Adults who grew up in the neighborhood can wax poetic about the smell of freshly baked bread that was part of their childhood, and enticing aromas are still wafting out the windows. Here they make rye bread, sweet bread, chruscik, a flaky bow tie–shaped pastry, kolacke, and crumb babka, a coffee cake. Prune punczke are a house specialty, and they also do pies, cookies, danish, and special occasion cakes.

▲

Foods available: baked goods ▪ Hours: Mon–Fri 7 a.m.–5 p.m., Sat 7 a.m.–4 p.m., Sun 7 a.m.–12:30 p.m. ▪ Cash only

JAWORSKI'S MEAT MARKET & DELI

Cleveland   Near East Side
5324 Fleet Ave.
☎ 271-4575

The Jaworski family has been making fresh and smoked kielbasa sausage here for 58 years. Stuffed cabbage and pierogies as well as hard-to-find Polish delicacies are also prepared on the premises, including flaczki (tripe) and czarnina (duck) soups; bigos, a stew of sauerkraut, kielbasa, tomatoes, and mushrooms; head cheese; and kabanose, a dried smoked sausage made with pork and garlic. Shelves are stocked with imported pickles, sauces, jarred peppers, and canned cabbage. There's a full deli with pierogi, cold cuts and salads, a nice choice of spices, and a limited selection of basic grocery items and fresh produce.

▲

Foods available: meat (fresh, frozen), produce, beans, flour, baked goods, spices, condiments, beverages, tea, prepared frozen foods, takeout meals ▪ Hours: Tue–Sat 8:30 a.m.–6 p.m.; closed Sun & Mon ▪ Cash only ▪ ₾ Full access

KRUSINSKI FINEST MEAT PRODUCTS

Cleveland   Near East Side
6300 Heisley Ave.
☎ 441-0100

This classic old-fashioned butcher shop in the heart of Slavic Village has been around for over 40 years, and is still owned and operated by the Krusinski family, who prepare their own flavorful garlic-laced sauerkraut. A wide variety of pierogies are made fresh daily, including potato, cheese, kraut, and fruit. Helen Krusinski and her staff also prepare smoked and fresh kielbasa, potato pancakes, blintzes, stuffed cabbage, and stuffed peppers. Other Polish specialty items include hurka (a rice and liver ring), jeternice (liver puddings), and krakowska (a lean meat cold cut similar to salami). They also sell all types and cuts of meat, deli meats, and cheeses.

▲
Foods available: meat (fresh), beverages, tea, wine, takeout meals ■ Hours: Mon, Tue, Thu, Fri, Sat 8 a.m.–6 p.m.; closed Wed & Sun (open Wed the week before a major holiday) ■ Cash only

NEW WARSAW EUROPEAN SUPERMARKET

Parma   Southwest
6163 State Rd.
☎ 885-1200

A European-style shop, this place has all the variety you'd expect in a small neighborhood grocery. Recently opened, they stock an international selection of imported canned and packaged foods, including syrups and jellies, cookies, and chocolates, with the emphasis on products from Poland and the other Eastern European nations. They prepare eight different kinds of fresh and smoked sausage, a variety of traditional pastries, and also have an extensive takeout menu that features Polish specialties such as stuffed cabbage and pierogies. There are also some non-ethnic foods and common household essentials.

▲
Foods available: meat (fresh, frozen), fish (fresh, frozen), produce, grains, beans, flour, baked goods, spices, condiments, beverages, tea, wine, prepared frozen foods, takeout meals ■ Hours: Mon–Fri 8 a.m.–7 p.m., Sat 8 a.m.–6 p.m., Sun 10 a.m.–4 p.m. ■ Checks accepted

PETER'S MARKET

Garfield Heights   Southeast
4617 Turney Rd.
☎ 341-5910

Peter's is a neighborhood meat market and grocery, with an emphasis on Eastern European foods and a good reputation that's grown by word of mouth. They carry cottage hams, head cheese, a variety of sausages and kielbasa, and canned and packaged products from Poland. There's a small selection of kitchen staples, plus deli meats. But the real specialty here are the pierogi prepared across the street, on Fridays only, 11 a.m.–7 p.m., at Sophie's Choice Pierogi (4631 Turney Rd.; 341-4150). The same people own and operate both businesses, and yes, there is a real Sophie who makes them. The little dough pockets come filled with potatoes, potatoes and cheese, sauerkraut, mushrooms, vegetables, apples, apricots, and prunes. Retail customers can stop by Sophie's and purchase traditional Polish homemade favorites to go, including soups, dumplings, blintzes, stuffed cabbage, and, of course, pierogi.

Other ethnic specialties: Polish

▲

Foods available: meat (fresh), produce, grains, beans, flour, baked goods, condiments, beverages, tea, coffee, wine, beer, prepared frozen foods, takeout meals ■ Hours: Mon–Wed 8:30 a.m.–6 p.m., Thu–Sat 8 a.m.–6 p.m.; closed Sun ■ Checks accepted ■ ¿ Full access

SAMOSKY HOME BAKERY

Parma Heights   Southwest
6641 Pearl Rd.
☎ 845-3377

Decorated to resemble an old-world bake shop with antiques displayed in a glass case, Samosky's has been in existence since 1910. And during that time they've continuously done what they do best: make traditional Polish baked goods, including hoska (a Polish bread traditionally served at Easter), punczki (doughnuts), kolacke, and flanceta. They also make a variety of cookies, cakes, and pies, strudel, nut and poppyseed rolls, plus brownies, danish, ladylocks, and Russian tea biscuits.

▲

Foods available: baked goods, beverages, coffee ■ Hours: Tue–Fri 6 a.m.–6 p.m., Sat 6 a.m.–4 p.m.; closed Sun & Mon ■ Checks accepted ■ ¿ Full access

T & T SAUSAGE MARKET

Cleveland   Near East Side
5901 Fleet Ave.
☎ 441-4022

Another Slavic Village establishment, this one specializes in homemade products, made fresh daily. "We cater in the old-country style," says Irene Chybowski, "to an ethnic, European clientele." With her father-in-law, Irene prepares everything from scratch on the premises including kiszka (blood sausage); krakowska (ham sausage); pasztet (liver pate); garaleta (pigs feet in gelatin); and kotleciki (little meat loaves) and four different types of kielbasa. They also sell heat-and-eat stuffed cabbage and pierogies.

▲

Foods available: meat (fresh), spices, condiments, takeout meals ■ Hours: Tue & Wed 9 a.m.–5 p.m., Thu & Fri 9 a.m.–7 p.m., Sat 9 a.m.–5 p.m.; closed Sun & Mon ■ Checks accepted

Polish, see also:
Buettner's Bakery (Eastern European Mix)
International Foods (Eastern European Mix)
K & K Meat Shoppe (Eastern European Mix)
Kathy's Kolacke & Pastry Shop (Eastern European Mix)

SLOVENIAN

MALENSEK'S MEAT MARKET

Cleveland   Near East Side
1217 Norwood Rd.
☎ 361-1037

This small, old-fashioned butcher shop almost qualifies as an official
Cleveland landmark. The Malensek family has been in business at this
same location for 78 years, and the third generation is currently on
hand to answer all your questions about Slovenian sausage, their specialty, including the traditional rice and blood versions. They prepare
smoked and fresh sausage, and a unique smoked sausage loaf that can
be sliced and used as lunch meat. They also cure and smoke a large
variety of pork cuts. According to Ken Malensek, their customers are a
mix of people who hear about the store by word of mouth and those
whose family have been shopping here for years. "Even people who
have moved away to other communities come back here to stock up
two or three times a year. And folks who never lived here themselves
come in, especially around the holiday times, to buy the traditional
meats they grew up eating."

▲
Foods available: meat (fresh) ▪ Hours: Mon, Tue, Thu, Fri 8 a.m.–5 p.m., Sat 8 a.m.–4
p.m.; closed Wed & Sun ▪ Cash only

SLOVENIAN

NOSAN'S SLOVENIAN HOME BAKERY

Euclid   East Side
567 E. 200th St.
☎ 481-5670

Family owned and operated for 50 years, this is a business so friendly
and accommodating that staff will even provide curb service for customers who have difficulty getting from their cars to the store. Whether
you come to them or they come to you, what you'll find is freshly baked
and genuinely ethnic products: three varieties of potica (a nut loaf);
flanceta (angel wing pastries), kroffe (Slovenian doughnuts), sharkael
(an egg dough and raisin bread), kolacke, and tortes. They also sell

their own homemade noodles. Customers can also purchase croissants, special occasion cakes, cookies, muffins, danish, and bread. A
second store of the same name is located at 6413 St. Clair Ave. in Cleveland (see next listing).

▲

Foods available: baked goods, coffee ▪ Hours: Thu–Sat 7:30 a.m.–4 p.m.; extended
days & hours during holiday seasons ▪ Checks accepted ▪ ⅙ Full access

NOSAN'S SLOVENIAN HOME BAKERY
Cleveland   Near East Side
6413 St. Clair Ave.
☎ 361-1863

See listing for Nosan's in Euclid for description.

▲

Foods available: ▪ Hours: Tue–Sat 6 a.m.-4 p.m.

PATRIA IMPORTS
Cleveland   East Side
794 E. 185th St.
☎ 531-6720

This is a fairly small store located in Cleveland's Old World Plaza shopping district. They carry imported cheeses, canned and "barrel" fish,
sprats (a smoked fish similar to sardines), chocolates, cookies, jams,
and preserves. Some household products and convenience items, plus
gift and "souvenir" objects such as amber, pictures, tablecloths, and T-
shirts. Parking lot in back.

Other ethnic specialties: Croatian

▲

Foods available: meat (fresh), fish (fresh), beverages, wine, beer ▪ Hours: Mon–Sat 9
a.m.–5:30 p.m.; closed Sun ▪ Checks accepted ▪ ⅙ Full access

WOJTILAS BAKERY
Euclid   East Side
897 E. 222nd St.
☎ 731-7080

Using family recipes his father brought over from Czechoslovakia,
Donny Wojtilas and his wife Barb prepare a variety of traditional
Slovenian pastries daily, including potica (a nut bread), flancete (often
called angel wings), and krofe (a sort of donut). They also offer a selection of non-Slovenian fresh breads, muffins, cookies, and cakes. They
opened the bakery with the idea of re-creating the kind of neighborhood shop Donny recalled from his childhood.

Foods available: baked goods ■ Hours: Tue–Fri 6 a.m.–6 p.m., Sat 6 a.m.–4 p.m., Sun 7 a.m.–1 p.m.; closed Mon ■ Checks accepted ■ & Full access

SLOVENIAN, SEE ALSO:
K & K Meat Shoppe (Eastern European Mix)
Raddell's Sausage Shop, Inc. (Eastern European Mix)

CHAPTER 5

Europe West of the Danube

FOR THE PURPOSES OF THIS BOOK, Western Europe includes Ireland and the United Kingdom, France, Germany, and Scandinavia. Grouping these countries together, even from a culinary point of view, is problematical, for each is as different as the languages they speak. But one thing they hold in common is a connection to Cleveland, both past and present.

It has been estimated that by 1860, 45 percent of the city's population were foreign born, and the majority came from Germany, Ireland, and the United Kingdom (England, Scotland, and Wales). They were poor, usually uneducated, and forced to accept backbreaking jobs at the bottom of the economic pyramid. So they labored to build canals and railroads, worked in the quarries, the steel mills, and at the docks, and manned the growing number of factories that transformed Cleveland from a rural outpost to an industrial metropolis. Swedes followed in the 1870s, and then the Danes and Finns. The French however, came one by one, as traders in the 1700s, nuns in the 1850s, and the brides of American servicemen after World War II. While the flow of immigrants from most other Western European nations tapered off, Germans continued to settle here in significant numbers well into the 20th century. Many were skilled craftsmen: jewelers, tailors, musical instrument and cabinet makers, and machinists.

Over the years, each of these nationality groups quietly transformed itself from immigrant outsiders to mainstreamed Americans. The Irish, especially, were eager to put aside all that reminded them of the poverty and despair that most had left behind. But what was kept by all were the rich folk traditions of their homeland, traditions that lived on in music, dance, storytelling, and, of course, food.

Though Ireland is renowned more for starvation than feasting, and for a cuisine of potatoes and boiled meat, those who know the food well insist that it is in its own way memorable. "I grew up on a little farm in County Mayo," said Celine O'Leary, who came here in 1952 at the age of 20. "Vegetables grew in our garden and my grandfather was a butcher, so we always had some meat. There were griddle cakes made over an open fire, soda bread, and scones with whole milk and fresh butter. We'd roast lamb or beef in a cast-iron pot oven. It would cook on hot peat coals in the hearth. And of course we ate plenty of potatoes and turnips. Our food was plain and nourishing, but now when I think of the things we ate, I think how good they were."

The British and the Irish eat much the same way. Bacon, oats, root vegetables and cabbage, dairy products and seafood are basic, along with tea, toast, and marmalade. Traditionally, cooking is done simply, and food is seasoned with a light hand. Pies filled with meat, rolls stuffed with sausage, and eggs with bacon may not be haute cuisine, but they are invariably satisfying.

Equally satisfying are the substantial dishes of old-fashioned German cooking, a genuinely meat and potatoes cuisine. Good, hearty breads, cheeses, wurst (cold cuts), sausages of all kinds, sauerkraut, and pickles are characteristic. Braten (roasted meat) is the national dish, and pork, both cured and fresh is the favored meat. "Our food," explained Dr. Robert Ward, a third generation German American, "is so much a part of the American way of eating, that most people don't even know they're enjoying German food. It was Germans, for example, who introduced Americans to sauerkraut and beer. In the 1850s, Germans started brewing beer in Cleveland. The Hofbrauhaus Restaurant is located in what was once a German neighborhood full of gasthauses (taverns) and outdoor beer gardens like those in Europe, and each one made their own brew."

The cuisines of the Scandanavian countries warrant little exposition here because there are no longer any restaurants that serve it and only a few stores sell some imported products or bake traditional breads. Like the other nationalities that make up this chapter, they use potatoes and pork extensively. Fish and cheese also dominate their table. Dill, as it is for the Germans, is the herb of choice.

And then, at last, there is French food, a cuisine that has had an influence on fine dining far out of proportion to the number of French people who have come to America. "The French live their food," said Marcie Barker, who, with her husband chef Ali Barker owns Cleveland's widely praised restaurant, Piperade. "They are passionate about cooking and eating."

French cooking at the professional level has long set the standard for chefs and gourmets in this country, and the precise techniques and methods of preparation they've perfected form the foundation of a good culinary education.

"French cuisine is organized and unified with a great respect for the character of each ingredient," said chef Donna Adams, who displays her skills at La Pomme, a French restuarant in Lakewood she owns with her husband Jim. "Once you've got the basics, they can be expanded in so many ways."

A well-stocked French larder includes butter, wine, cream, mustard, onions, garlic, shallots, leeks, potatoes, and wild mushrooms. Bay leaves, chervil, bouquet garni, tarragon, and parsley are favored herbs. Root vegetables, green beans and peas, fresh fruit, nuts, and cheeses are also important.

"Real French cooking," said Jeanine Mihallek, who came here from Paris in 1946, "is about the art of beautiful simplicity. We like to know what we are eating, and waste nothing. Even leftovers can look and taste like a feast. But we need our bread; good bread is everything."

Luckily for Jeanine and the rest of us, good French bread is indeed available in Cleveland, along with some other authentic examples of the French culinary art of beautiful simplicity.

RESTAURANTS

BRITISH

DERBY & FLASK, THE

South Euclid   East Side
4285 Mayfield Rd.   Casual
☎ 381-9999 $$$$$

This is a restaurant first, a drinking establishment second, and it does a good job at both. It's a warm, friendly place often crowded with regulars who come for the good food, imported beers, and musical entertainment. Once inside it's easy to forget you're just a few steps away from busy Mayfield Road in a Cleveland suburb and imagine you're drinking your bitters and eating your shepherd's pie in Dublin or London. Other house specialties include Welsh rarebit, Stilton pate, real English-style liver with onions and bacon, and Yorkshire pudding. They also do a nice rendering of steaks, chops, and fish. The place has a softly lit, cozy ambience in the tradition of a true British Isles pub. It's a nice setting for a casual night out with friends. There's a small parking lot in the rear of the restaurant.

Other ethnic specialties: Ireland

▲

Hours: Lunch Mon–Fri 11:30 a.m.–1:30 p.m.; Dinner Mon–Thu 6–10 p.m., Fri & Sat 6–11 p.m.; closed Sun ■ Reservations taken ■ MC, VS, AX accepted ■ Bar: beer, wine, liquor ■ Takeout ■ Not recommended for children

RITZ CARLTON

Cleveland   Downtown
1515 W. 3rd St.   Formal
☎ 623-1300 $$$$$

This is a place you choose when you want a setting for a very special occasion. I took my friend, Jean—a dedicated Anglophile—there for her birthday. We felt quite grand, sitting in comfortable, high backed chairs, sipping Earl Grey tea poured from a bottomless silver pot by an attentive server, and nibbling little finger sandwiches and cakes. It was just like the game "Ladies" I used to play with my younger sister, only better because the food is real. It's a beautiful room, with large windows, a fireplace, and consistently stunning arrangements of fresh flowers on a table in the center. The full afternoon tea includes elegant open-faced sandwiches and a three-tiered dessert tray that comes with a bowl of thick, sweet Devonshire cream. Light tea is the same, without the sandwiches. On Sundays, they offer a Children's Tea at which hot chocolate and Shirley Temples are also available. It's a great opportunity to make the kids dress up and experience what it's like to eat in a civilized manner. Tell them to think of it as a sort of off-season Halloween. For Americans, it's pretend, but English folk would probably feel at home, recognizing this as the best part of an almost bygone era. There's a small full-service bar for those not thoroughly into the etiquette of tea, and, on request, the bartender will produce a special gadget for trimming cigars. Practice crooking your little finger while holding a tea cup before arriving. You can park in Tower City's lot and walk through the mall to the entrance on the upper level, or drive to the front entrance of the hotel on West Third, and have your car parked by a valet—a complimentary service of the hotel for patrons.

▲
Hours: Tea: Mon–Sat 1–5 p.m., Sun 1:30–5 p.m. ▪ Reservations taken, for parties of 6 or more ▪ MC, VS, AX, Dis accepted ▪ Bar: beer, wine, liquor ▪ ⅃ Full access ▪ Non-smoking section

FRENCH

CHEZ FRANCOIS

Vermilion	Farther West
555 Main St.	Formal
☎ 967-0630	$$$$

Vermilion was once a fishing port, and long ago sails were made and nets were stored in the building that now houses this restaurant. The original hand-carved beams and exposed-brick floors and walls create a rustic ambience countered by coral-colored table linens and a classic French menu. Chef John D'Amico, who owns the place along with a partner—the maitre d'—uses reduction sauces made with cream, butter, and stock and tends toward grilling and poaching his meat, poultry, and seafood. "In keeping with contemporary tastes," he explained, "I try to make my sauces lighter than the traditional version, and flavor with fresh herbs that I buy from local farmers along with their fresh produce. Much of what I use is organically grown." At a customer's request, John will gladly prepare dishes with no saucing at all, and can compose interesting offerings for vegetarians with some advance notice. All the desserts, from Napoleons to sorbets, are made in his kitchen, too. In business since 1988, Chez Francois relies primarily on word of mouth to attract diners, many of whom willingly travel over an hour (it's a 45-minute trip from downtown Cleveland) for the experience. The patio garden overlooks the Vermilion River, and diners here sit amidst greenery under an awning. A few tables inside share this lovely view. At least three times a year there are scheduled events, such as wine tastings, Mother's Day celebrations, and a cigar party—the only time cigar smoking is permitted in the restaurant. Get on the mailing list to receive newsletters announcing these special activities.

▲
Hours: Tue–Thu 5–9 p.m., Fri & Sat 5–10 p.m., Sun 4–8 p.m. In warm weather months, patio opens at 2 p.m. on Sat & Sun; Restaurant closed December 31st–March 14th ■ Reservations taken, recommended, required for Fri & Sat evenings and patio ■ MC, VS, AX, checks accepted ■ Bar: beer, wine, liquor ■ Not recommended for children

LA POMME

Cleveland   Near West Side
10427 Clifton Rd.   Dressy
☎ 651-0001 $$$$$

Here's a small, bistro-type restaurant located in a lace-curtained store-front. Crisp cloth table linens, fresh flowers, and subdued blue-grey walls give the place an elegant feel, but jeans are as acceptable here as a coat and tie. The walls are decorated with posters from the Museum of Modern Art and the Metropolitan. While this is clearly not a family-style restaurant, patrons can feel comfortable bringing children old enough to sit in a chair and there's even a hamburger with French (but of course!) fries on the menu. You'll find a variety of French-inspired soups, like potage aux flageolets blanc au pistou (white beans with a garlic and herb puree), pates served with onion jam and small rounds of fresh walnut raisin bread, and entrees such as cassoulet (a mix of duck, pork, sausage, and white beans), medallions de pork (pork ten-derloin in a wine and cream sauce), and lapin du jour (rabbit prepared with the sauce of the day). Anyone who's interested in learning some of chef Donna Adams's secrets should ask about her cooking school, which meets in the restaurant after hours. The daily lunch menu includes an omelette, salads, quiche, and sandwiches. Each evening, in addition to the a la carte menu, there's a three-course prix-fixe (fixed price) selection. Desserts include Gateau Chocolat (a dense chocolate cake), profiteroles (a cream puff stuffed with vanilla ice cream), and dacquoise (a meringue cake filled with walnut butter cream). The handsome 12-seat bar lends itself to intimate conversation over drinks slowly sipped. On-street parking only.

▲
Hours: Lunch Mon–Fri Noon–3 p.m.; Dinner Mon–Thu 6–10 p.m., Fri & Sat 6–11 p.m.; closed Sun ■ Reservations taken, recommended ■ MC, VS, checks accepted ■ Bar: beer, wine, liquor ■ Takeout ■ ♿ Full access ■ Non-smoking section

PARKER'S RESTAURANT & CATERING

Cleveland

2801 Bridge Ave.

☎ 771-7130

Near West Side

Formal

$$$$$

The kitchen here is committed to the art of fine dining, and the well-trained serving staff understand their role in making the experience complete. So a meal here makes one feel elegant and urbane. Patrons enter the restaurant through the bar area (not greatly changed since its days as the Ohio City Tavern), a space that juxtaposes polished woods with exposed brick. A walk through the bar takes you to the teaching kitchen where restaurant owner and chef Parker Bosley trains others in this approach and the techniques of classical French cooking he has perfected. There are two small but attractive dining areas. Tables, dressed with crisp linens, are rather close together but it doesn't seem crowded. There are more forks and spoons at each place setting than most of us know what to do with. The menu is small but different each day. Quality rather than quantity, both in the number of offerings and the size of the portions, is what's emphasized. Dishes are created around the idea that truly good food is the result of simplicity married to seasonal foods and local, farm-fresh ingredients, many of them organically grown. So you might encounter Ohio-grown greens in a mustard vinaigrette, cream of turnip soup, a country terrine of pork, veal, and duck, medallions of pork tenderloin in black currant sauce, or a grilled breast of free range chicken in mushroom madeira sauce. Luncheon is a la carte, dinner prix fixe. Not surprisingly, the wine list is extensive, with many French imports, and the knowledgeable staff can help diners make a selection that will complement their meal. Parker's is located in historic Ohio City, a neighborhood behind the West Side Market where gentrification and decay battle for prominence. Parking is free and convenient in a lot across the street from the restaurant.

▲

Hours: A la carte Lunch Mon–Fri 11:45 a.m.–2:30 p.m., Prix fixe Dinner Fri & Sat 6–9:30 p.m.; closed Sun ▪ Reservations taken, required Sat ▪ MC, VS, AX, Dis, checks accepted ▪ Bar: beer, wine, liquor ▪ Takeout ▪ Not recommended for children ▪ No smoking

PIPERADE

Cleveland

123 Prospect Ave. NW

☎ 241-0010

Downtown

Dressy

$$$$$

Ali Barker, classically trained chef and owner, along with his wife Marcie, likes to think of his food as French and Mediterranean inspired. Though its not strictly ethnic, I felt compelled to stretch the definition so I could include this unusual restaurant, which has won numerous awards, been featured in both local and national magazines, and is one of the few Cleveland establishments to be listed in the 1994 Zagat Dining Guide. Barker prepares unique terrines and risottos daily, and his creative flair is apparent in menu items like Salmon Francaise, a filet sauteed in basil batter, and Veal Scaloppine "Napolean," a dish made with gruyere cheese and spinach. A dish of tasty black olives marinated on the premises arrives at the table with the fresh French bread. The wine list is thoughtfully chosen. The place has a New York supper club panache. Decor and table settings are as interesting as the food. Near Gateway and Tower City, the restaurant is housed in a beautifully rejuvenated old office building, and the Art Deco ornamentation has been stunningly restored. A stainless steel bank vault, circa 1928, is the setting for Piperade's Bar and Grill. There's a room for private parties and the restaurant also does catering. Complimentary valet parking at the Prospect Avenue entrance.

Other ethnic specialties: Mediterranean

▲

Hours: Lunch Mon–Fri 11:30 a.m.–2 p.m.; Dinner Mon–Thu 5:30–10 p.m., Fri & Sat 5:30–11 p.m.; closed Sun ▪ Reservations taken, recommended ▪ MC, VS, AX, Dis accepted ▪ Bar: beer, wine, liquor ▪ Takeout ▪ ⅁ Full access ▪ Not recommended for children ▪ Non-smoking section

FRENCH, SEE ALSO:
Georgio's (Mediterranean Mix, Chapter 3)
Sans Souci (Mediterranean Mix, Chapter 3)
Taste of Europe (Western European Mix)

GERMAN

DER BRAUMEISTER

Cleveland   Near West Side
13046 Lorain Ave.   Casual
☎ 671-6220 $$$$$

The decor is German gasthaus cum American rustic, and the atmosphere is warm, comfortable, and friendly. Many patrons are regulars and address each other, as well as the servers, by name. The 100-seat dining room works as a setting for a drink and a quick, light meal or a place to linger over a four-course dinner, and the Castle Room, which seats up to 75, is a popular venue for club meetings or private parties. The menu is a mix of German specialties like rouladen (filet of beef rolled around a stuffing laced with pickles, onions, and bacon), schnitzel (a thin veal cutlet), and schweinsbraten (braised pork roast), and more American-style dishes such as prime rib, pan-fried walleye, and roast duck. Portions are large. Appetizers, soups, salads, and snacks also reflect the blend of traditional German and thoroughly American favorites. There is a selection of German sausages and cold cuts for sandwiches, and side dishes like pickled cucumber salad and potato dumplings. German beers are on tap and imported wines are available by the glass or bottle. Easy to find with convenient parking on the well-lit side street and in the rear. A small German deli operates under the same name and roof (see market listings in this chapter for more information).

▲

Hours: Mon–Sat 11 a.m.–10:30 p.m.; closed Sun ▪ Reservations taken ▪ MC, VS, AX, Dis accepted ▪ Bar: beer, wine, liquor ▪ Takeout ▪ ♿ Full access ▪ No smoking

HEIMATLAND INN

Brunswick   Farther South
3511 Center Rd.   Casual
☎ 220-8671 $$$$$

"This," said one diner, "is some serious grub. I left the table in a delight-ful food coma." He went with a friend, whose father is from Germany, and his official word was that the Deutsche part of the menu is the gen-uine article. Evelyn Rowerstein, who opened the restaurant in mid-1994 with her partners, learned to cook from her German mother. She prepares spaetzle, potato salad, and dumplings from scratch to serve with sauerbraten, rolladen, knockwurst, bratwurst, and schnitzel. The marinated herring appetizer served with sour cream, raw onions, and cucumbers rates high on the ethnic richter scale, as does the red cab-bage side dish. There are other European dishes on the menu, a section for kids, and numerous non-German dishes that range from grilled chicken breast to chef salad. An ever-varied selection of European-style desserts is available. Breakfast is straight bacon and eggs. The building is made to resemble a mountain chalet. The dining room is narrow and deep, decorated with handpainted murals that depict var-ious Bavarian cities, European scenes, and distinctive town crests. Cur-rently the restaurant can seat about 70, but they are in the process of expanding to almost double that capacity. When they get their liquor license, they'll open a rathskeller and an outdoor biergarten. Service is that nice combination of friendly and efficient, and many employees are members of the owners' families. "Herzlich willkommen," they write on the menu: "With a warm heart, we welcome you."

▲

Hours: Tue–Thu 6:30 a.m.–9 p.m., Fri–Sun 6:30 a.m.–10 p.m.; closed Mon ▪ Reserva-tions taken, for parties of 12 or more ▪ Checks accepted ▪ Bar: none ▪ Takeout ▪ ♿ Full access

HENRY WAHNER'S RESTAURANT & LOUNGE

Kent
1609 E. Main St.
☎ 678-4055

Farther South
Casual
$$$$$

This family restaurant is well-known and loved by the German American community. The two sisters who own the place will often stop by tables to chat with diners, comfortable in either English or German. Many people have been coming here for years to celebrate their high-water marks—birthdays, anniversaries, and graduations—and the staff, too, have almost all worked here for a long time. Mixed in with a standard selection of steaks, chops, and seafood are some German classics: sauerbraten, rouladen, schnitzel, and kassler rippchen (smoked pork chops). Spaetzles, potato pancakes, German potato salad, and sauerkraut are also available, and the Deutsche combination plate offers a selection of German house specialties including home-made sausage. Portions are enormous. There is a children's menu, and half portions (which still tend to fill the plates to overflowing) are available during the early-bird-special hours between 4:00 and 6:00 p.m. The dining room is wood-paneled, the carpeting looks well-used, and the place doesn't offer much in the way of ambience or decor. Nonetheless, it attracts a crowd and it's easy to find, a freestanding building surrounded by a parking lot just past the Kent State University campus.

▲

Hours: Mon–Thu 5–9 p.m., Fri & Sat 5–10 p.m.; closed Sun ■ Reservations not taken ■ Checks accepted ■ Bar: beer, wine, liquor ■ Takeout ■ ᕦ Full access ■ Non-smoking section

HOFBRAU HAUS

Cleveland
1400 E. 55th St.
☎ 881-7773

Near East Side
Casual
$$$$$

The new entrance is no longer on 55th but around the corner on Stanard with parking in a lot across the street. It's a huge building with a small lounge, called the Jaegerstube, a sprawling dining room with German beer hall decor and the ambience of a Bavarian Octoberfest, and another room where the band plays and dancers two-step. Some of the servers, whose primary job is to smile, bring you your beer, and clear (this is strictly a self-serve buffet), wear traditional dirndls: white blouses, snug vests, and full skirts. Wrought-iron and stained-glass chandeliers hang from the high ceiling. There are many large tables to accommodate big groups. This is an all-you-can-eat deal, so when you belly up to the table you should have an appetite. There's plenty of simple, standard American dishes to choose from, but what gives the Hofbrau Haus its ethnic status are the German specialties: schnitzel, potato pancakes, rouladen (thin slices of beef rolled around a stuffing), sauer-braten, Koenigsburger klops (meatballs), strudel, Schwartzwalder kirschtorte (cake), and palatschinken (a desert crepe). The items on the buffet may vary from day to day, and the largest selection appears on the weekends. When my children were young they found this place infinitely interesting, loved being able to choose and eat only what they liked, and both the staff and other diners were always tolerant of their natural exuberance.

▲
Hours: Lunch Mon–Fri 11:30 a.m.–3 p.m.; Dinner Tue–Thu 5–9:30 p.m., Fri & Sat 5–10 p.m., Sun noon–8 p.m. ▪ Reservations taken, recommended on weekends ▪ MC, VS, AX, checks accepted ▪ Bar: beer, wine, liquor ▪ Takeout ▪ ♿ Full access ▪ Non-smoking section

GERMAN, SEE ALSO:
Cancun Restaurant & Lounge (Mexican, Chapter 6)
Taste of Europe (Western European Mix)

WESTERN EUROPEAN MIX

TASTE OF EUROPE

Twinsburg   Southeast
9149 Ravenna Rd.   Formal
☎ 425-7340 $$$$$

The chef is German, trained to prepare authentic dishes, using recipes that may be 200 years old, not only from his home country but from Austria, Switzerland, Italy, England, and France as well. No nouvelle cuisine here, but rather hearty and very traditional presentations of classic dishes like hasenpfeffer (German rabbit), kaiserfleisch (Austrian smoked pork), lammrogout (Swiss lamb stew), and poacher's pie (an English pot pie). Patrons tend to be well-traveled folks who enjoy the chance to rediscover the flavors of Europe closer to home. The atmosphere is similar to what you'd find at a small country inn on the Continent. From the outside, the building resembles a Bavarian chalet; inside, the ambience is quaint and comfortable, with soft subdued lighting and a working fireplace. The walls are decorated with posters and souvenir plates from all over Europe. The dining room seats 60 and a canopied deck and patio, open in good weather, has table space for 30 more. This is the sort of place you'd choose for a special, dress-up occasion. It attracts a business clientele at lunch and a mostly over-40's crowd for dinner.

Other ethnic specialties: Austrian, English, French, German, Swiss
▲
Hours: Lunch Tue–Fri 11:30 a.m.–1:30 p.m.; Dinner Tue–Thu 5–9 p.m., Fri & Sat 5–10 p.m.; closed Sun & Mon ▪ Reservations taken, recommended ▪ MC, VS, AX, Dis accepted ▪ Bar: beer, wine, liquor ▪ Takeout ▪ ♿ Full access ▪ Non-smoking dining room; smoking permitted at bar and on patio

MARKETS

BRITISH

SCOTT'S HOME BAKERY

Middlefield   Farther East
14855 N. State St.
☎ 632-1916

In business for 48 years, Scott's was located   downtown until they
moved in 1967 to their present site inside the Foodland Super Market.
The bakery offers some Scottish specialties that can be found nowhere
else in the area: fern cakes (cookie dough in cupcake shapes with
strawberry and yellow cake filling and iced with a fern leaf design),
abernathy and empire biscuits (two types of cookie), and currant
squares (pie crust with currant filling topped by puff pastry). People
stop in from all over the country to pick up the frozen meat pies and
sausage rolls. Also available are breads, pies, and pastry. Owner C.J.
Caldwell will also gladly make up party trays and bake wedding cakes.
Other ethnic specialties: Scottish

▲

Foods available: baked goods, tea, coffee, prepared frozen foods ▪ Hours: Mon–Wed 7
a.m.–7 p.m., Thu & Fri 7 a.m.–9 p.m., Sat 7 a.m.–6 p.m., Sun 9 a.m.–5 p.m.
▪ Checks accepted ▪ ♿ Full access

BRITISH, SEE ALSO:
Gaelic Imports (Irish)
Puritan Bakery (Western European Mix)

FRENCH

FRENCH BAKERY & BISTRO, THE

Cleveland   Downtown
The Galleria, 1301 E. 9th St.
☎ 241-4215

In the tradition of French rural bakeries, this thoroughly modern,
completely American-looking establishment prepares authentic
hearth breads. The steam-injected baking ovens have been imported
from France and the flours, free of all chemicals and preservatives, are
specially blended. French visitors and the well-traveled have verified
that the finished products are genuine in shape, color, texture, and
taste. Bakers arrive at 1:00 AM, and breads are ready between 8:00 and

9:00 AM. Also baked fresh daily on the premises are croissants, muffins, pastry, biscotti, cookies, and cakes. Some sandwiches, salads, and soups available for take-out or eating in the Galleria food court.

▲
Foods available: baked goods, beverages, coffee, takeout meals ■ Hours: Mon–Fri 7 a.m.–7:30 p.m., Sat 10 a.m.–7 p.m., Sun Noon–5 p.m. ■ Cash only ■ ♿ Full access

FRENCH, SEE ALSO:
Molinari's Food & Wine (International, Chapter 8)

GERMAN

BLACKFOREST PASTRY HAUS

Willoughby Hills   East Side
34351 Chardon Rd.
☎ 944-6464

Only all-natural ingredients are used in these old-world breads and European-style pastries and cakes, baked fresh daily. The bakery has its roots in Germany, where the ancestors of the current owners ran a bakery long ago. Shoppers can usually find as many as 25 varieties of bread.

▲
Foods available: baked goods ■ Hours: Mon–Fri 7 a.m.–6 p.m., Sat 8:30 a.m.–6 p.m., Sun 9 a.m.–2 p.m. ■ Checks accepted ■ ♿ Full access

DER BRAUMEISTER DELI

Cleveland   Near West Side
13046 Lorain Ave.
☎ 671-6220

This well-stocked deli is located inside Der Braumeister restaurant. It carries a variety of German food imports and many of the most popular German brands and products. Imported biscuits and cookies, mustards, jelly and jam, and pickles can be found here. There's a good selection of German wines and beers and a deli counter with traditional favorites such as head cheese, leberwurst, blood tongue, and other cold cuts. (See restaurant listing under same name in this chapter).

▲
Foods available: baked goods, spices, condiments, beverages, tea, wine ■ Hours: Mon–Sat, 11 a.m.–6 p.m.; closed Sun ■ MC, VS, AX, Dis accepted ■ ♿ Full access

GEILER'S MEATS

Parma   Southwest
5543 State Rd.
☎ 741-0027

Smoked meats and the sausage that Eric Geiler makes are their specialty at this butcher, family owned and operated for 20 years. They also prepare liverwurst, head cheese, Hungarian salami, and other Eastern European favorites, and some less-than-ethnic but nonetheless homemade smokies, jerky, and cottage hams. They maintain a stand in the West Side Market (G-7, telephone #241-5483); see listing in International chapter for more information.

Other ethnic specialties: Eastern European Mix

▲
Foods available: meat (fresh) ■ Hours: Tue 9 a.m.–4 p.m., Wed–Fri 9 a.m.–5 p.m., Sat 9 a.m.–3 p.m.; closed Sun & Mon ■ Cash only

HANSA IMPORT HAUS

Cleveland   Near West Side
2701 Lorain Ave.
☎ 281-3177

You can't miss this place. Built to resemble a Bavarian mountain chalet complete with white stucco and exposed wood beams, it's a standout in its West Side neighborhood. The Hanseatic League, from which this store gets its name, was a medieval trading association of merchants from northern German and neighboring areas, and like its namesake this store does a brisk business buying and selling German imports. They stock a variety of packaged breads, cakes, cookies, and Swiss as well as German chocolates; maintain a good selection of beers and wines; and the deli counter offers traditional German cold cuts, sausages and cheeses. In addition to food products, the store has a large number of German-language magazines and tapes, toiletries, and gift items such as nutcrackers, beer steins, and wall plaques. At Christmastime, they also stock traditional German tree ornaments.

▲
Foods available: baked goods, spices, condiments, beverages, tea, coffee, wine, beer ■
Hours: Mon–Sat 9 a.m.–5:30 p.m., open Suns in December only, 1–4 p.m.
■ MC, VS, checks accepted ■ ♿ Full access

MEAT MART

Parma   Southwest
10405 W. Pleasant Valley Rd.
☎ 845-4935

Much like a an old-fashioned butcher shop from days gone by, the Mart offers an assortment of cuts and deli meats. The many varieties of smoked and fresh sausage made on the premises are their real specialty. But this large store also has a selection of imported foods, including honey, packaged German breads, cookies, chocolates, and biscuits, plus bottled and canned foods like pickles and sauerkraut.

▲

Foods available: meat (fresh), baked goods ■ Hours: Mon, Tue, Thu, Fri 9 a.m.–7 p.m., Wed 10 a.m.–7 p.m., Sat 9 a.m.–6 p.m., Sun 10 a.m.–3 p.m. ■ Checks accepted

MICHAEL'S BAKERY

Fairview Park   West Side
4478 Broadview Rd.
☎ 351-7530

Best known for the past 20 years for their baked goods made from authentic old-world recipes, Michael's also offers a nice selection of other foods, imported primarily from Germany, including soups, pickles, peppers, and juices. They ship their heavy dark rye, German rye, crusty Vienna, and other old-fashioned European breads all over the country. The deli counter prepares sandwiches to order on this same freshly baked bread. A variety of tortes like mocha, chocolate, and rum are available as well as cookies, poppyseed and nut rolls, danish and doughnuts. Michael's has a second location at the West Side Market, (telephone 771-5757), open Wednesdays, Fridays, and Saturdays (see listing for West Side Market in International chapter for further information).

▲

Foods available: meat (fresh, deli), baked goods, beverages, tea, coffee, takeout meals ■
Hours: Tue–Fri 7 a.m.–6 p.m., Sat 7 a.m.–4 p.m.; closed Sun & Mon ■ Checks accepted

OLD COUNTRY SAUSAGE

Maple Heights   Southeast
15711 Libby Rd.
☎ 662-5988

Some of their customers come from the other end of the state or another state altogether just to get their genuine German-style meats and sausages. When the Neiden family took over the business in 1982, they brought in a German metzger (butcher) to teach George Neiden how to make sausages the old-world way. Now one of only a few stores left in Cleveland that actually prepare these products themselves, Old Country offers 40 different kinds of sausage and wursts including bratwurst, liver pate, metwurst (a spread made with smoked meats), and rohschinken (a smoked, aged ham similar to Italian prosciutto). They also stock a selection of cheeses, sandies, packaged cookies and pickles from Germany, bottled sauerkraut and red cabbage, and mixes for potato pancakes, dumplings, and spaetzle. "We're considered an authentic source of German food," says George, "even by people visiting Cleveland from Germany. Our spicings and flavorings are just like what you'd find there."

▲
Foods available: meat (fresh), baked goods ■ Hours: Tue & Wed 9 a.m.–5 p.m., Thu 9 a.m.–6 p.m., Fri 9 a.m.–7 p.m., Sat 9 a.m.–5 p.m.; closed Sun & Mon ■ Checks accepted

REINECKER'S BAKERY

Macedonia   Southeast
8575 Freeway Dr.
☎ 467-2221

Seven members of the Reinecker family run this business, which is primarily a wholesale operation. They've been supplying area grocery stores with German-style baked goods for 35 years. But if you're willing to make the trip to their place, they're happy to sell smaller quantities to individuals, too. They specialize in breads—rye is their particular triumph—and all five types of bread that they bake are natural whole-grain products with little sugar or fat. They are preservative-free, and most are made from recipes the family says are over 300 years old. Reinecker's is one of the only bakeries in the country to make these types of bread, and even their baking equipment is from Germany. They also make Christmas stollen, nut and poppyseed potica, and a variety of tortes. Note: there's no storefront to speak of; Heidi Reinecker, who says the casual, family-like atmosphere of the place means that most of their retail customers feel like old friends, suggests people use the back door.

▲
Foods available: baked goods ■ Hours: Mon–Fri 4 a.m.–6 p.m.; closed Sat & Sun ■ Checks accepted

SACHSENHEIM HALL

Cleveland   Near West Side
7001 Denison Ave.
☎ 651-0888

The exact date varies from year to year, but annually in November and December traditional bratwurst, made with and without garlic, is offered for sale. In February, there's liver sausage as well. They're prepared by hand by members of the Alliance of Transylvanian Saxons on a Wednesday and sold the next day. Call about one month in advance to find out the precise date. Orders must be placed about two weeks ahead. The freshly made sausages can be purchased in bulk and frozen.

Enter the Hall from the side door. There's a 300-car parking lot adjacent to the building.

▲

Foods available: meat (fresh) ▪ Hours: Three times/year (for one day in Nov, Dec, & Feb), 11 a.m.–7 p.m. ▪ Cash only ▪ ♿ Full access

IRISH

EMERALD IRISH IMPORTS

Euclid   East Side
199 E. 228th St.
☎ 261-2207

When owner Joan Flynn opened her original Irish import shop downtown under the name Emerald in the Flats in 1973, it was the first of its kind in Ohio. Now located in Euclid, she can claim hers to be the oldest Irish import store in the state. While it's not primarily a food store, there are always some Irish whiskey cakes on hand and a small but interesting selection of teas, jellies and jams, oatmeal, soda bread and scone mixes, and Irish cookbooks. The main offering, however, is unique Irish-oriented gifts and specialties: wool blankets and hand-knit sweaters and scarves, china, pewterware, and jewelry.

▲

Foods available: baked goods, condiments, tea ▪ Hours: Mon–Fri 11 a.m.–6 p.m., Sat 10 a.m.–5 p.m.; closed Sun, extended winter holiday hours ▪ MC, VS, AX, checks accepted ▪ ♿ Full access

GAELIC IMPORTS

Cleveland   Near West Side
4882 Pearl Rd.
☎ 398-1548

The shelves here are well-stocked with foods imported from Scotland, Ireland, Wales, and England. Brand-name products whose labels read like music to those who know them well include Bovril, Marmite, Branston Pickles, Alana Sauce (thought to be an essential condiment by some), Robertsons Jams, and Cadbury Candies. There's a good selection of marmalades, oatmeals, and teas. The store's own sausage is available frozen. Homemade meat pies, cornish pasties, and sausage rolls are available, too, and you can call ahead and find out when they'll be fresh out of the oven. Also made on the premises are bangers (a pork sausage), black-and-mealy pudding, and haggis (a dish you must have grown up with to fully appreciate, as it consists of minced sheep or calf innards mixed with suet and oatmeal boiled together). Baked goods are fresh, too, and include tarts, shortbread, scones, cakes, and biscuits. Some gift items are available, including wool blankets, hats, scarves, kilts, tartans, and even small bagpipes from Scotland—and some fine English china teacups. Convenient parking in back.

Other ethnic specialties: British

▲

Foods available: baked goods, spices, condiments, tea, prepared frozen foods, takeout meals ▪ Hours: Tues-Sat 10 a.m.-5 p.m., closed Sun and Mon ▪ Checks accepted

IRISH COTTAGE

Lakewood   West Side
18828 Sloane Ave.
☎ 221-6412

Three greenhouse rooms make up the Cottage, and its owners describe this shop as "filled to the gills" with unique items from Ireland. Shoppers can sit beside the fireplace in one of the rooms and enjoy tea and scones. Children love the wishing pond. The store stocks jellies, jams, and marmalades, packaged crackers and cookies, oatmeal, Irish sausage and bacon, and locally baked scones and soda bread, which arrive fresh from the oven on Mondays, Wednesdays, and Fridays. The focus, however, is more on non-food items; there's imported crystal and china, clothing, dolls, books, and Blarney Stones.

▲

Foods available: meat (fresh), baked goods, condiments, tea, coffee ▪ Hours: Mon–Wed 10 a.m.–6 p.m., Thu 10 a.m.–8 p.m., Fri & Sat 10 a.m.–6 p.m., Sun Noon–5 p.m.; extended winter holiday hours ▪ MC, VS, checks accepted ▪ ☖ Full access

WESTERN EUROPEAN MIX

BAVARIAN PASTRY SHOP

Lakewood   West Side
17004 Madison Ave.
☎ 521-1344

The scope of this bakery goes way beyond what its name indicates, and it has to be among the most uncommon shops in the region. Owner Carl Von Carlowitz draws on the baking traditions of all Europe and combines them with his own determination to offer healthy, high-quality baked goods. The result is one-of-a kind foods. He has a farm and raises chickens that supply all the eggs he uses; he grows organic plums, grapes, raspberries, apples, cherries, blueberries, and rhubarb that become the fillings and flavorings for his strudels, pies, and tortes; and he raises bees to supply him with honey. Eschewing the use of all chemical additives and preservatives, he bakes nutritious breads that are full of old-world flavor and goodness, and the variety is large: Vienna, white, flax seed, buckwheat, five grain, sunflower millet, rye, and amaranth. He does 25 different kinds of cookies, plus a special line for the holidays. He also prepares sausage rolls, pies, pastries, and special-occasion cakes and party trays. There is a second store in Chagrin Falls (see next listing).

▲

Foods available: baked goods ■ Hours: daily 9 a.m.–7 p.m. ■ Checks accepted

BAVARIAN PASTRY SHOP

Chagrin Falls   Farther East
100 North Main St.
☎ 247-4086

See Lakewood store listing for description.

▲

Foods available: ■ Hours: Mon–Sat 9 a.m.–7 p.m. (until 8 p.m. in December only), Sun noon-5 p.m.

CHARLES PETERS BAKE SHOP

Garfield Heights   Southeast
4608 Turney Rd.
☎ 641-6887

Only three different owners have run this bakery since it opened in 1929. The shop features specialties that span the European continent: Slavic sweet breads, Polish paczki (donuts), Hungarian nut rolls, and Italian eclairs. A large variety of breads including Bohemian rye, Viennese seedless rye, salt sticks, hard rolls topped with caraway seeds and salt, and a potato bread are baked in a brick oven. Professional baker Jeff Stadnik prepares authentic, made-from-scratch fruit tarts, tortes, strudel, kuchen, cakes, cookies, and pastries daily.

Other ethnic specialties: Eastern European Mix

▲

Foods available: baked goods ■ Hours: Tue–Fri 8:30 a.m.–5:30 p.m., Sat 7:30 a.m.–3 p.m.; closed Sun & Mon ■ Checks accepted

HAAB'S BAKERY

Cleveland   Near West Side
2108 W. 19th St.
☎ 781-8588

The bakery has been in business since 1957, and it's become a sort of landmark, rating a place on Lolly the Trolley's tour route. The building resembles a Bavarian mountain lodge, and on the back outside wall of the bakery (visible from West 20th Street) is a handpainted mural depicting an Alpine view complete with trees, stream, and snow-capped mountain peaks. Haab's offers a veritable cornucopia of freshly baked old-world breads, including a European sourdough, a dark, heavy Lithuanian rye, a Bohemian loaf, French bread, raisin bread, and sweet breads. They also make European-style tortes including Black Forest and Dobos; strudel, nut rolls, poppyseed rolls, French pastries, kolacke, doughnuts, and danish. During the Christmas holidays, a variety of special traditional European cookies are available. If you stroll in on a Saturday, you can get hot Bavarian-style pretzels, renowned enough to have garnered a write-up in *The Plain Dealer*, hot salt sticks and rolls, and pizza bread. They will also roast meats such as whole pigs or lambs for you in their ovens; you can bring your own, or they will arrange it for you directly with a butcher. They also have a few shelves stocked with imports like vanilla sugar and other baking products, potato dumpling mix, and candies.

▲
Foods available: baked goods, beverages ■ Hours: Tue–Thu 9:30 a.m.–6 p.m., Fri & Sat 8 a.m.–6 p.m.; closed Sun & Mon ■ Cash only

PURITAN BAKERY
Painesville   Farther East
15 S. St. Clair St.
☎ 354-3851

 This place is hard to classify. You couldn't go so far as to call Puritan a Scandinavian bakery, but they're the only ones in the area to carry some unusual Scandinavian specialties including a Finnish round bread, Finnish coffee cake, and Finnish toast. Manager Margaret McCormick is sure that each of these items has a Finnish name, but admits she has no idea how to spell them! It seems a baker previously employed there brought the Finnish recipes with him and taught the Puritan staff how to prepare them. You couldn't rightfully describe it as a Scottish bakery, either, but three or four times per year they have Scottish Week. The store is decorated with Scottish calendars and tapestries, and they feature Scottish specialties such as meat pies, sausage rolls, and scones. These can also be ordered at any other time, in large quantities, by calling in advance. Nor could you say this is an Eastern European bakery though they regularly bake Hungarian pastries filled with nuts, apricots, raspberries, and cheese. Non-ethnic muffins, doughnuts, and assorted cakes are regularly available, too. Many neighborhood regulars shop here, but some people make a special trip for Finnish products, especially around the holidays, and for the Scottish items. Everything is made on the premises, and has been for more than 30 years.

Other ethnic specialties: Eastern European Mix, Finnish, Hungarian, British Isles
▲
Foods available: baked goods, coffee ■ Hours: Tue–Fri 6 a.m.–6 p.m., Sat 6 a.m.–5 p.m.; closed Sun & Mon ■ Checks accepted ■ ♿ Full access

RUDY'S STRUDEL & BAKERY

Parma   Southwest
5580 Ridge Rd.
☎ 886-4430

Dessert strudel, fresh and frozen, is their signature item, and fillings are apple, cherry, cheese, poppyseed, nut, pineapple, blueberry, apricot, and peach. They also prepare gourmet dinner strudels—layers of flaky dough alternating with cabbage, broccoli and cheddar cheese, spinach and mozzarella, mushroom and onion, or potato, onion and bacon. Dobos, Sacher, and Black Forest Tortes are also available, and everything is all-natural and preservative-free. The business turned 45 years old in 1994, and to celebrate, the owners added a takeout line called Flavor of Europe featuring ready-to-eat ethnic dishes like goulash, paprikash, and 15 varieties of pierogi. Muffins, breads, danish pastry, crepes, and a variety of cakes are made fresh daily.

▲

Foods available: baked goods, coffee, prepared frozen foods, takeout meals ■ Hours:
Mon 8 a.m.–5 p.m., Tue–Fri 6:30 a.m.–6 p.m., Sat 8 a.m.–5 p.m.; closed Sun
■ Checks accepted ■ ♿ Full access

CHAPTER 6

Latin America

CULINARY PRACTICES form a living historical record, marking the political and economic events that have generated cultural exchange. Nowhere is this more apparent than in Latin America, which is represented in the Cleveland food community by Jamaica, Puerto Rico and the other island nations of the Caribbean, Mexico, and Brazil. For centuries these countries played host to pirate brigs and trading ships, slaves from Africa, conquistadors and explorers, expatriates from the far reaches of the British Empire, and immigrants from the war-torn nations of Western Europe. Over time, the foods of indigenous tribal peoples merged with the products and techniques these outsiders brought with them.

"How we Mexicans eat," explains Maria Galindo, a member of Cleveland's Hispanic Cultural Center, "reflects much of our history. You cannot separate the two. We were invaded, conquered, and colonized. And these people gave us language, religion, and culture. But behind that are the influences of our ancient ancestors which we never gave up, and it is from them we got the tortilla, the tostada, and our taste for hot and spicy food made with the hundreds of different types of chilies that grow here."

Chris McLaughlin, who is from Jamaica, tells the same story about her own country. "Our food is a mix of cultures and flavors, telling all about the people who've come to the Islands. You can taste Africa, India, and China, mixed in with what is native to the region."

So Jamaicans use ackee, a fruit first brought by a slave ship from West Africa in 1178; allspice and Scotch Bonnet chilies, which grow there in abundance; and think of curry as their own national dish. Mexicans eat flan, a custard dessert that came with the Spanish, and make moles using cocoa, an ingredient rooted in their Aztec past, which they serve with rice, a food that was introduced to them by Asian sailors and merchant ships.

As you'll discover if you visit the various restaurants that serve Latin food, each country and region has a unique way of preparing food, but most of the Caribbean island nations work with similar ingredients, which also appear in the cuisines of Central and South America, too. Rice, beans, garlic, onions, citrus fruits, thyme, and both sweet and hot peppers are widely used throughout the region. Where seafood is plentiful, it is an important part of the cuisine. Fruits like papaw (another name for papaya), mangoes, bananas, and coconuts are important ingredients in many dishes.

But there are obvious differences too. Jamaicans tend to cook with allspice, curry powder, and ginger, while Mexicans more often use cilantro, cinnamon, and cacao. For Brazilians, manioc flour made from cassava is a staple and, seasoned, it's a standard table condiment. Jerked meat is a strictly Caribbean specialty. A rich, fiery version of barbecue, it's said to have originated when escaped slaves, hiding in the jungle, survived by pit-roasting wild pigs and flavoring the smoked meat with the herbs and spices they learned to use from the local Arawak Indians. The addition of salt helped preserve the meat for long periods.

The people of Mexico and South America use tomatoes and corn in much of their cooking. According to Salvador Gonzalez, a Mexican of Indian descent who has lived here for 15 years, each area of his country has its own way of preparing tostadas, tamales, and tortillas. "Tortilla making by hand is an art," he says, "and they taste nothing like the packaged variety available in this country. In my family, they were made fresh every day, and sometimes I miss the taste of home."

The largest group of Spanish-speaking people for whom Cleveland is home are Puerto Ricans, followed by those from Mexico. Many make their home on Cleveland's West Side, where numerous Hispanic restaurants and markets are to be found. Like other immigrant groups past and present, people from Latin America have come to northeast Ohio to escape political instability and pursue economic advancement. They have filled the ranks of industry and agriculture, and increasingly in recent years have been attracted here by the wealth of educational opportunities.

The Club Azteca, a local Mexican social organization begun in 1923, now includes members from 21 different Latin American nations. "We try not to focus so much on where we've come from," explained Zulema Carreon, an active member for many years, "but on the fact that we all want to work together to share our cultures with Cleveland. We are proud of our pasts and don't want to lose what is our own. But it's also important to learn about one another. I get so excited when I have a chance to experience other people's ethnic customs, and I want them to feel the same about my heritage."

RESTAURANTS

JAMAICAN

DAILEY'S WEST INDIAN FOOD MART

Cleveland   Near East Side
3019 E 116th   Relaxed
☎ 721-7240 $$$$$

This come-as-you-are Jamaican eatery does not have a particularly inviting exterior, and even after you enter you'll think you made a wrong turn somewhere and ended up in a mini-mart. Orders are placed at the takeout counter in the rear of the store, where you can see the food that's been freshly prepared that day by Chris McLaughlin, who learned the art of Caribbean cooking from her grandmother when she was a girl living on a farm in Clarendon Parish on the island of Jamaica. Then you take a seat in a dining area at the back that looks rather like a windowless family rec room, usually populated with West Indians who are eating, visiting, hanging out at the small bar, or watching TV. The menu is surprisingly varied, each day featuring a different mix of selections. Some dishes are quite alien to the American palate: cowfoot and tripe, salt fish and ackee (cod stewed with fruit, onions, and other vegetables), beef skin, and oxtail (they're just what the names implies). But those who grew up on this food say it's got the real taste of home. More popular with native Clevelanders are jerked (spicy barbecued) chicken wings, curried chicken, fried snapper, rice with gungo (pigeon) peas, and peppered shrimp. There's a soup a day, and the variety is wide—from chicken and beef to conch, red pea, and mutton. One diner reports that this is not a place for the timid: unless you're West Indian or live in the neighborhood, both the food and the location demand a certain adventuresome spirit.

▲
Hours: Mon–Thu 8 p.m.–midnight, Fri–Sat 8 p.m.–2:30 a.m., Sun 8 p.m.–midnight ▪
Reservations not taken ▪ Cash only ▪ Bar: beer, wine, liquor ▪ Takeout
▪ Not recommended for children

L & R TROPICAL FOOD STORE

East Cleveland   Near East Side
2144 Noble Rd.   Relaxed
☎ 451-7622 $$$$$

The building has seen better days and there's nothing much pretty about this tiny restaurant, with its three plastic-covered tables and six-seat counter. But if you want to sample genuine Caribbean flavors then this is the place, since it caters specifically to the tastes of Cleveland's West Indian community. Each day features its own list of homecooked specials: Monday you can get curry goat or red pea soup; Tuesday stew chicken or cow foot; Wednesday offerings include tripe and beans or pepper pot stew; Thursday is for barbecue chicken or steamed fish; on Friday there's jerked pork and curry chicken; Saturday try oxtails or fish soup. In some long-ago incarnation this was probably a pharmacy with soda fountain, and an old glass-and-wood display cabinet is still in the middle of the room—now it contains packaged "remedies" from the Islands. And to drink with your meal, you can even order a tonic (on which most Jamaicans are raised) made from Irish sea moss. For an authentic Jamaican-style breakfast, you could try saltfish with steamed calaloo (it's a vegetable like spinach). The cook also whips up eggs and bacon, burgers, and fries.

▲
Hours: Mon–Thu 9 a.m.–11 p.m., Fri & Sat 10 a.m.–9 p.m.; closed Sun
▪ Reservations not taken ▪ Checks accepted ▪ Bar: none ▪ Takeout ▪ ♿ Full access

LATIN AMERICA / RESTAURANTS   163

TAB WEST INDIAN AMERICAN RESTAURANT

Warrensville Heights   East Side
20019 Harvard Rd.   Relaxed
☎ 295-2272 $$$$$

Much of Tab's trade comes via the West Indian grapevine. While you may run into a few folks from the neighborhood, most of the customers who eat and order out from here are clearly from the islands, and the food is meant to please their tastebuds. Offerings include curried goat, cow feet, jerk chicken, ackee (a popular Jamaican fruit) and codfish, mackerel and bananas, and Jamaican beef patties. Jamaican movies and reggae music videos are available for rental. Beyond that, there's not much to this little storefront eatery located in a short strip mall at Warrensville. Just nine plastic-covered tables, fake flowers, and a TV—plus a kitchen.

▲
Hours: Mon–Sat 8 a.m.–11 p.m.; closed Sun. ▪ Reservations not taken
▪ Checks accepted ▪ Bar: none ▪ Takeout ▪ ⅙ Full access ▪ No smoking

MEXICAN

CANCUN RESTAURANT & LOUNGE

Parma   Southwest
6855 Ridge Rd.   Casual
☎ 888-8900 $$$$$

One half of the husband-and-wife team that owns and operates the Cancun is from Germany; the other is Hungarian. Six years ago they decided to open a Mexican restaurant, and no, this is not a misprint. Georgie and Peter Mueritz simply loved Mexican food as well as what's usually referred to as Tex-Mex. For fun, in their first year in business they decided to celebrate Oktoberfest by occasionally slipping a few traditional German dishes into their list of daily specials. The move was so successful, with customers clamoring for more, that a German-Mexican restaurant was born. According to Peter, Mexico actually has a large German immigrant population and it's not unusual for restaurants there to have a menu that includes dishes from both cuisines. And to make it even more interesting, when Georgie is in the mood, she whips up something Hungarian that reminds her of home. So when they claim that the restaurant has something for everyone, they really mean it. Is there any other place in Cleveland where you can get a spicy chorizo sausage burrito while your tablemates enjoy bratwurst, goulash, and barbecued baby back ribs? Portions are large and the chips and salsa are plentiful. There's also selection of both German and Mexican beers. The atmosphere is casual, homey, and unpretentious, attracting customers who readily admit they come back regularly. They can handle about 112 diners at once, and seating is primarily in booths. The decor, which features dark wood, and a red, orange, and cream color scheme, has a mostly Mexican motif. It's located in a strip mall with nothing in its exterior appearance indicating what a unique and pleasant place is inside. A good choice for families and groups of friends.

Other ethnic specialties: German

▲

Hours: Mon–Thu 3:30–10 p.m., Fri & Sat 3:30–11 p.m.; Bar open until 2:30 a.m. daily; closed Sun ▪ Reservations taken, for parties of 5 or more only ▪ MC, VS, AX, Dis accepted ▪ Bar: beer, wine, liquor ▪ Takeout ▪ ♿ Full access ▪ Non-smoking section

EL CHARRITO

Wickliffe	East Side
30560 Euclid Ave.	Casual
☎ 585-2530	$$$$$

This doesn't look like much of a restaurant from the outside, with a neon sign advertising Mexican beer glowing in the window, but inside it has the pleasant feel of a south-of-the-border cantina. A family business, it was established in 1968 and has been at its present location since 1980. The small, cozy place seats about 48, and owners Olivia Jones and husband Bill, or one of their children greet guests at the door and serve as well. The homemade chips are so popular that they sell them for takeout by the bagful along with orders of their salsa. Many of their recipes, says Olivia, have been passed down among family members for generations, and in addition to tacos, burritos, and enchiladas, the menu features some very hot and spicy pascado (red snapper fillet), carne guisada (steak chunks), and pollo con mole (chicken). Most entrees include a generous dollop of sour cream or guacamole. The menu, which has a dictionary of Mexican food terms and dishes, also offers American sandwiches and special children-sized dinners. They prepare a special dessert that consists of a deep-fried tortilla folded over ice cream and they also offer Mexican coffee and coffee con leche (coffee with hot milk). There's only one table large enough to accommodate six; the rest seat four or two.

▲

Hours: Mon–Thu 11 a.m.–9:45 p.m., Fri 11 a.m.–10:45 p.m., Sat 3–10:45 p.m.; closed Sun ▪ Reservations not taken ▪ MC, VS, AX, Dis accepted ▪ Bar: beer, wine ▪ Takeout ▪ ♿ Full access

EL CHARRO RESTAURANT

North Royalton
13570 Ridge Rd.
☎ 237-6040

Southwest
Casual
$$$$$

No one could accuse this place of being trendy. It's just an easygoing neighborhood restaurant with a timeless quality, run by a family for families. The interior is a bit of mixed-metaphor pseudo-Southwestern with sombreros and bullfighting posters, but that's part of its charm. Patrons can sit at booths, tables, or the bar at the back. The menu has no big surprises but offers a broad and crowd-pleasing selection; Tex-Mex favorites plus classic Mexican combination plates, and popular dishes like quesadillas (flour tortillas with cheese and onions) and chili rellenos. The menu explains that foods are prepared with flavorful spices and are never hot unless you add the heat yourself. Service is fast and friendly, portions are substantial, and nachos with hot and mild sauce are complimentary. The bunuelo (light, fried dessert pastries with cinnamon and sugar), are a special after-dinner treat, because they are traditionally served mainly at New Year's. There's an all-you-can-eat lunch buffet daily and a Sunday brunch buffet. Park in the small lot out front or in the additional spaces in the rear. They also operate restaurants in Akron and Hudson (listed separately).

▲
Hours: Tue–Thu 11 a.m.–10 p.m., Fri & Sat 11 a.m.–11 p.m., Sun 10 a.m.–9 p.m.; closed Mon ▪ Reservations taken, for parties of 6 or more ▪ MC, VS, AX, Dis, checks accepted ▪ Bar: beer, wine, liquor ▪ Takeout ▪ ♿ Full access ▪ Non-smoking section

EL CHARRO RESTAURANT

Akron
491 E. Waterloo
☎ 773-4600

Farther South
Casual
$$$$$

See entry for El Charro in North Royalton for description.

▲
Hours: Tue–Thu 11 a.m.–10 p.m., Fri & Sat 11 a.m.–11 p.m., Sun 10 a.m.–9 p.m.; closed Mon ▪ Reservations taken, for parties of 6 or more ▪ MC, VS, AX, Dis, checks accepted ▪ Bar: beer, wine, liquor ▪ Takeout ▪ ♿ Full access ▪ Non-smoking section

EL CHARRO RESTAURANT

Hudson
180 W. Streetsboro, Rte. 303
☎ 656-2134 Cleveland/650-2134 Akron

Farther South
Casual
$$$$$

See entry for El Charro in North Royalton for description.

▲
Hours: Tue–Thu 11 a.m.–10 p.m., Fri & Sat 11 a.m.–11 p.m., Sun 10 a.m.–9 p.m.; closed

Mon ▪ Reservations taken, for parties of 6 or more ▪ MC, VS, AX, Dis, checks accepted ▪ Bar: beer, wine, liquor ▪ Takeout ▪ &. Full access ▪ Non-smoking section

EL CHARRO RESTAURANT

North Olmsted   West Side
30111 Lorain Rd.   Casual
☎ 779-9200 $$$$$

A pleasant place with a friendly atmosphere, rustic decor, and both Tex-Mex and more traditional Mexican fare. Seating about 180, the dining area and cantina-style bar with TV are done up with a Southwestern theme: stucco walls, exposed wooden beams, wrought-iron gates, cactus, weavings, and pottery. Lots of green plants fill the window that overlooks the parking lot and sit atop low dividing walls that separate tables. Servers wear traditional Mexican dress and are quick to bring fresh tortilla chips and two salsas, regular and mild, to the table when you sit down. The menu is extensive and has something for just about everybody. There's a full range of tacos, enchiladas, and tamales, and a few interesting and less-than-standard dishes such as papitas con chorizo y huevo (potatoes, sausage, and jalapeno peppers with scrambled eggs) and pork sabrosa (cubes of meat cooked with cactus). Just about everything comes with beans and rice and portions are hearty. A children's section has the likes of both burritos and burgers, as well as foods that give only a token nod to ethnic flavors, like charbroiled steaks and chicken. This is a good spot to pick when you want to get together over a meal with friends.

▲

Hours: Tue–Thu 11 a.m.–10 p.m., Fri & Sat 11 a.m.–11 p.m., Sun 1–9 p.m.; closed Mon ▪ Reservations taken, for parties of 6 or more ▪ MC, VS, AX, Dis accepted ▪ Bar: beer, wine, liquor ▪ Takeout ▪ &. Full access ▪ Non-smoking section

LA FIESTA

Richmond Heights   East Side
5115 Wilson Mills Rd.   Casual
☎ 442-1445 $$$$$

Antonia Valle began serving Mexican food to Clevelanders in 1952. Using many of the same family recipes, Antonia's children and grandchildren continue the tradition in a restaurant that features the cuisine of the central Mexican region of Michoacan, the area south of Guadalajara where Antonia came from. Diners will find many familiar Mexican dishes on the menu including tacos, enchiladas, burritos, and tamales, but the flavor is different than the Tex-Mex most Americans are used to. There are also some more unusual offerings like Lomo de Cerdo con Chipotles Y Ciruelas (roast pork loin stuffed with chipotle peppers and prunes and topped with orange gravy) and Chilaquiles (a mixture of beaten eggs, corn tortilla strips, cheese, and salsa). There's a large selection of items for vegetarians and special children's platters, too. The walls are peach-colored stucco, the floors are clay tile, and servers, who are knowledgeable about the food and glad to help, wear brightly colored skirts and white Mexican-style ruffled blouses. The overall effect is attractive and comfortable. Located in a retail strip adjacent to Richmond Mall, this is a relaxing place to eat and socialize.

▲

Hours: Lunch Tue–Fri 11:30 a.m.–2:30 p.m.; Dinner Tue–Sat 5–10 p.m., Sun 1–8 p.m. Bar is open between Lunch & Dinner; Happy Hour Fri 4–7 p.m.; closed Mon ▪ Reservations taken, recommended for parties of more than 5 ▪ MC, VS, AX, Dis accepted ▪ Bar: beer, wine, liquor ▪ ♿ Full access ▪ Non-smoking dining room; smoking in lounge

LOPEZ Y GONZALEZ

Cleveland Heights   East Side
2066 Lee Rd.   Casual
☎ 371-7611 $$$$$

Skylights, plants, and Spanish ceramic tiles on the walls and floor give this place an airy elegance. No mere taco and burrito joint (though these are available), this place offers dishes on the gourmet side of Mexican cuisine, plus a few unusual Spanish and southwestern items. The northern-style quesadillas are made with grilled chicken, chihuahua cheese, and mixed chile rajas and guacamole. Enchilada suizas are filled with chicken and baked in a green tomatilla sauce. Much of the menu is based on recipes collected by the restaurant's original chef during a year's stay in Mexico. Each night features at least two fresh fish specials. Meats are usually grilled and vegetarian dishes are available. The sampler plate gives a taste of a chicken taco, a cheese flauta, a bean and cheese burrito, rice, and refried beans. Among the more unusual entrees are marinated and chargrilled pork tenderloin and lamb, and mesquite-smoked free-range hen. Nine kinds of tequila are available and six brands of Mexican beer. Some booths tucked back away from the rest of the tables have a nice, almost private-room feel. Ambient noise can, on occasion, be an intrusion—the clattering of plates and other people's conversation just seems to ricochet off the walls and floors and land right at your table. Convenient parking adjacent to the restaurant plus additional space in the large supermarket lot behind.

▲

Hours: Lunch Mon–Fri 11:30–2:30; Dinner Mon & Tue 5:30–10;00, Wed & Thu 5:30–11, Fri & Sat 5:30–11:30, Sun 5–9 ▪ Reservations taken, only for parties of 6 or more; a private room that accommodates up to 12 people can be reserved ▪ MC, VS, AX, Dis accepted ▪ Bar: beer, wine, liquor ▪ Takeout ▪ Non-smoking section

LUCHITA'S MEXICAN RESTAURANT

Cleveland   Near West Side
3456 W. 117th St.   Casual
☎ 252-1169 $$$$$

A friend who has spent considerable time in Mexico says that a bite of Luchita's food transports her back there. The Galindo family has been preparing authentic regional dishes from central Mexico since 1981, and the only modification they make to traditional recipes is to substitute vegetable oil for lard. The menu, with glossary, explains what goes into each dish. There are some rarely encountered sauces such as mole (rich with chocolate), and suiza (tomatillos and cheese or sour cream), and specialties like puerco potosino (a simmered pork) and pollo sinaloa (a stew of chicken, potatoes, onions, and cactus) as well as burritos, enchiladas, and flautas (a stuffed tortilla rolled and deep fried). There is a good selection for vegetarians. The world beyond Cleveland is more familiar with this place than locals; its praises have been sung in airline magazines and international dining guides. But despite its fame, the atmosphere here is low-key, friendly, and comfortable. Both the bar, which serves Bohemia beer, a brand popular in Mexico, and 80-seat dining room are often populated by regulars. The building is vintage 1930s and, inside, the simple stucco walls, accented with Mexican ceramics, artwork, and figurines, form an ideal backdrop for the food which is the real attraction here.

▲
Hours: Lunch Tue–Fri 11 a.m.–2 p.m.; Dinner Tue–Thu 5–10 p.m., Fri & Sat 4–11 p.m., Sun 4–9 p.m.; closed between Lunch & Dinner; closed Mon ■ Reservations not taken ■ MC, VS accepted ■ Bar: beer, wine, liquor ■ Takeout ■ ৬ Full access ■ Non-smoking main dining area; smoking permitted at a few tables in the bar

MEXICAN VILLAGE RESTAURANTE Y CANTINAS

Cleveland   Near West Side
1409 Brookpark Rd.   Casual
☎ 661-3800 $$$$$

The building appears small from the outside, but inside there's actually room for up to 200 diners. The decor is traditional and attractive: tile floors, stucco walls decorated with masks, pottery, and blankets from Mexico, and arched tile-trimmed doorways. There's a separate barroom with a few tables. Established in 1962 and still family-owned, the Village features both traditional northern Mexican specialties and those Mexican-style dishes, like fajitas and chimichangas, found only on this side of the border. They offer tacos American-style or a more Mexican version. There's something to please those who crave Tex-Mex or those in search of truly regional dishes—like enchiladas in a mole or a tomatillo sauce, chorizo con huevos (sausage and eggs served with beans, rice, and tortillas), and chilies rellenos (poblano peppers stuffed with Mexican cheese). There are three classic desserts: flan, fried ice cream, and sopapillas (fried dough flavored with honey, sugar, and cinnamon). Downstairs, the Baja Cantina is open for drinking and dancing on Friday and Saturday nights. A DJ plays strictly Latin music, and the place is usually packed with people who know how to do the salsa, merengue, cumbia, and lambada, and those who want to watch. There's a small cover charge and no food is served in the cantina.

▲

Hours: Mon–Thu 11:30 a.m.–10 p.m., Fri 11:30 a.m.–11 p.m.; Sat 4–11 p.m., Sun 4–9 p.m. ▪ Reservations taken, recommended on weekends ▪ MC, VS, AX, Dis accepted ▪ Bar: beer, wine, liquor ▪ Takeout ▪ ら Full access ▪ Non-smoking section

NUEVO ACAPULCO

North Olmsted · West Side
24409 Lorain Rd. · Casual
☎ 734-3100 · $$$$$

Opened in 1995, Neuevo Acapulco, located close to Great Northern Mall, bills itself as a Mexican restaurant for families. There are simple, American steaks, hamburgers, and chicken dishes on the menu for those family members who'd rather not come face to face with a plate of camarones a la Diabla (prawns and mushrooms in a spicy red sauce) or quesadillas (flour tortillas stuffed with cheese, tomatoes, and chilies). Entree choices reflect cuisine from many regions of the country and the explanations on the menu will help even novices to understand what they're choosing. Staff, who greet guests in Spanish, are friendly and helpful. A dish of complimentary salsa arrives at the table before diners even place their order, and rice and beans (your choice of refried or cholesterol-free beans) come with most main dishes. The large, bright, colorful, open space seats about 130 and features beautiful murals and artwork with a Mexican motif.

▲

Hours: Mon–Thu 11 a.m.–10 p.m., Fri & Sat 11 a.m.–11 p.m., Sun 11 a.m.–10 p.m. ▪ Reservations taken, only on Friday and Saturday nights ▪ MC, VS, AX, Dis accepted ▪ Bar: beer, wine, liquor ▪ Takeout ▪ ら Full access ▪ Non-smoking section

VILLA Y ZAPATA

Cleveland · Near West Side
8509 Madison Ave. · Casual
☎ 961-1567 · $$$$$

There's no sign outside, but the building is easily identifiable by virtue of its tri-color paint job: the red, white, and green bands represent the Mexican flag. Inside, you'll find authentic Mexican food made from real hometown recipes served in a friendly, functional, unadorned setting with the feel of a neighborhood hangout. The restaurant seats about 75 at tables and booths, in two rooms; the one for smokers is also where the bar is located. Margaritas are available by the pitcher, and homemade tortilla chips are served with three different salsas, each with its own level of heat. The menu is made up of dishes from northern Mexico. Some, like sopes (tortillas filled with beans, carrots, and potatoes), are less familiar to most Americans than others, such as chile rellenos (stuffed chile peppers), enchiladas (corn tortilla rolled around a meat, cheese, or bean filling and topped with sauce), and Tex-Mex fajitas (marinated, sauteed beef or chicken). Two classic south-of-the-border desserts are available: flan (an egg-and-milk custard) and cajetas (sweet, caramelized goat's milk). Easy access from I-90; there's a fenced-in parking lot at the rear.

▲

Hours: Mon–Thu 11 a.m.–10 p.m., Fri 11 a.m.–midnight, Sat 5 p.m.–midnight, Sun 4–10 p.m. ▪ Reservations taken ▪ MC, VS, AX, Dis, checks accepted
▪ Bar: beer, wine, liquor ▪ Takeout ▪ ♿ Full access ▪ Non-smoking section

---

PUERTO RICAN

LOZADA'S RESTAURANT

Cleveland   Near West Side
1951 W. 25th St.   Relaxed
☎ 621-2954 $$ $ $ $

Carlos Baerga and other members of the Cleveland Indians baseball team love to come and sit in the 1950s-vintage red-vinyl booths and enjoy Puerto Rican and Latin house specialties. Nothing fancy here, and the place looks like a typical neighborhood joint complete with a counter, stools, and reasonable prices. But you won't be ordering a grilled cheese sandwich; the dishes are unlike what you'll find most anywhere else in town. The menu, in both English and Spanish, offers such items as pateles (a meat-and- green-banana pie), biste (a T-bone steak Puerto Rican-style with plantains), and bacalao arroz y haichuelas (codfish with rice and beans). There are soups, seafood salads, and unusual imported juices from South America. Fried banana balls are served like a vegetable, and daily specials might include goat stew or marinated beef tongue. Metered on-street parking, or use the municipal lot behind the West Side Market, which is nearby.

▲

Hours: Mon–Thu 10 a.m.–10 p.m., Fri & Saturday 10 a.m.–Midnight; closed Sun
▪ Reservations taken, recommended on Friday and Saturday night ▪ Cash only
▪ Bar: none ▪ Takeout ▪ Non-smoking section

RESTAURANTE EL COQUI

Cleveland

3156 W. 25th St.

☎ 398-4114

Near West Side

Relaxed

$$$$$

This spotlessly clean hole-in-the-wall eatery takes its name from the sound made by a frog common in Puerto Rico. A patron described it as wood-paneled nuevo retro, and was especially taken with what he said was the most complete array of mismatched plates and silverware he'd ever encountered in a restaurant. It's a true mom-and-pop place, and William and his wife Lydia do all the cooking, making everything fresh, each day, from scratch. The place is closed two days a week so they can shop and prepare some of the more time-consuming dishes. It's small—only 25 seats—and only a couple of years old. Most people probably wouldn't consider stopping here unless they already knew about the food inside. The menu, bilingual, gets high marks for variety and quality. The choice of appetizers alone includes alcapurrias (fried banana and seasoned ground meat), pastelillos (ground beef in a pastry shell), reyenos de papas (potato balls with meat in the center), and chicharrones (baked pork ribs). The entree selection is equally interesting, including a rotating and unpredictable array of daily specials. The pernil con guineos (roast pork with green bananas), for example, is soaked, then coated in a spice mix called adobo; the result is crisp and tangy on the outside, moist on the inside. Stews feature Puerto Rican vegetables. There are a few meatless dishes and some less-exotic fare, like a submarino sandwich or a maltas (malt). If you're unfamiliar or uncomfortable with this decidedly urban neighborhood, you might want to consider this as a lunch stop rather than a dinner place. On-street parking.

▲

Hours: Mon, Tue, & Thu 10 a.m.–8 p.m., Fri & Sat 10 a.m.–10 p.m.; closed Wed & Sun ▪ Reservations taken ▪ Cash only ▪ Bar: none ▪ Takeout ▪ ♿ Full access

 **MARKETS**

DAILEY'S WEST INDIAN FOOD MART

Cleveland   East Side
3019 E. 116th St.
☎ 721-7240

From the outside, this looks like a typical little neighborhood grocery. But inside it's filled with exotic, imported Caribbean foods, such as cans of pigeon peas or calallo (a Jamaican spinach), jars of guava jelly, soursop nectar (a fruit pulp), pickapeppa sauce, and many varieties of bottled jerk (a spicy barbecue sauce). Dailey's also stocks many different types of hot peppers, including the hard-to-find fiery Scotch Bonnets; unusual species of fish like conch and Caribbean snapper, plus dried salted codfish; and a large selection of fresh specialty produce, including chocho (a root vegetable that resembles a turnip), huge yams, coconuts (as well as canned coconut milk), and plantains, those hard green bananas so good for cooking. Traditional Jamaican foods like fried plantains, mutton soup, spiced shrimp, and jerked chicken are prepared fresh every day, and you can purchase a complete meal or just a single item ready to eat on the spot or take home. Irish moss, a seaweed used to make a sweet, invigorating drink that's reputed to be especially good for giving a guy's engine a jump start, is sold dried in bags. There are also tropical fruit drinks and Jamaican sodas, and freshly baked rum cake.

▲

Foods available: meat (fresh, frozen), fish (fresh, frozen), produce, grains, beans, flour, baked goods, spices, condiments, beverages, tea, wine, prepared frozen foods, takeout meals ▪ Hours: 8 a.m.–1 a.m. Sun–Thu, 8 a.m.–3 a.m. Fri & Sat ▪ Checks accepted

DAVE'S SUPERMARKET

Cleveland   Southwest
3565 Ridge Rd.
☎ 961-2000

This full-service grocery store caters to the Hispanic community, and just about anything you need for Latin cookery can be found here. They stock Goya, La Proferita, and Iberia brand canned goods; rice in 25-pound bags; salted codfish; Mexican cheeses like panela, anejo, manchego, ranchero, asadero, and chihuahua; chipotle chiles en adobo (dried smoked jalapenos in sauce); and a large selection of fresh produce, including plantains and hard green bananas, fresh chiles, tomatillos, and uncommon root vegetables. Produce specifically from the West Indies, such as malanga and breadfruit, is also in evidence, and there are unusual colas and fruit drinks from the Islands. If you don't see what you want, ask for it; if they don't have it, they'll try to get it. The store is in a newly renovated building, twice as large as the original Dave's on Payne, and has been open only since the end of 1993. It's spacious, modern, and convenient, with plenty of free parking.

▲

Foods available: meat (fresh, frozen), fish (fresh, frozen), produce, grains, beans, flour, baked goods, spices, condiments, beverages, tea, wine, prepared frozen foods ▪ Hours: Mon–Sat 8 a.m.–9 p.m., Sun 8 a.m.–6 p.m. ▪ MC, VS, checks accepted
▪ ♿ Full access

LA BORINCANA FOODS

Cleveland   Near West Side
2127 Fulton Rd.
☎ 651-2351

This is where to find a large selection of meats and sausages used in Caribbean cookery, and hard-to-find fresh produce like plantains, Scotch peppers, green bananas, and mountain parsley. There are also some unusual canned food products from Tobago, Trinidad, and the West Indies. Owner Rick Muniz calls it "the home of Caribbean food in Cleveland; one-stop shopping for all your Caribbean recipes." He also carries a wide variety of ingredients essential for preparing dishes from Puerto Rico, Mexico, Central and South America, and Spain. If they don't have it, they will find it for you and order it. Their place has the feel of a neighborhood store. They also stock Spanish-language newspapers and tapes, plus American grocery products.

Other ethnic specialties: Caribbean, Mexico, Puerto Rico

▲

Foods available: meat (fresh, frozen), fish (fresh, frozen), produce, grains, beans, flour, baked goods, spices, condiments, beverages, tea, wine, prepared frozen foods, takeout meals ▪ Hours: Mon–Sat 9 a.m.–8 p.m., Sun 9 a.m.–2 p.m. ▪ Checks accepted ▪
♿ Full access

CARIBE BAKE SHOP

Cleveland   Near West Side
2906 Fulton Rd.
☎ 281-8194

Started in 1969 by Andy Morales's father, who was born in Trujillo, this is the only Puerto Rican bakery in Ohio. And now that the shop has expanded to include grocery items, it can claim to be the only strictly Puerto Rican market in the city. There's a selection of almost all the canned products, seasonings, and packaged goods needed to stock an authentic Puerto Rican pantry. The store offers freshly baked breads and traditional sweets such as bread pudding, coconut candy, flan, and guava-filled turnovers. On weekends, Andy roasts salt pork and sells it, freshly sliced, by the pound. He also sets up a "hot box" Friday, Saturday, and Sunday that's loaded with meat-filled pastries, fried bananas, and potato balls.

▲

Foods available: meat (deli), grains, beans, flour, baked goods, spices, beverages, tea, takeout meals ▪ Hours: Tue–Sat 7:30 a.m.–6 p.m., Sun 7:30–3 p.m.; closed Mon ▪ Checks accepted ▪ ♿ Full access

CHAPTER 7

American Regional

THIS IS A SHORT CHAPTER, and the title is somewhat misleading. There are just three distinct food cultures included in this section, and only two, Louisiana Cajun/Creole and Southern soul, are actually tied to a specific geographic section of this country. The third, Jewish-style, is as placeless as, historically, the people who claim it is as their own. But each represents a way of eating that has become identifiably American, a blend of regionality and ethnic roots, combined with a hodgepodge of influences from around the world that could only happen in the United States. You could say that they are the best of what was once called, before it became politically incorrect, the melting pot.

The idea of one homogenous blend has been put aside. Now the dominant motif is a mosaic. Diversity is the buzzword, and celebrating it has become the new American way. Acknowledging our social and historical singularities is a way to express enthusiasm about one's own particular way of fitting into the big picture, and it's more than just fashionable. It speaks of how we are re-defining who we are as a culture and a country.

The word "ethnic" evokes images of folksy people in quaint costumes from a bygone era. And even though that view is outmoded, it does not seem out of place when applied to the cultures of other countries. It makes sense to us to go to restaurants and see waitresses in Tyrolean dirndls or Japanese kimonos. But in fact, the word really connotes any racial, religious, or social group with a common belief system. So while they are neither picturesque nor old-fashioned, existing very much in this time and place, the three groups assembled under this heading are also very definite and distinct ethnic entities. And their food, whether you view it as what comes from the melting pot or the tossed salad result of diversity, contributes to this city's cultural and culinary wealth.

The terminology can be perplexing. Should Hoppin' John (black- eyed peas with rice) and sweet potato pie be called African American, Southern, or soul? As far as many people are concerned, when you're talking about food there's not much difference. "Compare what are called soul food cookbooks with southern cookbooks, and you'll find that they are pretty much the same," said Dr. Lolly McDavid, director of the Cleveland chapter of the Children's Defense Fund. "White women of means didn't do their own cooking and many cherished southern recipes were actually created by the black women who cooked for them. And while the two races were segregated in their lives and lifestyles, they both ate the same things for Sunday dinners and celebrations. Even for blacks like me who have lived our entire lives in the North, home food, traditional food, is still what you'd call southern food."

"My father grew up on a farm where all the women cooked," she continued. "He met my mother at college and he had no idea she didn't know her way around the kitchen. It never even occurred to him. When he discovered that she couldn't cook, he sent her down to his family in Alabama so she could learn. The story goes that she followed the women around with a notebook, wanting to write down all their recipes."

But there were no recipes to write down. And an old expression explains why: "Frying pork chops is like drinking water—you either know how or you don't".

But Southern cooking is much more than fried chops and chicken. Cooks in the coastal states have countless ways to prepare seafood. Beaten biscuits, country ham, pan gravy, and stewed tomatoes are dinnertime favorites, along with cornbread and corn cooked any other way you can think of. Grits, greens, beans, and yams are staples. Echoes of a long-forgotten African past crop up in the way many dishes are prepared, and some scholars suspect that seeds of okra and sesame, which are not native to the area, came here with the slaves.

Much of what came out of the black kitchens of the South is inextricably linked to a culture of slavery and discrimination. Rice was originally viewed as poor folks food, unfit for higher society, and chitterlings, which have now acquired a certain down-home panache, were used because they were the leftovers that nobody else wanted. Once, you could get them by the bucketful for free. Now, even people who can afford prime rib eat them because they are a treasured taste from childhood.

Black families have been a presence in Cleveland since the settlement's earliest days, increasing in numbers gradually over the years: 1,300 in 1870, 3,000 in 1890, 8,500 in 1910. Most came from the South, and by 1930 they comprised the majority of the population in many of the inner-city neighborhoods once filled with immigrants from Europe. During the World War II years, many more came, lured by the opportunities in the city's expanding industrial economy.

As people migrated north, their cooking style was re-formed in the context of an urban and often poverty-stricken environment. It came to be associated with salty, greasy dishes, but true African-American cooking is neither. "Real southern cooking is both healthy and economical," explained Curtis English, owner of Fins and Feathers Catering. "It's about playing with what's available, figuring out how to make it pleasing with spices, and how to make a little bit of meat 'stretch' by using grains, beans, and vegetables. Many dishes were meant to be baked or simmered all day, and every meal included lots of fresh natural foods from the garden like tomatoes, onions, sweet peppers, and cucumbers. As a child, visiting family in Georgia, I remember eating slow cooked smothered chicken, yams, green beans, and okra. When I talk with my grandmother now, she tells me they used to eat stuff white folks didn't even know was edible."

Whether it's called Cajun, Creole, or New Orleans style, this purely Louisiana way of eating is a kissing cousin to southern cuisine. Cajun food is actually a very old form of French country cooking that came to the region with the Acadians of Canada, adapted to make use of all the game and wild foods indigenous to the area, like alligator and tabasco peppers. The result is etouffe (a sort of stew), jambalaya, and boudin (pepper hot sausage). Creole cooking is more citified, the New Orleans version of Cajun with its own unique accent that came from the variety of people who gathered there. Gumbo, for example, is an African word, and the file it's made with (the powdered leaves of the sassafras tree) was introduced to the Acadians by Choctaw indians. After the Civil War, Greek, German, and Italian immigrants added to the culinary mix. So you can get a mufalletta (an Italian-inspired sandwich unique to New Orleans), oyster loaves and shrimp po' boys, bouillabaisse and crawfish bisque, and praline pudding.

You can find a few of these dishes on some Cleveland restaurant menus, but it must be understood up front that none of it, no way and no how, can hold a candle to what you might encounter, if you were lucky, down in Bayou Lafourche or the French Quarter. That said, it's still an experience worth having if you want to learn something about hot sauce, 'gator, or red beans and rice.

In his book about Southern food, which explores the particularities of African-American and Louisiana kitchens, writer John Egerton sums up the heart and soul of it all this way: "Fix plenty, make it good, share it around."

As a motto, that's too homespun and folksy to be a good fit for Cleveland's Jewish community, but the same sentiments still apply. That sense of plenty coupled with a voluble sociability characterizes the Jewish-style delis listed in the following pages. All serve sandwiches almost too big to get your mouth around, a smear of cream cheese equals a mountainous slather, and the bowls of pickles on the tables seem bottomless.

What most of us think of as Jewish style is actually very European. Jews from Morocco eat quite differently from those whose roots are in Hungary. The Jews of Europe didn't eat bagels and lox, but we think of that as typically Jewish. The kind of deli food familiar to Clevelanders is actually Eastern European Jewish by way of New York. So how to define Jewish food?

"There's really no such thing as Jewish cooking," insists Rabbi Daniel Schur of the Heights Jewish Center. "Jews have lived in various countries, a minority among a majority, and historically, we have always adapted, and adopted new ways of cooking. What makes food Jewish is the fact that it's kosher, prepared according to precise and ancient dietary laws."

In the early part of the 19th century, the largest number of Jews arriving in Cleveland were from Germany. But by 1870, they were emigrating from Poland, Hungry, Romania, and Russia. Between 1905 and World War I, the flow became a flood as Jews from other parts of the area known as The Pale—Latvia, Lithuania, and Estonia—struggled to escape the pogroms. In recent years, there has been another flurry of immigration by Jews from the former Soviet Union. Though of different nationalities, Jews have always been, and to a great extent continue to be, an ethnically cohesive community because of their shared values, ideas, and practices, which spring from their religious traditions.

"We Jews are an interesting people," said Eva Cohen, who runs Personal Touch Catering. "There's a huge world contained in our history and customs. Jews from Poland eat Polish. Jews from Russia eat Russian. Each country where Jews have made their home has influenced what we call Jewish cuisine. We've always taken on something of the food culture where we live, and then taken it with us, wherever we go. In Cleveland, most people are of Eastern European descent, so pickled herring, matzo ball soup, kugels and kreplach, borscht and blintzes are what reminds us of our past, and that's the kind of Jewish food you'll find here in the delis and stores that cater to a Jewish clientele."

RESTAURANTS

AFRICAN AMERICAN/SOUTHERN

ANGIE'S SOUL FOOD KITCHEN

Cleveland	Near East Side
5215 Euclid Ave.	Relaxed
☎ 881-9400	$$$$$

This is the home of home-cooked soul food. "I can't say what's the most popular of my dishes," said Bernice Tolliver, who's been cooking in Cleveland restaurant kitchens since she came here from Alabama 35 years ago, "because everybody who comes here likes everything I cook." She admits, however, that folks seem to particularly enjoy her short ribs, chicken with dressing, and peach cobbler. Everything is made from scratch, and nothing served here has ever seen the inside of a can. Portions are generous, and freshly baked corn bread muffins come with meals. Things like pork chops, ham hocks, oxtails, or catfish come with a choice of two sides from a list including yams, beets, rice, okra, collard greens, mashed potatoes, applesauce, or macaroni and cheese. There's barbecue, cooked outdoors year round, on Friday. The daily menu is small, but it changes every day, and the Sunday buffet includes just about everything. In the words of one intrepid diner, this place is not for the unadventurous. On the corner of Euclid and East 55th St., in a decidedly inner-city neighborhood, the restaurant, which has no windows, appears to be boarded up and closed from the outside.

▲
Hours: Mon–Sat 8 a.m.–11 p.m., Sun 8 a.m.–9 p.m. ▪ Reservations taken
▪ Checks accepted ▪ Bar: none ▪ Takeout ▪ ᓂ Full access

ART'S SEAFOOD

Cleveland   East Side
16402 Euclid Ave.   Casual
☎ 681-2787 $$$$$

The big draw here is the live jazz, mostly local groups and occasionally one with national recognition, coupled with the fact that Art's is a Cleveland tradition. The original restaurant, started by current owner Bobbie Harrison's father, Art, was a fixture on Cedar Avenue for 35 years. A fire in 1983 caused the move to the present location. It's a mid-sized place, seating about 80 diners in a comfortably furnished dining room with booths and tables reflected in a large mirrored wall. There's a separate bar room off the dining area and a party room downstairs. A devoted crowd of regulars comes for the music and the socializing. The menu offers such soul food standards as smothered chicken, St. Louis-style ribs, and catfish, plus a side of macaroni and cheese, along with a middle-of-the-road mix of steaks, burgers, and fish. There are also some Louisiana dishes, including red beans and sausage, bouill-abaisse à la New Orleans, and shrimp jambalaya. They do a brisk take-out business, and party trays are available. Like so much of Euclid Avenue, this stretch has seen good times and bad, and the neighbor-hood may not be one where everybody feels at home. Some on-street parking and more in the rear.

▲
Hours: daily 11 a.m.–3 a.m. ▪ Reservations taken, for parties of 4 or more only ▪ MC, VS, AX accepted ▪ Bar: beer, wine, liquor ▪ Takeout ▪ ᓂ Full access
▪ Not recommended for children ▪ Non-smoking section

B & B RESTAURANT

Cleveland   Near East Side
1206 E. 105th St.   Relaxed
☎ 231-5729 $$$$$

The kitchen here turns out Southern-style stick-to-your-ribs food six days a week. Cleveland Mayor Mike White likes to come here to lunch on chef Maynard Bradley's smothered fried chicken, and he's just one of many regulars who frequent this five-table neighborhood hangout. Bradley says one of the Mayor's favorite dishes is black-eyed peas seasoned with smoked turkey. "It's usually made with pork," said Bradley, "but the turkey is a good, healthy substitute." The linoleum on the floor may be cracked, and an arcade game in the rear is the only decoration, but that doesn't seem to matter, because down-home eating is what this place is all about. It's small, with the look of an old, rough-around-the-edges luncheonette, but the selection is large, and there are many specials to choose from every day, including roast pork, fried catfish, greens, black-eyed peas, and mashed potatoes. As you walk in the door, there's a steam table behind glass to accommodate takeout customers; you might see baked short ribs of beef, oxtail stew, lamb shanks, crowder peas with okra, real macaroni and cheese, candied yams, and a colorful dish called rat-tat-to made with okra, corn, tomatoes, and onions.

▲
Hours: Mon–Sat 7:30 a.m.–8 p.m.; closed Sun ■ Reservations taken ■ Cash only ■ Bar: none ■ Takeout

BRADFORD RESTAURANT

Cleveland   Near East Side
17415 Harvard Ave.   Relaxed
☎ 991-0181 $$$$$

The restaurant seats 70, but most of the business here is takeout. Many neighborhood families are regulars, stopping in throughout the week to pick up orders of fried chicken, pork chops, barbecue, fried fish, blackeyed peas, macaroni and cheese, collard greens, mashed potatoes, and pinto beans. On Sunday there is baked chicken, plus sweet potato, apple, and peach pies. There isn't any decor to speak of, and Linda Bradford is the first to admit it. "People come here for the food, and that's what keeps everybody coming back."

▲
Hours: Mon 11:15 a.m.–9 p.m., Tue–Thu 11:15 a.m.–10 p.m., Fri & Sat 11:15 a.m.–11 p.m., Sun 12:30 p.m.–6:30 p.m. ■ Reservations not taken ■ Cash only ■ Bar: none ■ Takeout ■ ♿ Full access ■ Non-smoking section

LANCER'S BAR & LOUNGE

Cleveland   Near East Side
7707 Carnegie Ave.   Casual
☎ 881-0080 $$$$$

The city's oldest black-owned and -operated restaurant, Lancer's is
tantamount to a landmark. The original restaurant started by Fleet
Slaughter more than 50 years ago at this location had another name.
Back in those days, when every black celebrity who came to town came
to Lancer's to see and be seen, the waiters wore tuxedos. Over the years,
the place has grown considerably more casual. The restaurant is still a
watering hole for well-known athletes, performers, and politicians, but
the not-so-rich-and-famous are right at home here, too. Everybody
tablehops, glad-handing and backslapping friends and making new
ones. The place feels like a private club, though if you're not a "member," you can still drop by for a heaping plateful of perch, catfish, or
pork chops and cole slaw. In the South, frogs are abundant in the fresh-
water ponds and rivers, and frogs' legs are considered by some to be a
true delicacy. Which must be why they appear on Lancer's menu. Mr.
Dixon, whom I overheard hailed by patrons as "King George," regally
presides over his boisterous domain. Sometimes he's the host, other
times you'll find him in cook's whites manning the kitchen. His operating philosophy is "I do whatever it takes to make it all work." The
round-the-clock party atmosphere must mean he's doing it right.
Parking available in the rear.

▲
Hours: daily 11 a.m.–2 a.m. ▪ Reservations taken ▪ MC, VS, AX, Dis accepted
▪ Bar: beer, wine, liquor ▪ Takeout ▪ ௯ Full access

VEL'S ON THE CIRCLE

Cleveland   Near East Side
2201 Stokes Blvd.   Dressy
☎ 229-5050 $$$$$

Vel's looks like a cross between a Las Vegas night club and a party center more accustomed to hosting weddings than seating diners: it is
often used for special events and large private parties. One ballroom
seats 500; the other holds 200, and the outdoor patio can seat another
300-400 people in warm weather. This place defies categories. Thursday through Saturday nights, it's not exactly a restaurant—the menu is
only finger food and the focus is on dancing, music, and socializing.
But on Sundays the global soul food buffet features authentic down-
home southern cooking. It's a flat price all-you-can-eat spread that
always includes collard greens, candied yams, blackeyed peas, fried
chicken, baked ham, macaroni and cheese, peach cobbler, banana pudding, and pound cake.

▲

Hours: Soul Food Buffet Sun noon–5 p.m. ▪ Reservations taken ▪ MC, VS, AX, Dis, checks accepted ▪ Bar: beer, wine, liquor ▪ ⅃ Full access ▪ Non-smoking section

VIVIAN'S RESTAURANT

Cleveland   Near East Side
14222 Kinsman Rd.   Relaxed
☎ 751-8002 $$$$$

Located on a commercial block across from a McDonald's on a busy stretch of Kinsman, Vivian's presents a less than welcoming appearance from the outside. There are metal grates over the windows and door, and the white paint has seen better days. Truth is, you're not likely to stop in unless you're familiar with the neighborhood or the restaurant. But the menu is all southern comfort foods, portions are large, and conversation is always lively, with everybody jumping in to give their two cents worth, whether they're sitting at your table or not. The menu changes daily, so you might get ham hocks and black-eyed peas, beef tips and rice, and chicken done every which way one day, and meat loaf, salisbury steak, pigs' feet, and greens on another.

▲

Hours: Tue–Sat 9 a.m.–5 p.m.; closed Sun & Mon ▪ Reservations not taken ▪ Cash only ▪ Bar: none ▪ Takeout

JEWISH

CORKY AND LENNY'S

Woodmere Village   East Side
27091 Chagrin Blvd.   Casual
☎ 464-3838 $$$$$

The first thing you see as when you walk in is the mouthwatering display of brownies, cheesecakes, and rugele (little pastries). Then the eye moves on to the deli counter packed with pickled herring, gefilte fish, huge hunks of corned beef, and long salamis. Behind this counter are the deli men, trained professionals who understand that making a real sandwich is an art. The menu here is almost big enough to be a room divider and features every kind and combination of deli food ever imagined. You can eat light—a bagel with lox and cream cheese or a fruit platter; indulge in a house specials like beef and latkas (corn beef stacked on potato pancakes), or Three Little Tootsies (corn beef, chopped liver, and hot pastrami on small rolls); or go the whole nine yards with beef flanken (potted short ribs) or roast stuffed kishkas (don't ask what it is, you're better off not knowing, and as any traditional Jewish grandma would say, "Just taste it"). *Northern Ohio Live* magazine readers rated this the best deli in 1993. It's an intergenerational mink coat to jeans clientele—sometimes mink coats *with* jeans. Grateful parents will find an ample supply of boosters, pull-up-to-the table high chairs, and even hook-onto-the table seats for the very youngest diners. There is a kids' menu, dairy specials, daily specials, seafood, and burgers. Located in the Village Square Shopping plaza.

▲
Hours: Sun–Thu 7 a.m.–11:30 p.m., Fri & Sat 7 a.m.–midnight ■ Reservations not taken ■ MC, VS accepted ■ Bar: beer, wine, liquor ■ Takeout ■ ᕋ Full access ■ Non-smoking section

GOODMAN'S SANDWICH INN

Old Brooklyn   Near West Side
5164 Pearl Rd. (at Brookpark)   Casual
☎ 398-6885 $$$$$

Goodman's, which opened in 1950 and is still owned and operated by the Goodman family, may be one of the few delis left in town that still hand-cuts its corned beef. Though its small, narrow space seats only 31, and its menu is equally abbreviated, the place draws those in the know who visit Cleveland, including movie and sports stars, and it's not unusual to see a limo or a motorcade parked out front. Adult patrons often tell Dennis Goodman they remember coming in as kids with their parents. The lure is the corned beef, brisket, and pastrami sandwiches (hot or cold), which, according to one patron who's been a regular for 40 years, "are the finest deli sandwiches, bar none, anywhere in this city, even the country." Worth a mention, too, are the egg specials: they're prepared, pancake-style, with corn beef, pastrami, or salami. The biggest part of the business is takeout. Located in the Pearl-Brookpark Shopping Center, so parking is easy.

▲
Hours: Mon–Thu 8:30 a.m.–6 p.m., Fri & Sat 8:30 a.m.–6:30 p.m.; closed Sun ■ Reservations not taken ■ Checks accepted ■ Bar: beer ■ Takeout

JACK'S DELI & RESTAURANT

University Heights   East Side
2175 S. Green Rd.   Casual
☎ 382-5350 $$$$$

Jack's has undergone a recent facelift to update the original 15-year-old look to something more contemporary. The result is a comfortable, pleasant, unpretentious restaurant that looks very 1990s, but the waitresses still call you "Dear" and the many regulars who frequent this pace continue to feel at home. Black-and-white caricatures of classically famous Hollywood personalities adorn the walls, and if you look closely you'll also find the faces of owners Alvie Markowitz and his father Jack. Though the decor has changed, happily for us all the menu remains the same, loaded with traditional Jewish dishes of the Eastern European school. There's borscht (beet soup) with sour cream, blintzes (thin pancakes rolled around a cheese, fruit, or potato filling), potato pancakes, noodle kugel (pudding), and deli sandwiches packed with steak pastrami, turkey (roasted in-house and sliced off the bone), and pickled tongue. You can even order your already-thick sandwiches extra large. A bowl of pickles and pickled tomatoes is part of the standard table setting, like napkins and forks. Breakfast is served anytime, there's a kids' menu for those under 12 who can't handle the regular hefty portions, and standard fare like hamburgers, onion rings, and salads. Alvie says they also make the best-looking deli trays in town, but admits he may not be totally objective on this point since he assembles them himself. Located in a small strip mall off Cedar Road, parking is easy.

▲

Hours: Mon–Fri 6:30 a.m.–9 p.m., Sat & Sun 7 a.m.–9 p.m. ▪ Reservations not taken ▪ Checks accepted ▪ Bar: beer, wine ▪ Takeout ▪ ᕝ Full access ▪ No smoking

MAX'S DELI

Rocky River   West Side
19337 Detroit Rd.   Casual
☎ 356-2226 $$$$$

Owner Michele Anter-Kotoch describes her place as "a traditional New York–style deli with a California flair." So there's food for those who think watching cholesterol is just a fad that will soon blow over, and more health-conscious options for those who don't. You'll find your corned beef on rye, blintzes, potato pancakes, and chopped liver, but you can also choose from a large list of salads, pasta dishes, low-calorie plates, and vegetarian sandwiches. This is the west side source for true cure-what-ails-you Jewish chicken soup with matzo balls. Breads come from the Jewish bakeries on the east side, but everything else is made on the premises from scratch, including a truly awesome selection of desserts that range from a classic cheesecake to brownies, truffles, and fruit tarts. Clients are an eclectic mix, giving Max's an urbane and cosmopolitan feel, and it seems that almost everybody from families to dating couples, seniors to babes-in-arms, artists to accountants, feels at home here, and the place buzzes with lively conversation and energy. The walls are adorned with captivating murals by local artist Donna Drozda.

▲

Hours: Mon–Thu 11 a.m.–11 p.m., Fri 11 a.m.–midnight, Sat 8 a.m.–midnight (Breakfast menu available until 11 a.m.), Sun 8 a.m.–11 p.m. (Brunch buffet 9 a.m.–3 p.m.)
▪ Reservations not taken ▪ MC, VS accepted ▪ Bar: beer, wine ▪ Takeout
▪ ᕝ Full access ▪ Non-smoking section

SLYMAN'S DELI

Cleveland   Downtown
3106 St. Clair Ave.   Casual
☎ 621-3760 $$$$$

This is not a place you'd choose for either the decor or the ambience.
But even so, the line is usually out the door between 11:00 AM and 1:00
PM both for tables and takeout, because the deli-style sandwiches are
awesome. A Slyman's sandwich is so big that the average eaters simply
cannot get their mouths around one, and they are best known for their
unbelievably huge corn beef on rye. This small luncheonette, located in
an industrial area near the Innerbelt, has a counter and tables that seat
only about 46, and serves a clientele that runs the gamut from be-suited
business folks to truck drivers, who like to come in early for their eggs
and coffee.

▲
Hours: Mon–Fri 6 a.m.–2:30 p.m., Sat 6 a.m.–1 p.m.; closed Sun
■ Reservations not taken ■ Cash only ■ Bar: none ■ Takeout ■ ᕦ Full access

LOUISIANA CAJUN

BAYOU CAFE

Berea   Southwest
804 Front St.   Casual
☎ 891-9455 $$$$$

Something about Cajun cuisine seems inevitably to inspire an attitude
of fun, or as they say in New Orleans, "laissez le bontemps roullez" (let
the good times roll). And that's what the Bayou is all about. Servers
dress in t-shirts and shorts, and a mostly young jeans-style crowd is in
attendance. Lighting is at a subdued bar-level, tables and chairs are
simple wood, and it would be a just another upscale burger joint if it
wasn't for the Cajun specialties on the menu. There's a good dose of
spice and bite for those who like it, with extra hot sauce available at the
table and a selection of classic Louisiana dishes like catfish, red beans
and rice, gumbo, etouffee (a sort of stew made with your choice of
shrimp, crawfish, alligator, or flavorful Andouille sausage). You can
pretend you're in New Orleans and order a plate piled high with boiled
crawfish, a po' boy (a meal-sized, richly sauced and seasoned sandwich), or a muffaletta (another meal version of a sandwich that features
olive salad and Genoa salami). There is a four-item kids' menu. A
weekend brunch (Saturday and Sunday from 11 a.m.–2 p.m.) offers
Beignets (kin to a powdered sugar donut), chicory coffee reminiscent
of Cafe Du Monde in New Orleans, sweet potato flapjacks, and South-
ern-fried grits.

▲
Hours: Mon–Sat 11 a.m.–1:00 a.m., Sun 11 a.m.–7 p.m. ■ Reservations taken
■ MC, VS, AX, Dis accepted ■ Bar: beer, wine, liquor ■ Takeout ■ ᕦ Full access
■ Non-smoking section

 # MARKETS

AFRICAN AMERICAN/SOUTHERN

DAVE'S SUPERMARKETS
Cleveland   Near East Side
3301 Payne Ave.
☎ 361-5130

This is one of the few really large supermarkets within the city limits, and it's been around for 70 years. About 10 years ago they expanded to stretch the entire block and can now provide plenty of parking, too. Over the years their stock has changed to serve the needs of the changing ethnic makeup of the community. Currently they carry everything for Southern and soul food cooking, including a large selection of smoked meats and hams, hocks, neck bones, ribs, chitterlings, greens, and black-eyed peas, plus a variety of barbecue and hot sauces. They used to have many items for Latin American and Caribbean cooking, and still maintain a small selection at this location, but since the second store on Ridge Road was opened, most of those products are stocked there. The result has been that this Dave's is less crowded and cramped than it used to be, and there's a shorter wait in the checkout lines. (For more information on Dave's on Ridge, see the market listings in Chapter 2, Latin America).

▲

Foods available: meat (fresh, frozen), fish (fresh, frozen), produce, rice, baked goods, spices, condiments, beverages, tea, coffee, wine, prepared frozen foods ▪ Hours: Mon–Sat 8 a.m.–8 p.m., Sun 8 a.m.–6 p.m. ▪ MC, VS, Dis, checks accepted
▪ ⓚ Full access

OLD COUNTRY SMOKEHOUSE
Cleveland   Near East Side
4041 Payne Ave.
☎ 361-0276

"It smells like a smokehouse," says owner Gloria Carruthers, "and looks like an honest-to-goodness country store. You step in that door and feel like you've gone down South." Slabs of smoked meat are hanging from hooks, and the shelves here are filled with products like cornmeal, hoop cheese, and sausages. She carries not only the famous Smithfield hams but others from Kentucky, Virginia, Tennessee, and North Carolina, each made with a distinctive signature flavoring. She's got other smoked meat, too, including bacon, ham hocks, jowl, and pig tails. The store's been around for 30 years, and Carruthers been in charge since 1987. She ships her products all around the country and makes up specialized gift baskets full of her own version of Southern comfort.

▲

Foods available: meat (dried), flour, spices, condiments ▪ Hours: Mon noon–6 p.m., Tue–Sat 9 a.m.–6 p.m.; closed Sun ▪ MC, VS, checks accepted

JEWISH

ALTMAN'S QUALITY KOSHER MEAT MARKET
University Heights   East Side
2185 S. Green Rd.
☎ 381-7615

 Originally located on Chagrin Boulevard, Altman's has been in business 45 years, and at their present location since 1968. It's a meat market and grocery that also offers many Jewish-style foods prepared on the premises according to old Eastern European recipes. One longtime customer now in his seventies told me that going into Altman's takes him back 60 years, because the food tastes just like the kind he grew up eating. There's chicken soup, matzoh ball soup, kreplach (another version of ravioli) soup, mushroom barley soup, roast chicken, brisket, potato and noodle kugels (puddings), stuffed cabbage, and potato latkes (pancakes). Among the cold items are chopped liver, gefilte fish, potato salad, cole slaw, and pickles. They make their own salamis and hot dogs, including unusual veal and turkey dogs. Zucchini kugels and zucchini latkes are two of their own modern versions of traditional delicacies. The baked goods are from Unger's, and challah is delivered every Friday. The store has its own parking lot. Jack's deli is only a few doors away, so before you head home with dinner in a bag, you might want to stop off there for a "nosh".

▲

Foods available: meat (fresh), grains, beans, baked goods, spices, condiments, wine, prepared frozen foods, takeout meals ▪ Hours: Mon–Thu 8 a.m.–6 p.m., Fri 8 a.m.–3 p.m., Sun 8 a.m.–1 p.m.; closed Sat ▪ Cash only ▪ ♿ Full access

BORIS'S KOSHER MEAT
University Heights   East Side
14406 Cedar Rd.
☎ 382-5330

Boris's is primarily a butcher but does carry some of their own prepared Jewish-style specialties. Take home chicken soup, matzoh ball soup, mushroom barley soup, stuffed cabbage, matzoh balls, and stuffed chicken. In the freezer you'll find gefilte fish and blintzes. They also stock a small line of canned and packaged goods—basics that you might pick up to complete a meal, plus wine and beer, mostly imports, including some from Israel. They also have some baked goods from Unger's. (See entry for Unger's in this section.) Convenient parking in the strip. Their motto is "If we do not have it today, we will have it tomorrow."

▲
Foods available: meat (fresh, frozen), fish (fresh, frozen), baked goods, beverages, wine, beer, prepared frozen foods, takeout meals ▪ Hours: Mon–Wed 8 a.m.–6 p.m., Thu 8 a.m.–7 p.m., Fri 8 a.m.–2 p.m., Sun 8 a.m.–1 p.m.; closed Sat ▪ Checks accepted ▪ ♿ Full access

LAX & MANDEL KOSHER BAKERY & DELI
Cleveland Heights   East Side
2070 S. Taylor Rd.
☎ 932-6445

The bakery end of Lax and Mandel offers Jewish rye (which happens to be fat- and cholesterol-free), French, garlic, and potato breads, Russian raisin pumpernickel bread, challah (including one that's cholesterol-free), and corn rye on Sunday. They also bake rugelach, Russian tea biscuits, tortes, custom-made cakes, and a variety of cookies, doughnuts, and danish. The deli department has mushroom barley and chicken noodle soups to go, as well as a Jewish/Yemenite soup made with chicken and potatoes, and seasoned with cumin and turmeric. They also make falafel, hommus, tabbouleh, baba ghanouj, spicy eggplant, chicken breast schnitzel, fried and roasted chicken, stuffed cabbage, knishes, noodle and potato puddings, Israeli salads, and sandwiches. Metered parking on the street and in a municipal lot to the rear of the building.

▲
Foods available: meat (fresh, deli), baked goods, beverages, tea, coffee, takeout meals ▪ Hours: Mon–Wed 5:30 a.m.–10 p.m. (deli closes at 8 p.m.), Thu 5:30 a.m.–midnight (deli closes at 10 p.m.), Fri open 5:30 a.m.–closing time varies (call for information), Sat 9 p.m.–1 a.m. (bakery only), Sun 5:30 a.m.–8 p.m. ▪ Checks accepted ▪ ♿ Full access

UNGER'S KOSHER BAKERY & FOOD SHOP
Cleveland Heights   East Side
1831 S. Taylor Rd.
☎ 321-7176

Unger's is a bakery and a supermarket, with a deli counter that also features a selection of ready-to-eat entrees like kishka, roast chicken, and stuffed cabbage, plus cole slaw and other salads. I like to buy pickles, an essential part of a deli meal, here because they have both sour and half-sour, and pickled red peppers like those found on New York's lower East Side. Fresh baked breads include Jewish rye, challah, pumpernickel, onion rolls and bagels, plus cinnamon and raisin breads, and croissants. A variety of cakes, pies, danish, doughnuts, and cookies are available, but among the especially Jewish-style treats (some of which bear a strong resemblance to those of Eastern Europe) are Dobos torte, kichel, honey and sponge cakes, Russian tea biscuits, cinnamon-, nut-, or chocolate-laced coffee cakes called babkas, and Hungarian nut slices. On the shelves, along with regular grocery store items, are food imports from Israel, and packaged Israeli-style salads. The store is bright and modern. They've got their own parking lot, recently enlarged.

▲

Foods available: meat (fresh, frozen), fish (fresh, frozen), produce, baked goods, spices, condiments, beverages, tea, coffee, wine, beer, prepared frozen foods, takeout meals ▪
Hours: Sun–Wed 6 a.m.–10 p.m., Thu 6 a.m.–11 p.m. Fri 6 a.m.–closing time varies (call for information); closed Sat (sometimes opens on Sat night, after sunset; call to confirm)
▪ MC, VS, Dis accepted ▪ ⅚ Full access

CHAPTER 8

International

THERE IS NO HISTORICAL LEAD-IN appropriate for this chapter, no groups of people to write about or "palette" of ingredients to explain. This section is devoted to all those restaurants and markets that defy a single, simple ethnic definition (yet still have some definite ethnic characteristics).

This category could devolve into a grab bag of restaurants that offer a vaguely defined cooking style borrowing from a variety of traditions and techniques. But that is not my intention. Included here are restaurants that successfully prepare a variety of dishes from many different food traditions, while staying true to the origins of each. There are only a few, but they do what they do so well that they deserve a place of their own in this book.

Interest in ethnic ingredients is growing rapidly and those ingredients are assuming an increasingly prominent role in contemporary American cooking. The markets listed in this section are important resources. They offer convenience, variety, and a global array of choices so busy shoppers can get what they need to stock a multicultural kitchen at a single location.

Zona Spray's Cooking School in Hudson, Cleveland's oldest, is one place to learn how to use, and taste, all these ingredients. Chefs from around the world teach classes in everything from making Greek phyllo dough and classic French sauces like bordelaise and chasseur, to Indian garam masala spice blends and the dashi (fish broth) basic to Japanese cookery.

Zona's approach to food, with its respect and enthusiasm for all traditions, seems especially appropriate to introduce this chapter. "The art of cooking is about more than just food, and that's what I really love. In it you can see the history, politics, economics, psychology, and culture of a country. No other single thing encompasses so many aspects of living."

Restaurants and markets with an international flair reveal our current preoccupation with diversity, pluralism, and what has been called our "tossed salad" society, a recently coined term meant to replace the old "melting pot" concept. The idea is that as a society we no longer want to see ourselves as a bland, homogenized American whole but instead wish to keep what is our own and strive for an interesting, eclectic, all-inclusive mix.

The story behind Sergio's is apropos. Sergio Abramof's grandparents left their home in Russia, heading for South America. His father was born en route, aboard a ship in French waters off the African coast, making him a French citizen. Sergio's mother was Brazilian, but her work as a medical researcher brought her to America. Sergio grew up in Cleveland, spending summers in Brazil. He perfected his cooking skills in the kitchen of one of Cleveland's premier Italian restaurants. The dishes he prepares now at his new restaurant in University Circle reflect this personal, cross-cultural history.

At a time when borders are changing rapidly and national allegiance can be a highly charged issue, restaurants and markets whose offerings transcend the divisions of geopolitics are a sort of cultural oasis, a metaphor for peaceful coexistence.

 # RESTAURANTS

LORETTA PAGANINI SCHOOL OF COOKING

Chester Township   Farther East
8613 Mayfield Rd.   Casual
☎ 729-1110

Technically speaking, Paganini's is a cooking school, not a restaurant, but each year the school sponsors a series of ethnic dinners prepared both by staff and visiting chefs. A recent calendar, for example, highlighted the foods of Bohemia in Central Europe, Brazil, Italy, the American Southwest, Poland, Scandinavia, and Japan. The dinners are not exactly workshops, but they're definitely not your regular out-to-eat experience, either. Each features the cuisine of a different country or region, and diners learn a bit about the area, discuss recipes, and actually watch the meal being prepared. Although it is not really meant to be a hands-on event, sometimes the chef invites participation. The evening takes place in the school's large and comfortable classroom cum dining area. The room is brightly lit, and a mirror hangs over the stove and work area so that no matter where you sit you can see what's going on. Long tables seat six or more. To attend, you must sign up beforehand and pay in advance. Call for more information.

▲
Hours: A couple of times per month, evening ■ Reservations taken, required ■ MC, VS, checks accepted ■ Bar: none ■ Not recommended for children ■ No smoking

RUTHIE & MO'S DINER

Cleveland   Near East Side
4002 Prospect Ave.   Casual
☎ 431-8063 $$$$$

I knew that this unique restaurant deserved a place in this book, but for a long time I couldn't decide exactly where it belonged. Ruthie Hellman, who owns the place with her husband Mo (a man people line up to talk to), does the cooking and is self-taught, with a natural flair for flavor that asserts itself no matter what culinary tradition she tackles. They call the place a diner and promote the real home-cooked quality of the food. The key word here is home, and the question is, whose home? Because whatever ethnic dish Ruthie puts a spoon to turns out to be the real thing; her matzo ball soup is as good or better than anybody's Jewish bubby (grandma) ever made, and her wedding soup is as Italian as it gets. The same is true of her Greek salad, Indian mulligatawny, Hungarian beef goulash, Creole chicken gumbo and cornbread, and Thai noodles in peanut sauce, any of which might be the daily special. Then again, she'll blend the best of two worlds and make something with a contemporary twist, like white chicken chile or turkey burritos with jalapeno sauce. Or, she might just bake pans of simple, creamy macaroni and cheese. And it's all served up, in booths or at the counter, in a genuine old restored diner, circa 1930s. They've recently undergone an expansion, with the addition of a second car, brought in from Pennsylvania, vintage 1950s, which brings their seating capacity up to 80. The only way to classify this popular restaurant is to view it as an international, cross-cultural, down-home joint. Many people regard it as their own private club, stopping by daily for food and friendly banter with Mo, the ultimate front man, which must be why *The Plain Dealer's* Steven Litt dubbed it "a social landmark as well as an architectural one." American-style breakfasts are served until 11:00 a.m. The regular lunch menu also offers hamburgers, sandwiches, and salads; and Ruthie's homemade desserts are in a class all their own.

▲

Hours: Mon–Fri 6 a.m.–3 p.m.; closed Sat & Sun ▪ Reservations not taken ▪ MC, VS, AX, Dis accepted ▪ Bar: none ▪ Takeout ▪ ᕼ. Full access ▪ No smoking (except one section at breakfast)

SERGIO'S IN UNIVERSITY CIRCLE

Cleveland   Near East Side
1903 Ford Dr.   Casual
☎ 231-1234 $$$$$

This is surely one of Cleveland's most interesting places to eat. It's one of the newest, having only opened, in a historic carriage house in University Circle, in January, 1995. Chef Sergio Abramof, who owns the restaurant with his wife Susan, draws upon a truly international culinary palate for his inspired cross-cultural offerings, which reflect both his own personal history and philosophy of cooking. His grandparents were Russian Jews, his father a French citizen, his mother Brazilian. Born in Brazil himself, Sergio lived in America for much of his life after age seven. A graduate of Cleveland Heights High School, for 14 years he served as Executive Chef at Ristorante Giovanni's. All these influences come into play in his kitchen, but he aims for uncomplicated dishes prepared so that the flavors stay true to the culinary tradition they spring from. And while there are some decidedly Italian interpretations, with a variety of unusual pasta dishes, some bursts of the Asian, and even mashed potatoes, the dominant theme here is Brazilian. Camarao baiana is made with shrimp, coconut milk, fresh toma-toes, and hot malaguetta pepper. There's Amazon River fish, and the beef tenderloin is served with black beans and rice and farofa (a fla-vorful topping made with flour from the cassava, sauteed in butter with onions, olives, and parsley). Frango passarinho (small pieces of chicken marinated and grilled on a stick) is served with a hot green sauce or carioca relish for dipping. They prepare Brazil's national drink, caipirinha, made of sugar cane liquor with lime and sugar, and a non-alcoholic tropical drink called guarana. The decor echoes the gaiety and zest of the tropics with splashes of bold, primary color, and clean modern lines. It's small, seating just 46 in close quarters, but there are plans to open a 30-seat patio for outdoor dining during warm weather. Take your chances finding a parking spot or use their valet service.

Other ethnic specialties: Brazilian

▲

Hours: Lunch Mon–Fri 11:30 a.m.–2:30 p.m.; Dinner Mon–Thu 5:30–9:30 p.m., Fri 5:30–10:30 p.m., Sat 5:30–10:30 p.m.; closed Sun ▪ Reservations taken, strongly recommended ▪ MC, VS, AX, Dis accepted ▪ Bar: beer, wine, liquor ▪ Takeout ▪ Not recommended for children ▪ No smoking

WEST POINT MARKET

Akron   Farther South
1711 W. Market St.   Casual
☎ 864-2151

This small, 40-seat cafe is an informal in-store eatery where diners can look into the kitchen and watch the chefs at work. There's no set menu (offerings change weekly), and diners choose from whatever's available in the bakery and at the deli counter plus specials the chefs are prepar-ing that day. Items are also available to heat-and-eat at home. Making use of the array of international ingredients featured in the store, offer-ings are an eclectic mix of regional cuisines and flavors. Meals are served at tall round butcher block tables, and diners sit on high stools. There are a few lower tables to accommodate patrons in wheelchairs and high chairs. A popular spot with busy executives, harried shop-pers, and parents with children.

▲

Hours: Mon–Fri 8 a.m.–7 p.m., Sat 8 a.m.–6 p.m.; closed Sun ▪ Reservations not taken ▪ MC, VS, Dis, checks accepted ▪ Bar: wine ▪ Takeout ▪ ♿ Full access ▪ No smoking

MARKETS

EUCLID MEAT & SAUSAGE SHOP

Euclid   East Side
821 E. 222nd St.
☎ 261-9006

This is a full-service meat market offering all the regular meats and cuts, plus custom cutting. They are also a virtual sausage boutique, and that's their claim to ethnic fame. They carry traditional Italian, Mexican, Hungarian, Lithuanian, and German links; Slovenian smoked sausage, and rice and blood rings made with a combination of beef, pork and rice stuffed in a casing and tied in a circle; fully cooked Irish-style potato-pork-veal sausage; and the Andouille, which is a must for Louisiana cooking. They also have a small selection of meat-related products such as barbecue sauces, marinades, and steak sauces. This is a family business, open for seven years; the family also operates a stand at the West Side Market called the Euclid Sausage Shop.

▲

Foods available: meat (fresh), spices, condiments ▪ Hours: Mon–Fri 9 a.m.–6 p.m., Sat 9 a.m.–5 p.m.; closed Sun ▪ Checks accepted

LAKE ROAD MARKET

Rocky River   West Side
20267 Lake Rd.
☎ 331-9326

This gourmet specialty grocery store is owned and operated by three brothers, Jim, Alan, and Sal Rego who grew up in the food business. They've made it a source for unique foods from around the world, as well as a quality full-service food market. Shoppers can find one of the area's largest selections of sauces and seasonings from the island nations of the Caribbean; pastas, cheeses, and olive oils from Italy; and products from France, England, Germany, Greece, and the Middle East, such as mustard of Provence, Devon cream, and European butters. They bake their own French bread, which has gotten rave reviews from French visitors.

▲

Foods available: meat (fresh, frozen), fish (fresh, frozen), produce, grains, beans, flour, baked goods, spices, condiments, beverages, tea, coffee, wine, takeout meals ▪ Hours: Mon–Fri 9 a.m.–9 p.m., Sat 9 a.m.–7 p.m., Sun 9 a.m.–6 p.m. ▪ Checks accepted ▪ ⅙ Full access

LORETTA PAGANINI SCHOOL OF COOKING

Chester Township   **Farther East**
8613 Mayfield Rd.
☎ 729-1110

This is an all-gourmet specialty store housed in a cozy, converted old home fondly known as The Gingerbread House. It offers a large and eclectic selection of imports and hard-to-find items, especially baking ingredients and supplies. There's vanilla sugar and almond paste from Germany, cannoli forms from Italy, and cloves from Madagascar. Everything is personally selected by owner, chef, and cooking school teacher Loretta Paganini, including a variety of pastas, rice, oils, vinegars, sauces, and European cooking mixes. This is the place to find obscure ingredients like jalapeno jelly, pickled ginger, and chestnut honey, and equally obscure utensils such as a cherry stoner, a tortilla press, fancy tart molds, a marble mortar and pestle, and tools so esoteric I couldn't even guess their use. There are also many ethnic and international cookbooks for sale, and sometimes authors visit and the shop hosts book signings. Everything is neatly crammed together in a very small but nonetheless delightful space at the front of the Paganini's cooking school, with lace curtains at the window, an Oriental rug on the floor, a stereo in the fireplace, and China from England gracing the old wooden mantel. For more information about this location see listing under the same name in the restaurant section of this chapter.

▲

Foods available: grains, spices, condiments, tea, coffee ■ Hours: Mon–Fri 10 a.m.–5 p.m., Sat 10 a.m.–4 p.m., also during class; closed Sun. ■ MC, VS, checks accepted

MEDITERRANEAN IMPORTED FOODS

Cleveland   **Near West Side**
1975 W. 25th St.
☎ 771-4479

Your first impression on entering Maria and Costa Mougiano's store is that they've tried to stock this small place with everything from everywhere, and that's not too far from the truth. This tiny corner shop, which can be entered either from within the West Side Market building itself or off West 25th Street, is crammed with an almost all-world selection of food: there's candy from England, chocolate from Belgium, saffron from Spain, coffee from Turkey, beans from Jamaica, rice from India, and tinned fish from Norway. A deli case is packed with a variety of Greek and Italian cheeses and olives. Shoppers will find imported mustard, jam, sauces, and honey; black, blossom, and herbal teas; a wide selection of gourmet oils, including walnut, hazelnut, almond, and rapeseed, as well as safflower and olive and almost as many vinegars; dried fruits and mushrooms; pasta; canned salmon, caviar, and herring; crackers, biscuits, breads, and cookies. Rice, bulgur wheat, buckwheat groats, barley, chickpeas, and oatmeal are available in bulk quantities. And still, that's not all. There are meat grinders, tomato strainers, cheese graters, and coffee makers too. A visit here isn't just a shopping trip, it's an education. Metered parking on the street or use the Market's lot, which is a good city block away at the opposite end of the West Side Market building.

▲

Foods available: grains, beans, flour, baked goods, spices, condiments, beverages, tea, coffee, prepared frozen foods ■ Hours: Mon 9 a.m.–4 p.m., Wed 8 a.m.–4 p.m., Fri 8 a.m.–6 p.m., Sat 7 a.m.–6 p.m.; closed Sun, Tue, Thu ■ Checks accepted
■ ♿ Full access

MILES FARMERS MARKET

Solon   Southeast
28560 Miles Rd.
☎ 248-5222

Known among the cooking cognoscenti as The Place To Shop if you're searching for the freshest, most exotic gourmet foods or hard-to-find imported ingredients, Miles Farmers Market is a huge, bright, noisy grocery store packed with products from around the world. Many people come here for an outing and the notion that shopping is a leisure-time activity is reinforced by the pot of serve-yourself coffee that's just inside the door. The selection of produce is vast and it's not uncommon to see such exotica as Asian pears, starfruit, or papayas. An olive bar, set up like a salad bar, allows shoppers to select and package their own combinations. The variety of beans is staggering; French falgeolet, calypso, tongues of fire, giant limas, five different kinds of lentils, plus all the more standard sorts like garbanzo, fava, pinto, and black. There's a full deli with meats, cheeses, and warm-at-home entrees, and a full bakery. It's impossible to list all the products Miles stocks, but rest assured that whether you need crumpets or grape leaves, pickled peppers or pasta, sausage or salsa, you'll surely find it here. And if your salivary glands just can't take all the stimulation, there are even a few booths available where you can sit down and eat some of their prepared foods.

▲

Foods available: meat (fresh), fish (fresh), produce, grains, beans, flour, baked goods, spices, condiments, beverages, tea, coffee, wine, prepared frozen foods, takeout meals ■ Hours: Mon–Fri 9 a.m.–8 p.m., Sat & Sun 9 a.m.–6 p.m. ■ MC, VS, checks accepted ■ ♿ Full access

MOLINARI'S FOOD & WINE

Mentor   Farther East
8900 Mentor Ave.
☎ 269-1230

This gourmet shop, which is also a restaurant and wine bar, (see Mediterranean chapter for restaurant) has a chic, upscale look and an extensive selection of both specialty foods from around the world and unique regional and Ohio products. The choice of wines is large, including the best from Italy, France, Australia, and California, and the knowledgeable store staff are happy to advise shoppers. There are also many imported and local micro-brewery beers. Home cooks will find ingredients for Mexican, Italian, and French cuisine: plus many importsed relishes, sauces, dressings, pates, pastas, crackers, chocolate, and cookies. A gourmet deli counter features cheeses, desserts, and freshly baked bread, including Molinari's fat-free French loaf. They offer attractive preassembled or customized food gift baskets. Most of the food on the restaurant menu is also available for takeout. When you visit the store, be sure to pick up one of their quarterly newsletters listing special food events they'll be hosting in the shop.

Other ethnic specialties: French, Italian, Mexican
▲
Foods available: grains, beans, flour, baked goods, spices, condiments, beverages, tea, coffee, wine, takeout meals ■ Hours: Mon–Thu 9:30 a.m.–10 p.m., Fri & Sat 9:30 a.m.–11 p.m. ■ MC, VS, AX, Dis, checks accepted ■ 占 Full access

PAT O'BRIEN'S OF LANDERWOOD

Pepper Pike   East Side
30800 Pinetree Rd.
☎ 831-8680

Pat O'Brien has been in business for 24 years and calls his shop A "quality of life store" that carries unusual, exotic, imported gourmet foods and wines. He personally invites people to come and savor the ambience of his place. "You must visit," he says "to fully appreciate the variety." Visitors will find an interesting selection of cheeses, olive oils, vinegars, pasta, sauces, caviar, and bottled pickles, olives, and peppers. There are many brands of jam and jelly from around the world plus cookies, crackers, biscuits, chocolate, and candy. A few non-food items such as corkscrews and wine racks.
▲
Foods available: beans, flour, baked goods, spices, condiments, beverages, coffee, wine, beer, prepared frozen foods ■ Hours: Mon–Sat 9:30 a.m.–6 p.m.; closed Sun ■ MC, VS, AX, Dis, checks accepted ■ 占 Full access

WEST POINT MARKET

Akron   Farther South
1711 W. Market St.
☎ 864-2151

This is a full-service grocery store for adventurous cooks. The focus is on specialty gourmet products from all over the country and the world. Shoppers will find most everything available in a regular grocery store—and then some. So when looking for rice you can choose from Uncle Ben's white, jasmine, or Indian basmati rice. There may be only one brand of paper towels on the shelves but 50 different olive oils from France, Italy, Greece, and Spain. The Market hosts international food fairs throughout the year that highlight a country and its cuisine with lectures, cooking demonstrations, and tastings. They regularly stock hard-to-find products like Devonshire clotted cream, piccalilli, and treacle from England; Swedish crispbreads and Scandinavian lingonberries; wine kraut from Germany; and the rose and orange waters used in Greek and Middle Eastern cookery. Uncommon produce is common here, and fresh herbs are available year round. Bakers come in at midnight to prepare made-from-scratch old-world breads. With over 3,000 labels in stock, they boast the largest selection of premium imported wines in the state, and the choice of cheeses is equally impressive: imports like Italian parmesan reggiano, French triple brie, Dutch gouda, Greek feta, and English lancaster plus products from small American regional cheesemakers. Using an international array of ingredients, the kitchen, staffed by eight chefs, prepares a variety of entrees to take home or enjoy in the Market cafe. (For more information about dining in, see West Point's listing in the restaurant section of this chapter.) There are always samples of new and unusual food products for tasting, and a flyer, published every two weeks, lets you know about upcoming events.

▲

Foods available: meat (fresh), fish (fresh), produce, grains, beans, flour, baked goods, spices, condiments, beverages, tea, coffee, wine, prepared frozen foods, takeout meals
▪ Hours: Mon–Fri 8 a.m.–7 p.m., Sat 8 a.m.–6 p.m.; closed Sun
▪ MC, VS, Dis, checks accepted ▪ ⅃ Full access

WEST SIDE MARKET

Cleveland   Near West Side
1995 W. 25th St.
☎ 664-3386

Back in the 1860s, this corner was known as Market Square, a place where farmers brought their produce and city dwellers came to shop. The present building on this spot, dedicated in 1912, is an architectural landmark, and the West Side Market is one of the few remaining municipal markets of its kind in the country. The 115 tenants, and 80 stands in the outdoor fruit and vegetable arcade, include families who trace their ethnic roots back to 22 different nationalities. Many of the stands have been operated by the same family for three or four generations, serving customers whose own families have been shopping there just as long. Specialty produce items for many types of cuisine, from pomegranates and star fruit to bean sprouts and green bananas, will be found outside, along with just about any other fresh fruit or vegetable you can imagine. The same huge variety is available inside along the main concourse. The following list highlights some of the merchants (with their stand numbers) who offer ethnic products. There is free parking in a lot east of the building.

Patricia Hauser (A-12), homemade pierogies

Jerry Chucray (B-10 & B-6), homemade Ukrainian sausage

Pat Delaney (C-2), Slovenian meats

Scott Kindt (C-9), Mexican chorizo sausage

Brent Seabrook (C-13), exotic spices, small quantities or bulk

Michael Mitterholzer (D-2), Eastern European Bakery

John Bistricky (D-11), lamb, goat, halal meats

Sherry Belohlavek (D-13), Hungarian strudel

Carmen Messina (E-11), Italian imports and homemade Italian salads

Angela J. Dohar Szucs (F-1 & F-2), homemade Hungarian sausage

Frank Ratschki (G-3, H-3), bratwurst

Theresa and Erich Geiler (G-7), homemade sausage and cold cuts

Freddy Graewe (G-10), German sauerkraut

Stamatios E. Vasdekis (H-12), gyros

Husam Zayed (Grocery Department #1,2), Middle Eastern foods

▲

Foods available: meat (fresh, deli, frozen, dried), fish (fresh, frozen, dried), produce, grains, beans, flour, baked goods, spices, condiments, beverages, tea, coffee, wine, takeout meals ▪ Hours: Mon & Wed 7 a.m.–4 p.m., Fri & Sat 7 a.m.–6 p.m. ▪ Cash only

Indexes

Index by Name

(Markets in italic)

Index by Location

(Markets in italic)

Idea Index

Have a special need? Can't decide what you want? Here are some fun suggestions to try when you're not sure where to go. This is by no means a comprehensive list, but it should get you started.

Take the Kids

10 Restaurants where the atmosphere is tolerant, the staff accommodating, food includes things kids are sure to eat, and prices won't require a bank loan:

Fanny's, 122
Parma Pierogies, 118, 119
Mama Santa's, 87
Nuevo Acapulco, 169
Seoul Hot Pot & Deangelo's Pizza, 37
Frankie's Italian, 84, 85
Sforzo's Italian Family Restaurant, 94
Balaton, 117
Max's Deli, 185
Hofbrau Haus, 146

Romance

6 spots where the atmosphere encourages hand-holding and the whispering of sweet nothings in each other's ears:

Lu Cuisine, 30
Portofino Ristorante, 93
La Pomme, 142
Georgio's, 96
Chez Francois, 141
The Greek Isles, 77

The Sophisticated Side of Cleveland

8 locations for impressing out-of-towners and entertaining business associates:

Johnny's Bar, 86
Massimo da Milano, 89
Sans Souci, 97
Ristorante Giovanni's, 93
Piperade, 143
Saffron Patch, 59
Lu Cuisine, 30
Parker's Restaurant, 143

Eat Al Fresco

5 restaurants offering seating in the great outdoors(when the weather obliges):

Taste of Europe, 147
Chez Francois, 141
Maria's, 88
Sergio's, 194
Marinko's Firehouse, 117

Perfect for Parties

7 with private party rooms or facilities and services suitable for large groups:

Lopez Y Gonzales, 167
Frankie's Italian, Westlake, 85
Gintaras Dining Room, 118
Bo Loong, 26
Der Braumeister Restaurant & Deli, 144
Theo's Restaurant, 80
Mr. Z's, 90
Piperade, 143

After Midnight

Places where it seems the kitchen almost never closes and you can get anything from a snack to a full meal long after the dinner hour:

Bo Loong, 26
Li Wah, 29
Mardi Gras, 79
Bayou Cafe, 186
Lancer's, 182
Art's Seafood, 180
The Plaka, 79
Corky and Lenny's, 183

By the Dawn's Early Light

Early morning eats for those with the get up and go to get up and go there :

Ruthie and Mo's, 193
Slyman's, 186
Corky and Lenny's, 183
Jack's Deli, 184
Heimatland Inn, 145

Cheap Eats East & Downtown

Dinner Entrees Under $10.00:

Aladdin's Eatery, 62
Marie's Restaurant, 116
Dailey's West Indian, 161
Angie's Soul Food Kitchen, 179
The Greek Express, 77
Nam Hing, 42

Cheap Eats West:

Dinner Entrees Under $10.00:

Minh Anh, 41
Thai Kitchen, 39
El Coqui, 171

Tell us where to go!

Do you know of an *authentic* ethnic restaurant or market in Greater Cleveland that should have been included in this guide but wasn't? Well, that's what second editions are for! Tell us about your favorite place using the form below. If we add it to a future edition, you'll receive a free copy when it's published.

Restaurant / Market (cirle one)

_____
Ethnic Cuisine

_____
Name

_____
Address

_____
City, State Zip

_____
Phone Number

_____
Owner or Manager (if you know)

Your Name & Address:

_____
Name

_____
Address

_____
City, State, Zip

Mail this form to:
Cleveland Ethnic Eats
Gray & Company, Publishers
11000 Cedar Avenue · Cleveland, Ohio 44106

CLEVELAND
Guides & Gifts

If you enjoyed *Cleveland Ethnic Eats*, you'll want to know about these other fine Cleveland guidebooks and giftbooks ...

Neil Zurcher's Favorite One Tank Trips

At last! TV's "One Tank Trips" in a book. Ohio's travel expert shows where to take delightful mini-vacations close to home. Hundreds of unusual getaway ideas.
$12.95 softcover • 208 pages • 5 ⁄" x 8 ⁄"

Cleveland Discovery Guide

The best family recreation in Greater Cleveland collected in a handy guidebook. Written by parents, for parents; offers detailed descriptions, suggested ages, prices, & more.
$12.95 softcover • 208 pages • 5 ⁄" x 8 ⁄"

Cleveland Golfer's Bible

Describes in detail every golf course, driving range, and practice facility in Greater Cleveland. Includes descriptions, prices, ratings, locator maps.
$12.95 softcover • 240 pages • 5 ⁄" x 8 ⁄"

Cleveland Garden Handbook

Advice from local experts on how to grow a beautiful lawn and garden in Northeast Ohio. Filled with practical tips and good ideas.
$12.95 softcover • 264 pages • 5 ⁄" x 8 ⁄"

Cleveland On Foot

Follow these walking tours and discover Greater Cleveland's historic neighborhoods, distinctive suburbs, glorious Metroparks, and surrounding nature preserves (and get some great exercise, too!) Step-by-step directions.
$12.95 softcover • 264 pages • 5 ⁄" x 8 ⁄"

Cleveland: A Portrait of the City

105 brilliant color photographs capture Greater Cleveland in all seasons. Familiar landmarks and surprising hidden details. A handsome hardcover giftbook.
$35.00 hardcover • 96 pages • 8 ⁄" x 10 ⁄"

Best Things in Life: *236 Favorite Things About Cleveland*

A fun collection of thought-provoking quotations by Clevelanders about Cleveland.
$5.95 softcover • 144 pages • 6" x 4 ⁄"

Color Me Cleveland

The All-Cleveland coloring book. For all ages and skill levels. Use crayons, markers, pencils.
$4.95 softcover • 32 pages • 8 ⁄" x 11"

Available at Your Local Bookstore.

These and other Gray & Co. books are regularly stocked at most Cleveland-area bookstores and can be special-ordered through any bookstore in the U.S.

For information, call:

Gray & Company, Publishers
11000 Cedar Avenue • Cleveland, Ohio 44106
(216) 721-2665